An
ELEGANT
ART

PLATE 1   Dress (cat. no. 25).

PLATE 2   Coat (redingote; cat. no. 27).

Organized by Edward Maeder

Essays by
Edward Maeder
Alicia M. Annas
Natalie Rothstein
Nikki Scheuer
Anne Ratzki-Kraatz
Anna G. Bennett
Aileen Ribeiro

An

Fashion & Fantasy in the Eighteenth Century

ELEGANT

Los Angeles County Museum of Art Collection of Costumes and Textiles

ART

Los Angeles County Museum of Art in Association with

Harry N. Abrams, Inc., Publishers, New York

Copublished by the
Los Angeles County Museum of Art
5905 Wilshire Boulevard
Los Angeles, California 90036
and
Harry N. Abrams, Inc.
110 East 59th Street
New York, New York 10022

Edited by Phil Freshman, Dorothy J. Schuler, and Barbara Einzig
Designed by Tina Davis Snyder
Photographed by Lawrence S. Reynolds, Peter Brenner, Kent Kiyomura, and Jack Ross
Text set in Baskerville type by Set to fit Photo-Typography, Inc., Greenwich, Connecticut
Printed in an edition of 3,000 hardcover and 15,000 softcover, on
128 gram Fukiage Matte Coated paper, by Nissha Printing Co., Ltd., Japan
Bound by Taikansha Book Binding Co., Ltd., Japan

Library of Congress Cataloging in Publication Data
  Los Angeles County Museum of Art.
  An elegant art.

  Bibliography: p.
  1. Costume—History—18th century—Exhibitions.
  2. Fashion—History—18th century—Exhibitions.
  3. Fashion and art—History—18th century—Exhibitions.
  I. Maeder, Edward.   II. Title.
  GT585.L64   1983   391 .009′033074019494   82-11531
  ISBN 0-8109-0864-6 (Abrams)
  ISBN 0-87587-111-9 (pbk.)

Exhibition Dates: March 8 – June 2, 1983
This exhibition was organized with the aid of a grant from the National Endowment for the Arts

Cover illustration:
Panel (cat. no. 400)

CONTENTS

FOREWORD

The acceptance of costume as a legitimate art form and the emergence of costume history as a solid academic discipline are relatively recent developments in the field of art history. It is, therefore, highly gratifying to be able to note the exceptional strength and vitality of the Los Angeles County Museum of Art's Department of Textiles and Costumes; its ever-expanding collection both enhances the holdings of other departments and helps broaden our awareness of the sensibilities of periods far removed from our own.

One such period was the eighteenth century, a time characterized by a widespread dedication to the attainment of beauty and artistry in all realms of life. As this catalogue and exhibition richly demonstrate, that dedication was perhaps most revealingly expressed in the dress of the age. The art historian and layman alike will gain insight and pleasure from the way in which this catalogue's authors have sought to interrelate the costumes and social currents of the time. The exhibition, planned with perception and enthusiasm by Curator Edward Maeder, seeks to make eighteenth-century dress vivid and accessible to contemporary museum visitors.

The catalogue and exhibition together are the culmination of more than a quarter of a century of collecting and nearly four years of scholarly research and preparation. In this regard, we are deeply grateful to the National Endowment for the Arts for providing a grant that greatly facilitated presentation of the exhibition. We are confident that this publication, both as a document of the exhibition and as a contribution to the literature on the period, will be of lasting significance.

Earl A. Powell III
DIRECTOR
LOS ANGELES COUNTY MUSEUM OF ART

PREFACE AND ACKNOWLEDGMENTS

This exhibition and catalogue formally began life in October 1979, when the first planning discussions took place and the initial letters of inquiry were written. Seeds were informally sown, however, more than a decade ago, when I began studying the costumes and people of the eighteenth century—the Age of Elegance.

When I undertook this project it was not possible to foresee that its success would finally derive from the sustained efforts of a virtual army of devoted individuals. Though I can certainly praise some of those people here, I cannot adequately express my appreciation for their help.

Mention must first be made of Stefania Holt, founding curator of the Museum's Department of Textiles and Costumes, and of her husband, Eugene. Between 1954 and 1966 they acquired outstanding examples of the eighteenth-century costumer's art. The Museum's Costume Council, organized in 1954 in part to assist in this endeavor, has over the years lent the kind of support and funding necessary to form the world-class collection this institution has today.

Also essential to this project's creation were the influence, inspiration, and information supplied by a number of great teachers, curators, and collectors. Stella Newton, Courtauld Institute of Art, University of London, and Pegaret Anthony, lecturer and writer, Central School, London, put me on the proper path of study. Jean-Michel Tuchscherer, Director, Musée Historique des Tissus, Lyon, and Gabriel Vial, an analyst at the same institution, let me study at first hand costumes of the period. Mr. and Mrs. Werner Abegg, Abegg Foundation, Bern, Riggisberg, Switzerland, graciously granted me extended exposure to their remarkable collection. The one and only Cora Ginsberg allowed me access to her extensive collection, permitting me to study and photograph it at will. Janet Arnold's publications were a source of inspiration, and the staff of the Textile Department, Victoria and Albert Museum, was a source of encouragement. June Swan, Central Museum and Art Gallery, London, expertly identified items in our Museum's shoe and buckle collections.

It has been an honor and a privilege to work with the six scholars whose essays grace this catalogue: Alicia M. Annas, Associate Professor of Drama, San Diego State University; Natalie Rothstein, Department of Textiles and Dress, Victoria and Albert Museum; Nikki Scheuer, writer and lecturer; Anne Ratzki-Kraatz, Lace Consultant, Musée des Arts Décoratifs, Paris; Anna G. Bennett, Curator of Textiles, The Fine Arts Museums of San Francisco; and Dr. Aileen Ribeiro, Head of History of Dress Department, Courtauld Institute of Art, University of London. Their erudition and infectious enthusiasm for the eighteenth century have helped make this volume one that anyone interested in the period can approach and enjoy.

On behalf of Anna G. Bennett, I want to thank Guy Delmarcel and Maurice Hudkins for their advice and The J. Paul Getty Museum, Malibu, for making its records available to her. Her special thanks go to Edith A. Standen, whose command of the tapestry field is equalled only by her generosity.

My gratitude to the Museum's Department of Textiles and Costumes staff for their tireless efforts on behalf of this project is immeasurable. Curatorial Assistant Claire Polakoff collaborated with me in the difficult task of formulating the essay "The Elegant Art of Dress." Curatorial Assistant Florence Karant, a veritable Sherlock Holmes, tracked down fugitive acquisition information and composed hundreds of photographic orders. Curatorial Assistant Nola Ewing, with her intimate knowledge of the collection, unearthed treasures that had been buried during the rapid growth of the department's holdings. Departmental secretary Rae Avrutin typed endless pages of manuscript and handled the formidable correspondence this project entailed. Research Assistant Nancy Gardner was relentless in her pursuit of bibliographic minutiae and in the verification of information included in this catalogue's glossary. Research Assistant Dale Gluckman's help, in a host of areas, was essential.

I am particularly indebted to supervising editor Phil Freshman and to staff editors Dorothy J. Schuler and Barbara Einzig for their indefatigable, meticulous, and highly professional work on this catalogue. Its organization, fluidity, and consistency are a direct result of their expertise. The catalogue also owes much to the astute, graceful design of Tina Davis Snyder, and to the production coordinating skills of Nora Beeson of Harry N. Abrams, Inc.

Photography Supervisor Lawrence S. Reynolds and his staff, Peter Brenner, Kent Kiyomura, and Jack Ross, produced splendid, sensitive images while remaining flexible in the face of extensive demands. The Museum's textile conservators, Pat Reeves, Fernande G. Jones, Nancy Conlin Wyatt, and Catherine C. McLean, performed miracles of rejuvenation on several hundred objects featured in the exhibition and catalogue. Registrar Renée Montgomery and her staff were helpful and patient at every stage. And Assistant Director Myrna Smoot was a major support in areas too numerous to name.

Thanks go, too, to the Museum's Curator of European Paintings, Scott Schaefer, who helped select and secure paintings which complement and add special depth to the exhibition. Designer Herb Camburn provided brilliant guidance in the creation and fulfillment of the exhibition plan. He was instrumental in securing for us the services of wigmaker Vikki Wood and sculptor Clare Graham; together they have produced mannequins that are perfect in every respect.

The exhibition has been made more meaningful by the efforts of Head of Museum Education William Lillys and his staff, who have gathered an array of eminent scholars for the lecture series connected with *An Elegant Art.* I am also deeply grateful to the Museum's Operations staff for their fortitude during all phases of the exhibition installation.

This project would not have been accomplished without the selfless help of a regiment of volunteers. Evelyn Ackerman spent some six hundred hours compiling material for the glossary; she was also a vital consultant on several of the essays. Anna Lee Binder, Louise Coffey, Jeanne de Coster, Tom Fender, Jon Gluckman, Lia Jantz, Myra Kornfeld, Dorothy Laupa, Peter Monsour, Victoria Newhouse, Lorraine Olson, May Routh, Joan Rudman, Joan Severa, Doris Sosin, Candy Van Woerkom, and Fern Wallace all contributed enormously in the areas of research and exhibition preparation. The volunteer energies and financial and moral support of the Needleworkers and Preservation Group of the Costume Council have likewise been essential throughout the last three and one-half years.

Finally, I would like to extend my thanks to the remarkable people of the eighteenth century who wrote the notes, memoirs, diaries, and novels from which we have learned so much, as well as to the people who created the costumes which have survived to our time—monuments to taste, craftsmanship, and elegance.

Edward Maeder
CURATOR OF TEXTILES AND COSTUMES

EDWARD MAEDER
CURATOR OF TEXTILES AND COSTUMES,
LOS ANGELES COUNTY MUSEUM OF ART

THE ELEGANT ART OF DRESS

"…comfort was neither understood nor expected but even the most ordinary objects of everyday use were required to be artistic."

MAX VON BOEHN,
MODES AND MANNERS:
THE EIGHTEENTH CENTURY, 1935

Artistry revealed itself in many ways during the eighteenth century and in no area was this more apparent than in the elegant art of dress, which epitomized the period's aesthetic ideals. The completed picture of an Elegant[1] evolved from the carefully composed and arranged basic artificial costume silhouette to the minutiae of surface decoration, elaborate accessories, powder, paint, and posture. A perfection of form was attempted by restructuring the human body through the use of clothing and either reducing or expanding the existing shape. Functional objects of everyday use such as fans, stockings, stomachers, aprons, and workbaskets became artistic creations through the use of the craftsman's art and the embroiderer's needle (plates 3, 4; cat. nos. 212, 82). These embellished accessories perfected the desired appearance of the completed composition.

Though it is impossible within the confines of this essay and this catalogue to discuss fully the fascinating and varied events that shaped the lives and attitudes of the people who actually wore the clothing and used the accessories displayed here, it is possible to look for an answer to a basic question: What spawned a fashion of such extremes?

Dress, as a symbol of social position, was a major concern of both seventeenth- and eighteenth-century societies. It reflected the influences of a powerful political atmosphere, an atmosphere perhaps best represented by the notion of absolute sovereignty. People believed that mere physical proximity to the monarch—his power and supremacy established through the divine right of kings—would elevate them to a higher social level. And dress, of course, had to be appropriate to the elevation. After all, the ordinary man could not bask in the sunshine of common brown wool cloth; he basked in the sunshine of the king's sumptuous cloth of gold, silver embroidery, and jewels.

Yet as the seventeenth-century Baroque gave way to the eighteenth-century Rococo, certain other powerful influences came into play; the eighteenth century became marked by duality and contradiction. In this overfertile age, sharply contrasting attitudes existed side by side: profound faith and devastating skepticism; rejection of law and strict observance of method; intoxicating feeling and icy logic. Three main trends—enlightenment, revolution, and classicism—coexisted. Each predominated in a given period, but all three were found throughout the century, so that the entire age was permeated by these currents.[2]

The Enlightenment was marked by a warm receptivity to inquiry and change; the social rigidities and restrictions of earlier periods were being broken down. Literacy spread.[3] Nothing was thought to be beyond the reach of human reason and inventiveness.

The spirit of the Enlightenment is perhaps best exemplified by the scientific advances of the period, which built upon and enriched the achievements of the seventeenth century. Mechanical creations aroused enthusiasm and pride and sparked further investigation. The same inventive hands and mind that engineered a desk which miraculously transformed itself into a bed were also capable of perfecting the complicated side hoops required by fashion. These artificial hips, extending several feet from either side of the wearer, were made manageable through a collapsible support mechanism whose ingenuity stands as a tribute to man's creativity. Symbolic of the Enlightenment, too, was one of the first successful ascents of the hot air balloon, by Jean François Pilâtre de Rozier and the Marquis d'Arlandes, on November 21, 1783;[4] the mind of man had even conquered the air.

The scientific changes of the period were closely related to the social revolution which began about the middle of the century. Brought about in part by the Industrial Revolution, which was just then getting under way, the social revolution also had roots in the writings of Jean Jacques Rousseau. In his discourse on *The Origin and Bases of Inequality among Men* (1754), Rousseau indicted private property and the political state as causes of inequality and oppression, and, praising the "noble savage," urged a general return to nature.

At this time, the rising bourgeoisie, a new middle class created by the Industrial Revolution, was straining to climb to a higher stratum of society. They wished to attain, or even surpass, the refined and elegant manner of their superiors. Meanwhile, the blasé members of high society, having tasted everything, began to delight in the charm of "naturalness" and "simplicity." Enthusiasm for country life became fashionable. Costume of this period reflected the enthusiasm for the natural, yet could not escape the artificiality of former extravagances.

In England, the commercial and industrial revolutions were undermining authority and the standards of previous eras. In France, the deepening abyss between the court and aristocracy and the masses intensified social uneasiness. Heart and head were both rebelling against the aristocratic way of life, and by the time Louis XVI ascended the throne of France in 1774, even the aristocrats themselves, though not yet fully aware of it, craved the security and peace that direct contact with the earth and "naturalism" seemed to promise. Of course, it was too late. The most they could attain was a superficial kinship with nature, and so they played at being shepherds and shepherdesses (cat. nos. 183, 184).

Classical values, especially those evolved by the Greeks, were held in great esteem during the Enlightenment. The Greeks were praised as balanced, rationalistic philosophers and were seen as having been masters of unity and simplicity. This return to the classical resulted from a fundamental need, in an age of multiplicity and para-

PLATE 3
Sewing Basket (cat. no. 212).

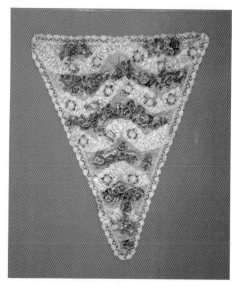

PLATE 4
Stomacher (cat. no. 82).

dox, to find respite and relief in a world of pure proportions, clear order, and self-limitation. Whether the Greece of antiquity was actually like this was beside the point; this was what the eighteenth-century man believed it to be.

In every age dress is the expression of the ideal picture which people make of their own appearance. In the eighteenth century dress was the premier symbol of one's wealth and station in life. Thus an understanding of the meaning held by particular elements of dress is vital in order to know how eighteenth-century people wished to see themselves. The wig, for example, was not, as one might assume, a means of concealing a lack of natural hair (although it could be), but was instead an important article of dress. It was used to adorn a person's outward appearance in much the same way as a plumed hat did. Through its use, the wearer created an impression of grandeur and importance, of dignity and gravity.

Like the wig, the use of powder (both for the hair and the face) was no mere frivolity of fashion. By ordering white hair for all, the Rococo imparted a kind of universal agelessness at a time when the age of forty represented, for most, the end of life. The use of powder for the hair became so widely accepted that it was even dutifully recorded in portraiture, where it appeared deposited on the shoulders of worthy gentlemen of fashion.[5] On the other hand, in this age of contradiction, the popular practice of pow-

dering and rouging one's face was a means of disguising signs of the aging process. Even the silhouette of the gown assisted in furthering the illusion of eternal youth. The foundation of laced corsets, pulled to extremes, lengthened and slimmed the waist, heightening the appearance of a youthful figure. The wide skirts, with their hidden foundations of hoops, served to accentuate the slim waist even more.

After its earliest appearance, in the second half of the fifteenth century in Spain, the hoop traveled into Northern Italy via Naples, at that time under the ownership of Spain. Conservative clergymen railed against this artificial expansion of the skirt as early as 1507, in Treviso. These attacks continued for the next two centuries, ignited by Protestant enthusiasms and other conservative elements. In the October 1724 edition of the *Journal de Verdun*, side hoops were accused of being "a fashion conducive to false modesty."[6] Such assaults on this bastion of fashion might seem to indicate that the hoop was a stylistic aberration. However, the enlargement of the human form through dress is a device that has been used throughout history to impress; the use of the hoop in the eighteenth century suited this purpose admirably.

Court dress, commonly believed to be the promulgator of high style, retained the exaggerated, expanded silhouette created by the hoop. While the ungainly, cumbersome, and often dangerous side hoop was

discarded by the fashion-conscious in the 1750s, it actually remained *de rigueur* for court dress in England as late as the first decade of the nineteenth century. The means by which these puffed and puckered protuberances were controlled is described at length in the essay "The Elegant Art of Movement."

The costliness of court dress led to the introduction of the court "uniform," first worn by both men and women during the reign of George III. This was an attempt by the monarchy to reduce the huge clothing allowances for members of the court. These uniforms followed dictates as rigid as those imposed on court dress. An example of this type, the Windsor Uniform, was widely discussed and was described by one contemporary as being worn by the court "at the ball at Windsor given on the King's recovery" in 1789 (fig. 1).[7] In France, in contrast to England, Louis XIV required new court dress at every formal function, forcing less wealthy courtiers into bankruptcy. Embroidery designs became so elaborate they even strained the resources of the royal coffers.[8] French court dress in the Regency remained so encrusted with heavy gold and silver embroidery that it was described by one contemporary as resembling a state bed on casters (plates 5, 6; cat. nos. 5, 79). Outward appearance masked the cultivated interior it was intended to reflect.

It is obvious that not everybody dressed in the rich fabrics and elaborate styles seen

PLATE 5
Dress (open court robe and petticoat; cat. no. 5).

PLATE 6
Stomacher (cat. no. 79).

in this catalogue and exhibition. In the eighteenth century there certainly existed a large lower class and a rising middle class, most of whose members were unable to extend their resources in the procurement of such vanities. Servants were furnished with clothing as part of their annual wage (plate 7; cat. no. 216). References are common in which servants mention clothing that suits their station in life. At the death of her mistress, Richardson's heroine Pamela receives handkerchiefs and aprons, as well as a suit of clothes and even stockings and shoes, of which she says, "The clothes are fine silk, and too rich and too good for me, to be sure."[9] Poor and middle-class people felt that common sense and morality ought to be reflected in one's dress. Again, Pamela speaks: "O how I wished for my grey russet again, and my poor honest dress, with which you fitted me out."[10] Regrettably, few examples of common clothing from this period have survived. This is because they were simply worn out or cut up and used for other purposes,[11] or, as seen in wills of the time, were handed down to friends and relatives even less fortunate.

Some of the richest sources of information on dress in the eighteenth century are personal diaries, journals, and letters (plate 8; cat. no. 196). Letter writing, in fact, became the period's dominant form of communication. The century saw the beginnings of the classic letter and memoir literature as we know it today, with its lengthy self-descriptions, great confessions, and dawning interest in psychology. Unlike those of today, letters of that time were not strictly intended as a way of conducting private and intimate business. Often they were meant for a wide circle of readers, and, as such, were circulated to be read in dozens of different places. They often took forms as contrived and convoluted as the costumes of the time, and could become quite long; letters of twenty-six pages were not uncommon. The two most important items in a lady's boudoir were her bed and her writing desk. Since polite society did not require her to be dressed until two-thirty or three in the afternoon, she was free in the morning to indulge in the crush of correspondence.

This epistolary preoccupation in the eighteenth century is strongly evidenced by the fact that *Pamela* (1740), generally considered to be the first modern English-language novel, was constructed in the form of a series of letters. The importance of clothing is confirmed in page after page of *Pamela*, with descriptions relating clothing to financial status or social appearances. In her letters Pamela refers to earlier fashions as ugly, a concept that has remained with us to this day that everything not currently in vogue, especially styles of the recent past, seems particularly unattractive.

Although a wealthy person's station was certainly obvious from the rich brocaded silks and embroideries that adorned the most elaborate dress of the period, at the outset of the century it was accessories and jewels that distinguished the truly wealthy from the pretenders. However, as noted above, the Industrial Revolution produced a new wealthy class that arose about the middle of the century, and they could also afford luxury goods. This threat to the aristocracy's supremacy caused them to instigate and cultivate complex forms of elaborate social ritual and manners that subtly distinguished them from the rising bourgeoisie.

There were many ways to embellish costume, either through richly brocaded fabrics, delicate laces, or multitudinous forms of elaborate embroidery. Embroiderers' samples were well-known and plentiful in the eighteenth century, and designs were made up for professional tailors and mercers. The customer could then choose a type of embroidery, which was subsequently placed on special order. Another alternative was a waistcoat already embroidered in the form of a length of fabric. This could then be cut and tailored to the specifications of the customer (fig. 2). There is also strong evidence that miniature garments were made on a reduced scale to show the kinds of fabrics and decorative possibilities available. One of these diminutive coats with an attached waistcoat, approximately one-third size, was recently discovered in a private collection in Lyon.[12] Although carefully executed and accurate to the most minute detail, it consisted of only half a

FIG. 2
Daniel Chodowieki (German, 1726–1801)
The Tailor with His Helpers, 1770
Engraving on paper
4¼ x 3¼ in.

PLATE 8
Dispatch Case (cat. no. 196).

PLATE 7
Livery Suit (coat, waistcoat, and breeches; cat. no. 216).

completed garment. Such miniatures were certainly used by merchants as samples and could easily be shipped to other countries.

Embroidery techniques were applied to many objects of daily use during the eighteenth century, but with the possible exception of state beds, costume was the major showcase for the embroiderer's palette. An extraordinary understanding of both medium and execution was required to produce, for example, the masterworks of embroidery displayed on the costumes of the moving works of art who glided through Vauxhall Gardens or the Tuileries.

Although embroidery techniques were extremely refined and complex, actual sewing methods for the construction of garments were quite simple. For a large part of the century, the basis for a luxury costume was a luxury textile.[13] A modern misconception is that handwork is always slow and tedious. Actually, it took much less time to fashion a garment in the eighteenth century than one might think. Direct evidence comes from *Pamela*:

Monday. I had a good deal of employment in chosing patterns for my new clothes. He thought nothing too good; but I thought every thing I saw was; and he was so kind to pick out six of the richest for me to chose three suits out of...One was white, flowered with silver most richly. And he was pleased to say, that, as I was a bride, I should make my appearance in that the following Sunday. And so we shall have in two or three days, from several places, nothing but mantua-makers and tailors at work....He made me also choose some very fine laces, and linen; and has sent a message on purpose, with his orders, to hasten all down, what can be done in town, as the millinery matters &c to be completed there, and sent by particular messengers, as done....All to be there and finished by Saturday afternoon, without fail.[14]

The inherent richness of the costumes was usually based in the fabric itself, which was often heavily brocaded with metal threads and complicated floral forms (cat. no. 381). The large expanse created by the side hoops helped to display rich silks such as this one to their best advantage.

Modern conservators often find it difficult to sew through eighteenth-century silks; the mere insertion of a needle through two pieces of heavy taffeta can require great physical strength. So sturdy was Italian silk taffeta, for example, that fifteen layers of it were used in the making of a plastron to protect the Sovereign of France from possible assassination when he appeared in public on July 14, 1792.[15]

Technical virtuosity allowed the weaver to translate the artist's designs into rich brocades, damasks, and brocatelles and partially freed the seamstress or tailor from the rigors of elaborate cutting and sewing techniques. The fabrics, lace, and trimmings at the time were so sumptuous that it might seem as though the actual construction of the garment was equally elaborate. For the most part, however, garment construction was straightforward and relatively uncomplicated.

All fashionable costume shapes, whether

for court or country, were the result of a buildup of layered foundation garments. In an age of questionable hygiene, when daily dress was sometimes unlaunderable, the logical way to protect these costly coverings from the forms they covered was by using a protective barrier which could not only be washed but could also withstand repeated boilings and subjections to harsh lye soaps. Laundry day, which only occurred every five weeks or so, was a major event often requiring three or four days' labor, as documented in *The Diary of a Country Parson*[16] (fig. 3).

An unending array of chemises, petticoats, fichus, and laces[17] were necessary in order for the fashionable lady to maintain the freshness of that part of her outward appearance which enabled her to resemble the flowers she wished to emulate. This emulation was further enhanced by floral fragrances that helped mask other less pleasant odors.

The importance of undergarments can be seen in workmanship that included stitches so minute as to be nearly invisible to the naked eye. These stitches were executed with a precision and regularity that could shame one of man's most important modern inventions, the sewing machine. Girls were taught from the earliest age to wield the needle. Even in boarding school, certain times were set aside when girls sat in a regular formation on a long bench, stitching shirts and undergarments.[18] Children began wearing simple white under-

garments as overgarments after the middle of the century. These were subsequently adapted and adopted by adults and even, by the end of the century, found their way into court wear.

The constant movement and change in fashion characterizing the period are emphasized by a series of strange contrasts. Though traditionally fashions began among the socially elite, in this age of enlightenment, with its attempted return to nature, a number of fashions were taken up by the aspiring bourgeoisie from the lower classes (plate 9; cat. no. 45). Among these adaptations, aprons, truly utilitarian in nature, became purely decorative (plates 10–12; cat. nos. 2, 109, 111). In the 1720s and 1730s, silk aprons were lavishly embroidered, with gold threads and silken representations of the most popular flora. As the century progressed, the sheerest of cotton muslin aprons increased in popularity among the bourgeoisie. Subtly embroidered, white on white, they were so fine and elaborate that the original purpose of the apron—protection of the garment underneath—was completely lost. It should be noted, however, that the early forms of embroidered aprons were never worn by the true aristocracy, who considered them middle class. As the century progressed, however, the newly fashionable, zephyrlike cotton aprons became so popular that they were even worn by members of the British royal family.

When thinking about the eighteenth century, what strikes us most forcefully are its seeming extremes of superficiality and self-love. Its outward manifestations, including its dress, often appear artificial and exaggerated. Yet these aspects both conceal and peculiarly express the period's profound need for self-analysis and for critical examination of the external world. Apart from the scientific advances we have mentioned, philosophical investigations concerning social justice and the interrelationship of classes within society, as well as discussions based upon the rediscovery of past great societies, were topics of daily conversation among the educated.

We have discussed here in general terms the life-style that arose from this atmosphere, a life-style that could hardly be more removed from the one prevailing in the United States of America of the 1980s. In succeeding chapters, we continue our critical examination of the dress and manners of a complex age. We invite you to share our interpretations.

FIG. 3
Daniel Chodowieki (German, 1726–1801)
Women's Room for Sewing, Washing, and Ironing,
1770
Engraving on paper
4¼ x 3¼ in.

PLATE 10 Dress (closed robe; cat. no. 2).

PLATE 11
Fichu (shaped; cat. no. 109, detail).

PLATE 12
Apron (cat. no. 111).

NOTES

1
The terms Elegant, Macaroni (see Costumes and Accessories Glossary), and *Incroyable* distinguished specific fashion movements of the eighteenth century. An Elegant was a fashionable person whose mode of life was marked by grace, propriety, and refinement. In France, *Les Incroyables* (literally translated: the Incredibles) were characterized by their extremes in dress, which included collars of grotesque height and greatly extended width; tightness of both coats and breeches; bunches of loops at the outside of the knees, replacing buckles; huge buttons; conspicuous watch fobs; cravats that brushed the earlobes and cradled the chin; and gypsylike earrings.

2
British rule was established in India in the middle of the century. This probably was the single most important factor in the forging of a new social class of *nouveaux riches* merchants who now had the means and leisure to acquire an education, once only the prerogative of the aristocracy and church.

3
The most important literary event for the awakening middle classes was the rise of the English weekly magazine. The ornamented and metallic surfaces employed in the period's costumes were paralleled by the need of those who wrote for these magazines to be stimulating and brilliant.

4
L. Salmon, "Ballooning: Accessories after the Fact," *Dress*, 2:1, 1976, p.1. J. Woodforde, *The Diary of a Country Parson*, ed. John Beresford, 2: 1782–87, Oxford, 1968, p. 142. In early July 1783, Reverend Woodforde noted fashion's homage to the world's first aeronauts with a reference to "...a neat genteel and pretty Baloon hat."

5
Frederick A. Pottle, the editor of Boswell's journal, clarifies Boswell's notation, "I dressed myself in my second-mourning suit, in which I had been powdered many months," by adding this note: "A dark suit but less sombre than one for first or full mourning. This one happened to be Boswell's oldest or shabbiest suit, and as he had worn it while his hair was being powdered, it had grown more shabby." F. A. Pottle, ed., *Boswell's London Journal 1762–1763*, New York, 1950, p. 272.

6
M. A. Challamel, *History of Fashion in France; or The Dress of Women from the Gallo-Roman Period to the Present Time*, trans. C. Hoey and J. Lillie, New York, 1882, p. 152.

7
The country parson recorded on Wednesday, August 5, 1789, that "The King was in his Windsor Uniform, blue coat with red Cape and Cuffs to the Sleeves, with a plain round Hat with a black Ribband round it..." Woodforde, *Diary*, 2:1782–87, p. 128.

8
C. de Saint-Aubin, *L'Art du Brodeur*, Paris, 1770.

9
S. Richardson, *Pamela*, New York, 1958, p. 10.

10
Ibid., p. 18.

11
It is commonly assumed that patchwork objects were always made from leftover scraps. But the country parson, for one, purchased lengths of new printed cotton to be used specifically for that purpose, which he dutifully recorded in his ledger: "November 19, Tuesday (1789)...To Mr. Aldridge for 7 yrds of purple Cotton to make me a morning Gown at 2/o per yrd pd 0.14.0....To Ditto for patch-work for my Niece." Woodforde, *Diary*, 3:1788–92, p. 150.

12
While the author was engaged in research in the fall of 1976 at Le Musée Historique des Tissus in Lyon, a large collection of textile and costume items was offered to that museum for purchase. This fascinating item was part of that collection. Unfortunately, it could not be photographed.

13
For a detailed analysis of textile design and production in the eighteenth century, see the essay "The Elegant Art of Woven Silk" in this catalogue.

14
Richardson, *Pamela*, pp. 499–500.

15
I. de Saint-Amand, *Marie Antoinette and the Downfall of Royalty*, trans. E. G. Martin, New York, 1900, p. 248.

16
Woodforde, *Diary*, 4: 1793–96, p. 320. "Washing Week, 1796, Nov. 28. '...Washing Week.'" (Editor's footnote): [1] The last entry of 'Washing Week' was on October 24. The next entry after November 28 was made on Jan. 2, 1797, and the next on February 6. Presumably this indicates that the Washing of personal linen &c. was a five-weekly event in the late eighteenth century."

17
Lace of this period possessed a durability which allowed for frequent cleaning. This subject is discussed in depth in the essay "The Elegant Art of Lace" in this catalogue.

18
E. Ham, *Elizabeth Ham, by herself 1783–1820*, intro. and ed. E. Gillett, London [1945], p. 37.

ALICIA M. ANNAS
ASSOCIATE PROFESSOR OF DRAMA,
SAN DIEGO STATE UNIVERSITY

THE ELEGANT ART OF MOVEMENT

"…one should always put the best foot foremost. One should please, shine, and dazzle, wherever it is possible."

LORD CHESTERFIELD, 1752

The elegant art of eighteenth-century movement, an integral part of daily living, was strongly influenced by how costumes were cut and how they were worn. In motion, these were superbly elegant; movement brought them to life!

While the modern idea of movement is a fairly simple one—the process of changing position, place, or posture—the eighteenth-century concept was far more complex. For our purposes, we may consider it to have consisted of four categories:

CARRIAGE OR BODY POSTURE: standing in repose;
MOTIONS: changing from one position to another, that is, walking, sitting, dancing, etc.;
MANNERS: performing social rituals;
ADDRESS: bearing of the body during conversation.

Each of these categories had precise standards of performance which were subtly reinforced by costumes. There was, however, an incredible variety in the actual execution of movement, since every eighteenth-century man and woman interpreted these standards according to his or her individual social standing and personality. For example, although the highly embellished French styles of movement, performed with effortless self-possession, were second nature to the upper classes, at times they chose to execute them perfunctorily or to ignore them completely. Upper- and middle-class fops were very frenchified, taking all movement to extremes. The urban middle classes tended to simplify movement, performing in a straightforward, if occasionally self-con-

scious manner, while country middle-class movement was often laboriously proper. Servants who imitated the movement of their masters too closely were criticized severely for "aping their betters." Those of all classes who were old-fashioned in their beliefs clung to the rigid formality of their seventeenth-century childhood.

To this highly class-conscious era, movement was the ultimate status symbol. "At court even, a graceful address, and an air of ease, will more distinguish a man from the crowd, than the richest cloaths that money may purchase."[1] At the beginning of the century, elegant movement was the hallmark of the aristocracy. But as the century progressed, the ambitious middle classes steadily expanded their economic and political bases of power, and began to challenge the social supremacy of those above them, driving the upper classes to retreat behind an invisible social barrier of manners rather than wealth. Movement became the final rung on the eighteenth-century social ladder. It was one art which could not be purchased; it had to be learned—a painstaking process requiring time and practice. There were rules for every conceivable type of movement—from entering a room to passing someone on the street, fighting a duel, dancing a minuet, or drinking a cup of tea. These rules were gleaned from three main sources: dancing masters, etiquette books, and costumes. By the end of the century, all three sources were being directed toward fur-

PLATE 13
Dress (sack-back closed robe; cat. no. 15).

thering the upward mobility of the middle classes.

Upper-class standards of movement originated in seventeenth-century France during the reign of Louis XIV. Although in the eighteenth century these rules were somewhat relaxed and refined, they were nevertheless continually regarded as the epitome of courteous behavior and elegant movement until the French Revolution. From the time they could walk, upper-class eighteenth-century boys and girls were tutored by French-trained dancing masters who regularly visited the fashionable homes of their charges to teach the latest bows, curtsies, and dances (fig. 4). Between visits, each child was expected to practice his lessons daily and, if necessary, in front of a mirror.

Less affluent parents sent their children to dancing schools or taught them at home from one of the many books on conduct and dance, which contained step-by-step instructions and often illustrations. One such text, *The Man of Manners: or Plebeian Polish'd*, was written in 1768 "chiefly for the Use and Benefit of Persons of Mean Births and Education, who have unaccountably plung'd themselves into Wealth and Power."[2]

Whether acquired from dancing masters, conduct manuals, or costumes, the elegant art of movement was something of a paradox. On the one hand, it depended upon a highly complex and precise set of rules whose execution required consider-able bodily discipline, while, on the other, it required an "easy" or apparently effortless manner of performance. A child learned very early just how much effort it took to appear effortless, in much the same way as does a classical ballet dancer today.

At first glance, the wearing of eighteenth-century costumes may not look so difficult. But if we could be transported back to the world of the costumes displayed in this catalogue and exhibition, we would be astonished by the many ways these clothes would affect our normal posture and ability to move. Today's woman would discover that she could not slump or bend forward without getting poked by her corset. Her ballooning skirt would make it hard to turn around without bumping into people or knocking over things. On her first attempt at sitting down in a chair, she would likely miss the seat altogether!

Today's man could find himself the model of this description by Lord Chesterfield, one of the century's foremost exponents of etiquette:

He is at a loss what to do with his hat, when it is not upon his head; his cane...is at perpetual war with every cup of tea or coffee he drinks; destroys them first, and then accompanies them in their fall. His sword is formidable only to his own legs....His clothes...constrain him so much, that he seems rather their prisoner than their proprietor.[3]

Such costumes obviously had a purpose other than comfort, reflecting a way of thinking different from our own. This relationship between mental attitude and movement in costume is significant because costumes were, and are, worn by the mind as well as the body—to grasp fully the significance of the costumes and movement of any era, we must look beneath the surface to the attitudes that generated them.

KEY ATTITUDES

The look of status always outweighed the desire for physical comfort. Witness this excerpt from the Duchess of Devonshire's letter to a friend in 1778: "...my new French stays...are so intolerably wide across the breast, that my arms are absolutely sore with them; and my sides so pinched—But it is the 'ton'; and pride feels no pain ...to be admired, is a sufficient balsam."[4] Fashionable men and women willingly suffered physical discomfort and deliberately sacrificed freedom of movement—so dear to the twentieth-century life-style—for the elegant look of status (plates 13–15; cat. nos. 15, 127, 135).

One of the main goals in eighteenth-century life was the pursuit of pleasure. Even the Declaration of Independence went so far as to proclaim the pursuit of happiness, a form of pleasure, as one of man's inalienable rights. Note, however, that *pursuit*, not attainment, was the guarantee. This was a century oriented toward process rather than goal, in which people believed that pleasure "was important...worth taking trouble about, and could be given some of the quality of art."[5] One of the most

PLATE 14
Corset (cat. no. 127).

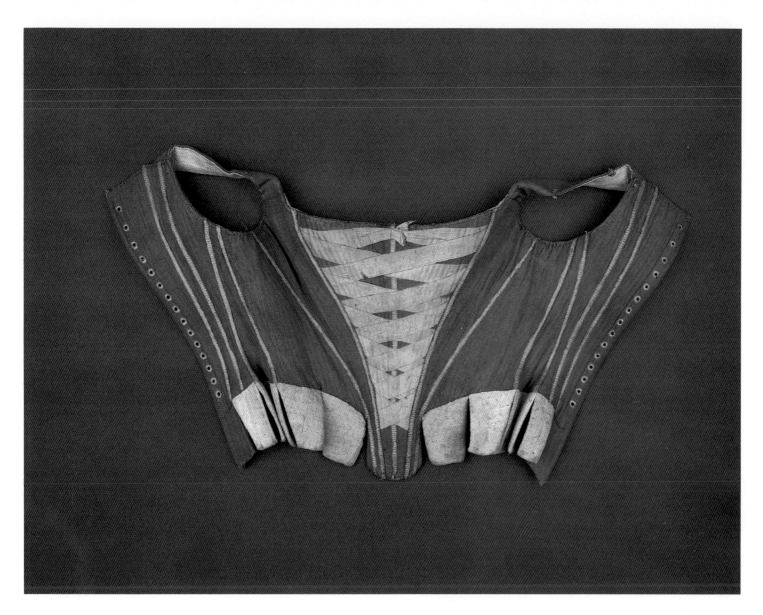

PLATE 15
Corset (cat. no. 135).

unusual aspects of the era's aesthetics was the conviction that if properly dressed and in sufficient command of movement, an individual could be transformed into a work of art. "Let us imagine ourselves, as so many living Pictures drawn by the most excellent Masters, exquisitely designed to afford the utmost Pleasure to the beholders," declared Kellom Tomlinson in *The Art of Dancing*.[6] Costumes, movement, and speech were all spectator-conscious. Every movement was artfully calculated to charm an audience, to show oneself off to best advantage with seeming effortlessness.

The S-curve of William Hogarth (1697–1764), the English painter and engraver, functioned as an aesthetic ideal; this asymmetrical serpentine line was proclaimed the perfect line of beauty. Its languid curve decorated every aspect of eighteenth-century life, from clothing to furniture, interior design, architecture, and landscaping, and also served as an integral part of movement. People walked, stood, and even gestured in S-curve patterns, a far cry from the dominant straight lines so popular today.

Intellectually, individuals derived great satisfaction from the belief that they were the epitome of rational beings. In this age of enlightenment, they were firmly convinced that anything could be accomplished if one's mind were put to it. They delighted in creating, in almost oriental fashion, contradictory but simultaneous levels of meaning—juxtaposing rapid speech with languid

movement, the language of words with the nonverbal language of fans, the performance of difficult movement with apparent ease, or mental vigor with frivolously embellished costumes.

Although feelings ran deep, they were carefully held in check by the intellect. The head ruled the heart in the eighteenth century. Interestingly, the major outlet for feelings and emotions was conversation, itself a highly developed art. The most admired conversation was both elaborate and balanced, abounding with themes and variations, well-turned S-curve phrases, epigrams, and double entendres. From gossip to philosophy to letter writing, the eighteenth-century man or woman was never at a loss for words. Whether conversing in salons, coffeehouses, or clubs, there was never a hurry to get to the point.

Such key attitudes combined to influence the fashionable eighteenth-century individual to choose costumes that challenged the body to a level of control and performance, the mastery of which gave pleasure to the mind. These attitudes also insured that, no matter how dazzling or elaborate the costume, one's personality would always dominate it.

Generally speaking, all four categories of eighteenth-century movement—carriage, motions, manners, and address—began with a disciplined body. To meet the criteria for elegance, movement had to be free and graceful; it could not be angular or stiff. Movement required time to be performed

and appreciated. Both performer and recipient developed a complex mutual rhythm of performance/acceptance that was never ignored or rushed, haste being the sign of a servant or rustic.

CARRIAGE

Proper carriage or body posture was the cornerstone of eighteenth-century movement (fig. 5): one had to learn to pose with studied ease. The basic rule of deportment taught to every child stated: "In order to attain a graceful manner in moving, it is first necessary to know how to stand still."[7] And, indeed, it required considerable self-possession and control to stand without fidgeting for extended periods of time, subject to others' "measuring" (looking one up and down). Elegant carriage consisted of artfully positioning the head, torso, and limbs in an easy, unaffected manner. The body, lifting from the base of the spine, should at all times express a light, floating quality, almost as if it were filled with helium, barely able to stay on the ground (plates 16, 17; cat. nos. 14, 161).

Elegant carriage began with the head which, as the seat of the intellect, was the focal point of the figure. If the head was held properly, all other movement followed naturally. "Hold up your head...let it stand free and easy; to be stiff is almost as bad as to stoop," was the general directive given in *The Polite Academy*.[8] Women were allowed to tilt their heads slightly to one side, forming a gentle S-curve with the torso, as long

FIG. 4
Daniel Chodowieki (German, 1726–1801)
Dance Master Teaching Correct Movement, 1770
(detail)
Engraving on paper
3 3/16 x 4 3/16 in.

FIG. 5
Daniel Chodowieki
(German, 1726–1801)
Advisers to the King, 1770 (detail)
Engraving on paper
3 1/4 x 4 1/4 in.

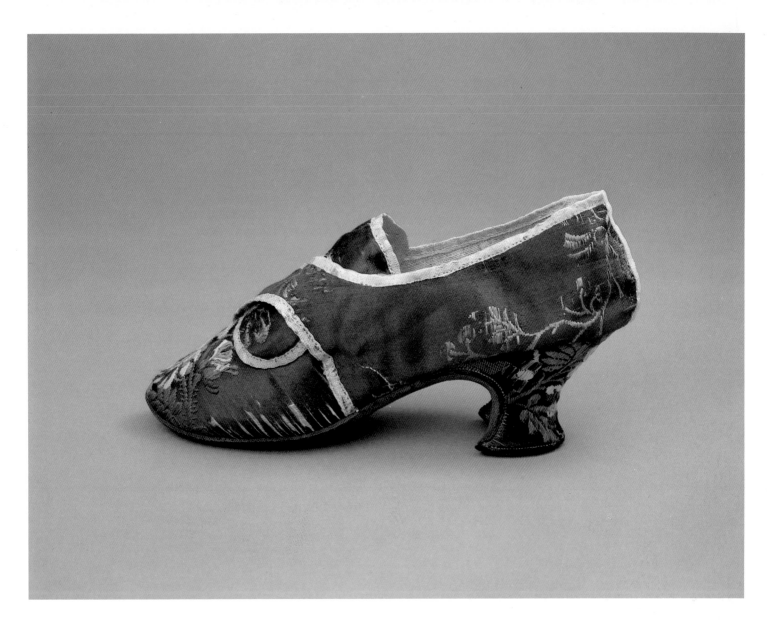

PLATE 17
Shoe (cat. no. 161).

PLATE 16
Dress (open robe and petticoat; cat. no. 14).

F<small>IG</small>. 6
Dress (open robe and petticoat, detail; cat. no. 14).

as they avoided all "affected motions of the head, all wanton...glances of the eyes, all ogling or winking, dimpling of the cheeks, or primming of the lips."[9] Wigs were the major costume item affecting head placement. In and out of fashion for both men and women throughout the century, wigs forced the head upright and limited its turns.

For carriage to be considered elegant, the shoulders and arms had to look relaxed, the upper arms curving gently away from the torso, not dropping straight down at the sides like servants or rustics. Correct placement of the hands was critical. A woman lightly rested them palms up, one on top of the other; they were turned slightly in toward the body at the front point of her bodice. The sleeves of the women's dresses in this catalogue and exhibition may be observed to be carefully shaped to reinforce this curved-arm stance (fig. 6; cat. no. 14, detail)—some cup under the back of the elbow, while others are darted at the inside elbow. Long before Napoleon, it was the practice for a man to place one hand (usually the right) lightly into the bosom of his waistcoat, which was left unbuttoned, except for three buttons at the waist. The other hand was placed under the side flap of the waistcoat above the swordhilt. Because the armholes of bodices, vests, and coats were cut very high under the arm, it was physically far more comfortable to hold the upper arms slightly away from the torso; to drop the arms straight down at the sides made the armholes bind. With his coat buttoned, a man could raise his arms up over his head and his coat would not ride up (fig. 8). These sleeves actually gave him more freedom to move in an upward direction than the coat sleeves of modern men's suits. Thus, both men's and women's sleeves were instrumental in supporting the elegant carriage of the arms.

The feet were always turned out. Not only did this throw the legs into an S-curve position, it also made an eighteenth-century gentleman "stand firm, easy, and graceful."[10] Encased in knee breeches, skintight stockings, and shoes with one- to three-inch heels, he cultivated a modified fourth-position ballet pose, displaying to all the world, and the ladies in particular, his well-developed, well-turned calves.

If a gentleman led with his calves, a lady, supported by her corset, led with her bosom. In this status-conscious century, corsets instantly proclaimed class distinction. The more severe the cut and boning of the corset, the higher the lady's class, provided that it was worn with apparent ease. It could not be laced too tightly, lest it produce stiff posture and awkward movement, which were both inelegant and unendurable. Actually, when correctly worn, the corset did most of the body display work for the lady; it obviously straightened her spine. Boned high in the back, it flattened the shoulder blades which, in turn, rounded and forced back the shoulders, resulting in a fashionably narrow back and uplifted or "prominent" bosom (fig. 7). The instant a lady started to slump, a gentle prod from the corset bones reminded her to straighten up. Although from today's point of view nothing could be physically more restrictive than a corset, to the eighteenth-century lady the corset conferred a degree of social security far more satisfying than physical comfort. The posture of status was consciously built into the corset's shape—no wonder it was such an essential part of her costume! As soon as she could walk, a little girl of the eighteenth century was put into training stays (less rigidly boned) which disciplined her young body to "naturally" develop that sought-after "air of good breeding," that correct and elegant posture which was the unmistakable stamp of the upper class.

Corsets were by no means restricted to girls. Aristocratic young boys were put into similar training stays (although usually without a front point) to mold their bodies into the fashionable shape and upright carriage expected of them as adults. At approximately age ten or eleven, boys discarded their stays, their chests by that time fashionably full and round.

Children spent long hours practicing the elegant art of carriage, assisted by such costume pieces as wigs, sleeves, shoes, and corsets. Having mastered this art, they proceeded to our second movement category, that of motions: walking, sitting, dancing.

FIG. 7
Nicholas de Launay (French, 1739–1792)
He Applied a Kiss to My Hand, Which I Sensed, 1777
Engraving on paper
7⅛ x 5½ in.
Los Angeles County Museum of Art, Mary B.
Regan Bequest
A.2674.31–143e

Wirklich, da hatte die Mama recht.
Ma foi, maman avoit raison.

II. Aufz. 5r Auftr.

FIG. 8
Daniel Chodowieki (German, 1726–1801)
Actually, Mother Was Right, 1784
Etching
3½ x 2 in.
Los Angeles County Museum of Art, Gift of Mr.
and Mrs. Fred Grunwald

FIG. 9
Daniel Chodowieki (German, 1726–1801)
Scenes from Life, 1770 (detail)
Engraving on paper
6⅜ x 8½ in.

MOTIONS

The motion of walking was so admired in the eighteenth century that all fashionable people spent a portion of each day publicly promenading in a park where, while nonchalantly strolling and conversing, they could display themselves and observe others displaying themselves to best advantage. Since walking began with the feet, the costume item that most influenced this movement was the shoe. Lacking arch supports, eighteenth-century shoes made the muscles of the feet and ankles work overtime. The higher the heel of the shoe, the more the weight of the body was thrown forward onto the balls of the feet, thereby shortening the stride; the narrower the heel, the more likely the ankle would wobble (plates 18a,18b,18c; cat. nos. 148,152,164). One was expected to maintain the same elegant carriage in walking as in standing still (fig. 9): "The rate of walking should be moderate, neither too quick or too slow. One suggests heedlessness, the other indolence; avoid these two extremes."[11] A gentleman was urged to take smooth steps, moderate in length, with legs turned out. He was cautioned to keep at least two yards away from ladies to avoid bumping their skirts or trampling their trains. A lady also was advised to walk smoothly, "swimmingly," but with steps shorter than a man's and without jostling her skirts.

The skirt, in fact, was the most challenging item of costume to manage in motion. Of the three fashionable eighteenth-century skirt shapes—round hoop, panniers, and bustle, each of which enlarged some aspect of the lady's hips—panniers were, undoubtedly, the ultimate status symbol. Extending up to four feet on either side of the hips, panniers caused traffic jams in the streets, riots over seats in the playhouses, and general consternation in such varied locales as parks, ballrooms, carriages, and church pews (fig. 10). Yet ladies were delighted with this fashion, which not only added dignity and grace to the figure, but set the wearer physically apart from the crowd, highlighting her to perfection as a work of art. To manage panniers successfully, the lady had to think *before* she moved. For example, if she found herself walking toward a too-narrow doorway, she would have to decide, long before reaching it, whether to turn gracefully and walk through it sideways or to collapse the sides of the panniers appropriately and, *without stopping*, smoothly translate her decision into action.

Panniers posed challenges to those surrounding the lady as well. Consider the dilemma of the gentleman accompanying a lady in panniers on a promenade or dance floor. Should he stand next to her where, in order to barely reach her hand, he would have to lean at an aesthetically awkward angle, or in front of her where her skirt would annoyingly bump up against him, or behind her? Usually this last was the most satisfactory solution for both parties (fig. 12).

Lord Chesterfield believed it was easier

to stand and walk gracefully than to sit gracefully. Certainly, sitting successfully in panniers—something of a cross between docking a boat and parallel parking—bears this out, as does the story of Baron Karl von Lyncker, page to the Duchess Anna Amalie of Prussia, who "conceived the brilliant notion of stretching the sides of his mistress's dress well out through both windows of the glass coach in which she went driving on Sundays."[12] Unfortunately for us, Lyncker neglects to describe how the duchess got into and out of this conveyance with grace.

Once seated, the lady's ability to move was regulated by her corset. She could bend sideways or backward, providing her corset cleared the waistline at the necessary points. But the length and stiffness of the corset front often prohibited her from bending forward at the waist or from crossing her thighs without doing herself serious damage (fig. 11). Consequently, a seated lady was most comfortable either perching on the edge of her chair or reclining sideways or backward, one elbow leaning on a table or furniture support, in an S-curve pose. If she accidently dropped a handkerchief or fan, she relied on a servant or gentleman to pick it up. Short-legged ladies, reclining backward on deep-seated chairs, often positioned a cushion or footstool beneath their feet to relieve the strain on their legs.

Chesterfield offered gentlemen this advice on sitting:

Awkward ill-bred people, being ashamed, commonly sit bolt upright and still; others too negligent...[wallow in their chairs]...but a man of fashion makes himself easy, and appears so, by leaning gracefully instead of lolling supinely; and by varying those easy attitudes, instead of that stiff immobility of a bashful booby.[13]

A gentleman never sat on the stiffened back skirt of his coat.

Of all the motions, dancing was the most formidable and most admired. It not only was a favorite leisure activity, but also provided the body with exercise, and when well done gave a "natural, easy, and graceful air to all the [other] motions of your body."[14] The most popular dance of the entire eighteenth century was the minuet. A stately, disciplined dance, it required exquisite timing, superb body control, intense concentration, and apparent effortlessness. Combining complex S-curve figures with improvised interludes, it demanded of the body a firm waist and controlled torso together with S-curve embellishments of the arms, hands, legs, and feet. The most elaborate minuet was danced at court by one couple at a time, for as long as seven minutes. It was a dance superbly designed to display the elegant motions and costumes of the performers to a highly appreciative and critical audience. From dance manuals we learn that a lady was allowed to take hold of her skirt at the sides—but only with her forefinger and thumb. Usually, she was not supposed to touch her skirt at all. Among the tales of danger on the dance floor comes that of

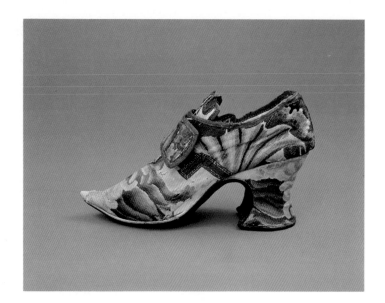

PLATE 18a
Shoe (cat. no. 148).

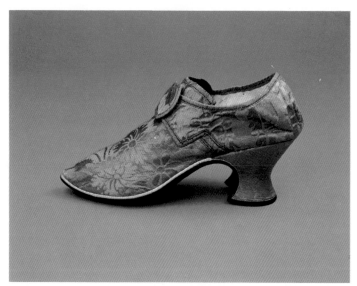

PLATE 18b
Shoe (cat. no. 152).

PLATE 18c
Shoe (cat. no. 164).

FIG. 10
Daniel Chodowiecki (German, 1726–1801)
Women in Church Pews, 1770 (detail)
Engraving on paper
3⅛ x 8¼ in.

FIG. 11
Daniel Chodowieki (German, 1726–1801)
Woman Seated at Table, 1770 (detail)
Engraving on paper
3³⁄₁₆ x 4¼ in.

Kluge Wahl!

PLATE 19 Dress (open robe; cat. no. 26).

PLATE 20   Dress (open robe and petticoat; cat. no. 34).

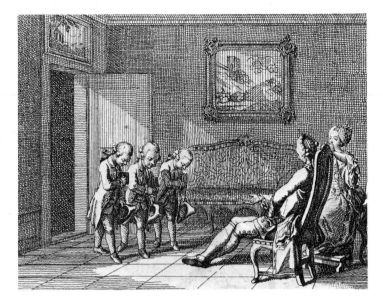

FIG. 13
Daniel Chodowieki (German, 1726–1801)
Children Thanking Their Father for Gifts, 1770
Engraving on paper
3³⁄₁₆ x 4¼ in.

"the Duke of Gloucester's [shoe] buckle [which] became tangled in Lady Bridget Lane's shoe rose in 1767, pulling the shoe off."[15]

The motions of walking, sitting, and dancing had several features in common. They each required a careful assessment of the physical dimensions added to the body by costumes; they involved a surprising degree of leg control to perform with "ease"; and they required the gentleman to give the lady some practical physical assistance.

MANNERS

Manners, our third category of movement, were expressions of feelings through accepted social rituals. While seventeenth-century manners were "marked by chivalry, grave dignity, formality: the manners of the throne room; [eighteenth-century manners] were characterized by gallantry, refinement, grace, and intimacy: the manners of the boudoir."[16] Manners included such salutations as the bow, the curtsy, and the kissing of the hand. Formal stationary bows and curtsies were exchanged when entering and leaving a room, beginning and ending a dance, and giving objects or receiving them (fig. 13). Less formal moving bows and curtsies were made in passing someone by barely dipping the body without stopping. These courtesies were performed smoothly and in keeping with a person's status. The higher the rank or the greater the regard in which a person was held, the deeper the bow or curtsy he or she received. Countless variations were possible.

Two methods of kissing the hand were in fashion. In one, still practiced in Europe today, the gentleman raised the back of the lady's hand to his lips. The other, now extinct, was an eighteenth-century form of blowing kisses. It was the most emotionally powerful gesture one could make, and was usually combined with a bow or curtsy. The procedure was to bring the forefinger of the right hand in a curved direction toward the lips and, without touching them, to reverse the curve and extend the hand outward and down in a continuous flowing motion.

Elegant manners required perfect timing, expert execution, and precise knowledge of the status of the person being complimented, so as to judge the degree to which the compliment should be paid.

ADDRESS

Our final category of movement is address: elegant bearing during conversation. As we have seen, conversation in the eighteenth century was a vital outlet for ideas and feelings. People engaged in both verbal and nonverbal conversations, often at the same time.

Verbal address consisted of speaking distinctly, gracefully, and briefly, without displaying anger, self-consciousness, or undue excitement. While it was desirable for the mind and speech to be agile and animated, the body had to remain quite still. Chesterfield cautioned his son: "Never hold anybody by the button, or the hand, in order to be heard out; for if people are not willing to hear you, you had much better hold your tongue than them."[17] He gave his godson this formula for checking the excess of passion: "Do everything in Minuet time, speak, think, and move always in that measure, equally free from the dulness of slow, or the hurry…of quick time."[18] And he further encouraged his son with this observation: "The characteristic of a well-bred man is, to converse with his inferiors without insolence, and with his superiors with respect and ease. He talks to kings…without the least concern of mind, or awkwardness of body."[19]

One of the most fascinating aspects of eighteenth-century address was the potential nonverbal language of such costume accessories as fans, snuffboxes, and handkerchiefs. A person might say one thing with words and just the opposite with a fan position or a pinch of snuff. The accessory that most clearly symbolized the ideal of eighteenth-century nonverbal address was the fan (plate 21; cat. no. 4). "Women are armed with fans as men with swords and sometimes do more execution with them," warned Addison in 1711.[20] A lady without her fan was considered undressed. It was her dear and constant companion, revealing the secrets of her head and heart to all who could read the language of the fan, which could assume a thousand different fleeting moods. Without saying a word,

FIG. 14
Jan van Grevenbroeck (Italian, 1737–1807)
The Huntress, c. 1780
Watercolor on paper
from Grevenbroeck's *Gli Abiti de veneziani di quasi
ogni eta con diligenza raccolti e dipinti nel secolo
XVIII,* vol. 1.

a lady could use it to flirt outrageously one minute and severely reprimand a lover the next. According to Addison, the mere flutter of a fan was fraught with drama.[21]

The manipulation of accessories like the fan required great dexterity of the fingers and wrists. They added a rich, silent vocabulary to the art of conversation and were indispensable to the art of flirtation.

The elegant art of eighteenth-century movement was sophisticated, charming, and varied. It reflected both the attitude and the personality of the individual who performed it, and extended even to riding costume (plate 22; cat. no. 48; fig. 14). In order to appear "easy," its performance required surprisingly intense mental concentration and bodily discipline, particularly of the legs. For its sustained effect it relied on the support of eighteenth-century costumes, whose surfaces concealed intriguing potentials for movement, that subtle yet significant dimension of the behavior of those elegant ladies and gentlemen who preened, glided, flourished, and flirted over the canvas of the eighteenth-century world, themselves the premier works of art.

PLATE 21   Dress (gown and petticoat; cat. no. 4).

PLATE 22 Riding Habit (cat. no. 48).

NOTES

1
A. Petrie, *The Polite Academy*, 8th ed., London [178-], p. 60.

2
J. Levron, *The Man of Manners: or Plebeian Polish'd*, 3rd ed., London [1768], title page.

3
P.D.S. Chesterfield, *The Letters of Philip Dormer Stanhope, 4th Earl of Chesterfield*, ed. B. Dobrée, London, 1932, 4:1408, letter of Sept. 27, 1749.*

4
N. Waugh, *Corsets and Crinolines*, London, 1954, p. 68.

5
K. Clark, *Civilisation*, New York, 1969, p. 240.

6
K. Tomlinson, *The Art of Dancing*, London, 1735, p. 3. Tomlinson notes in his introduction that the text was written considerably prior to publication in 1724.

7
Petrie, p. 35.

8
Ibid., p. 36.

9
Ibid., p. vi.

10
Ibid., p. 36.

11
P. Rameau, *The Dancing Master*, trans. C.W. Beaumont, 1931; reprint ed., New York [1970], p. 4. The original French text was published in 1725.

12
M. von Boehn, *Modes and Manners*, trans. J. Joshua, London, 1935, vol. 4, *The Eighteenth Century*, p. 164.

13
Chesterfield, 4: 1748, letter of June 10, 1751.

14
Petrie, p. xxxi.

15
J. Swann, *Shoe Buckles*, Northampton, 1981.

16
M. Baur-Heinhold, *The Baroque Theatre: A Cultural History of the 17th and 18th Centuries*, trans. M. Whittall, New York, 1967, p. 7.

17
Chesterfield, 4: 1245, letter of Oct. 19, 1748.

18
Chesterfield, 6: 2692, letter of Dec. 12, 1765.

19
Chesterfield, 3: 1151, letter of May 17, 1748.

20
Addison, *The Spectator*, Cincinnati, 1857, letter no. 102, June 27, 1711, p. 150.

21
Ibid., pp. 150–51.

*Throughout these notes, all dates of Chesterfield letters are Old Style.

NATALIE ROTHSTEIN
DEPUTY KEEPER,
DEPARTMENT OF TEXTILES AND DRESS
VICTORIA AND ALBERT MUSEUM

THE ELEGANT ART OF WOVEN SILK

"For many years past the manufacturers of silks have puzzled both their own and tortured the pattern-drawers' brains to contrive new fashions."

G. SMITH,
THE LABORATORY, OR SCHOOL OF ARTS, 1756

A fine gentleman stands in the Accademia in Venice; his concern for the tourist is minimal. His weary elegance personifies the informal fashions of his day, yet the silks he wears are decorated with some of the most extraordinary patterns to be seen in the West before the extravagances of art nouveau. Count Valetti was painted by Vittore Ghislandi in about 1709 (fig. 15). By comparison, Mrs. Siddons, one of the most popular and fashionable actresses of her day, painted by Gainsborough seventy-six years later, is dressed with great restraint (fig. 16). The disparity between the two images dramatizes the vicissitudes of fashion, which determine not only what should be worn and by whom, but which group of artisans will flourish as a result.

If we think of eighteenth-century silks it is almost automatically of their use in costume rather than in furnishings. In order to see why this should be so, we must look at some of the many uses for fine silks in this period. While the eighteenth-century silk designer/weaver built upon two thousand or more years of experience, the European textile printer of the time had had only about twenty years of trial and error on which to look back; until the late 1740s the patterns of fashionable materials were woven and not printed. During this century silk designers and manufacturers attained a mastery of their technique, a mastery most clearly seen in the work produced by the silk industries of those traditional rivals, England and France. Surviving examples

of this rivalry, which include a dated series of English and some French designs, enable us to follow in great detail developments in style as they unfolded.

LYON AND LONDON

Lyon is today one of the greatest industrial centers of France, with only tenuous links with the silk industry of its past—even though a few of the oldest and most distinguished firms continue in business. It was an important city even before Louis XIV's minister Colbert gave protection and encouragement to the Grande Fabrique in the second half of the seventeenth century. The silk industry was highly organized during the eighteenth century, with strict regulations governing work methods and cloth quality. Unfortunately, the rival interests of the *maîtres marchands*, who sold the cloth, the *maîtres fabricants*, the master weavers, and the *canuts*, the journeymen weavers, resulted in constant friction and much industrial strife; new regulations were passed throughout the seventeenth and eighteenth centuries, as first one faction and then another prevailed. In addition, the economic stresses of the Ancien Régime made production hazardous: there were internal customs duties to be paid between different cities and import duties on raw materials (France had to import much of her silk; the silk for the warp came largely from Piedmont and that for the weft from the Levant), to say nothing of the

FIG. 15
Vittore Ghislandi (Italian, 1655–1743)
Portrait of Count G.B. Valetti, c. 1709
Oil on canvas
89 x 54 in.
Accademia di Belle Arti, Venice

FIG. 16
Thomas Gainsborough (English, 1727–1788)
Mrs. Siddons, 1785
Oil on canvas
49³/₁ x 39¹/₁ in.
The National Gallery, London

protective measures taken by the British against the French. Not surprisingly, there were many bankruptcies, of which many records survive to provide us with a rich source of information about this oppressive atmosphere.

But despite a succession of wars, despite national bankruptcy in 1707, despite the loss of its chief customers during the French Revolution, despite the century-long upheavals which followed the Revolution, and despite the ultimate extinction of the European silkworm in the nineteenth century, the Lyon silk industry survived until the mid-twentieth century. Up to that time, the demands of fashion, and their own superb quality, ensured that Lyon silks retained their leadership throughout the world. French silks carried off prizes in the international exhibitions of the nineteenth century as they had won markets in the eighteenth century. Indeed, France began holding industrial exhibitions in 1799, under Napoleon. Through personal and official orders, Napoleon did much to offset the ravages of the Revolution in Lyon.

In the eighteenth century, France was ahead of other nations in founding training schools for both craftsmen and designers. The artists who worked for the French silk industry appear to have been attached to individual firms rather than working free-lance, as most of those in England did at this time. Though their names and some signed designs have come down to us, these designers have, apart from such well-known

artists as Jean Revel (1684–1751) and Philippe de Lasalle (1723–1805), remained shadowy figures. The economic facts about the Lyon silk industry are much easier to discover and assess.[1]

The London silk industry grew from small beginnings in the City of London in the seventeenth century to become the main rival of Lyon. Protected by the Navigation Acts and British control of the seas, it received its real boost during the Wars of the Spanish Succession at the beginning of the eighteenth century. As the industry grew so did the district of Spitalfields, which became forever associated with it. Many Huguenot refugees settled there and entered the industry before the revocation of the Edict of Nantes in 1685, and later, in the 1720s and 1730s. Most had never had any connection with silk in France, for Huguenots were forbidden to enter the Grande Fabrique in Lyon. In any case, many of these workers came from farming country in Normandy and Bas Poitou.

From the outset the Flowered Silk Branch of the industry dominated its affairs, and the survival of over one thousand dated silk designs by James Leman (1688–1745), Joseph Dandridge (1666–1747), Christopher Baudouin (settled in England in the late seventeenth century, died before 1736), and Anna Maria Garthwaite (1690–1763), inscribed with dates, technical details, and the names of their customers, have permitted us to establish a complete picture of the English silk industry of this period.

The Warner Archive of pattern books, largely from the firm of Batchelor, Ham and Perigal, enables us to follow the development of design throughout the eighteenth century.[2] Economic conditions in London differed very greatly from those in Lyon. The London industry benefited from its proximity to Parliament, to the Commissioners for Trades and Plantations and later the Board of Trade, to the Court, to the City, and to the center of fashion. Its most important overseas markets were the American colonies, and many of its silks have been preserved to this day on the eastern seaboard of the United States.

THE DRAWLOOM

To make a pattern that is not geometrical and is on a large scale it is necessary to control the warp threads individually, or at least in small bunches of two-to-ten threads at a time. The mechanism created to do this was the drawloom (fig. 17). Apart from two major modifications, discussed below, it remained unchanged from the early Middle Ages until the late eighteenth century. It was upon the drawloom that all of the patterned, woven materials seen in this exhibition and catalogue were made.

The pattern for the drawloom was preselected for each line of the design, and the lashes (fig. 18), which picked out the required threads to be lifted, were arranged in sequence so that the design could be repeated at will. The weaver

FIG. 17
Bernard (French, second half of 18th century)
Drawloom for the Making of Ciselé Velvet, 1777
Engraving on paper
8⅞ x 13⅜ in.
from Diderot-D'Alembert, *Encyclopedia on the Weaving of Silk Fabrics*
Los Angeles County Museum of Art, Gift of the Costume Council
M.82.24.5–135

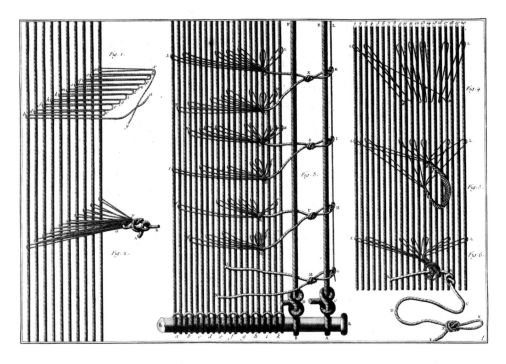

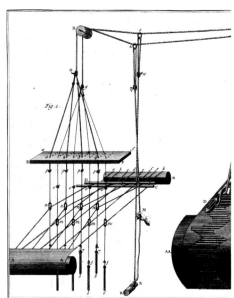

FIG. 18
Bernard (French, second half of 18th century)
Lashes, 1777
Engraving on paper
8⅞ x 13⅜ in.
from Diderot-D'Alembert, *Encyclopedia on the Weaving of Silk Fabrics*
Los Angeles County Museum of Art, Gift of the Costume Council
M.82.24.5–135

FIG. 19
Bernard (French, second half of 18th century)
Figure Harness, 1777 (detail)
Engraving on paper
12½ x 18¼ in.
from Diderot-D'Alembert, *Encyclopedia on the Weaving of Silk Fabrics*
Los Angeles County Museum of Art, Gift of the Costume Council
M.82.24.5–135

Fig. 20
Christopher Baudouin (English, b. France, d. before 1736)
Textile Design, 1724
Watercolor on paper
Victoria and Albert Museum, London
No. 5973/18

opened the shed by pressing his foot on the appropriate treadle while the drawboy or girl pulled hard on the group of lashes for the particular line of the design. It was an essential feature of the loom that the warp threads were under a dual control, from the shafts to determine the weave and from the lashes to make the pattern. As far as is known, only two major modifications were made, probably in the early seventeenth century—the comber board and the simple. The comber board, placed above the figure harness (fig. 19), permitted the pattern to be repeated across the textile in an even sequence. By tying the cords for each repeat at the neck of the pulley above the comber board the total number was reduced. The simple was then attached to these cords and the lashes were attached to the simple. It thus became possible for the drawboy to work from the side of the loom.

The design was first drawn freehand (fig. 20) and then redrawn on "rule" or point paper (fig. 21) in a particular proportion suitable for the thread count of the intended material. If the wrong paper were chosen, the design would be distorted. From this draft the lashes were tied, a line at a time (fig. 18). The loom was set up in the normal way, but the weaver often took the warp threads from two beams, one for the main or ground warp and one for the binding warp, which was generally only controlled by the shafts. Its function was to bind the wefts pushed to the face of the

textile by the warp threads controlled by the figure harness. This binding warp was set up in the loom in a regular proportion to the ground or main warp. When all this was completed the weaver would run through the pattern, stopping to retie incorrect lashes or to correct other faults. In spite of this care, mistakes are found in surviving textiles. It could take a weaver and his apprentice from three to six weeks to set up the loom, tie the lashes, and run off a trial sample.

Although we can group possible silk-weaving techniques into neat, orderly classes, the eighteenth-century designer and manufacturer were not concerned with such categorizations. They frequently combined technical effects, each one adding to the price and the time it took to weave. The painting of silks is in one sense the simplest technique, yet it is the one requiring the most skill by the individual workman. Chinese craftsmen painted dress silks for the European market, filling the orders of the East India Companies of England, France, and Holland. Such materials could not be legally sold or worn in France or England, but as Prohibited Goods they were legally exported and sold in the American colonies, and many of these have survived in the United States. Catalogue number 395 (plate 23) is a pastiche of a woven silk design of about 1740 that could well have been painted at any time within the following ten or fifteen years.

It is possible to construct a design to be

Fig. 2

FIG. 22
Panel (cat. no. 405).

Verd

Jeaune

Lilas clair.

Lilas foncé.

Violet

Pieds.

1   2   3   4

FIG. 21
Bernard (French, second half of 18th century)
Textile Design, 1777 (detail)
Engraving on point paper
12½ x 18¼ in.
from Diderot-D'Alembert, *Encyclopedia on the Weaving of Silk Fabrics*
Los Angeles County Museum of Art, Gift of the Costume Council
M.82.24.5–135

FIG. 23
Panel (cat. no. 396).

brocaded without any binding warp to hold the motifs in place. In such a material the floats must be short if they are not to catch on other surfaces and break. Catalogue number 405 (fig. 22) is, therefore, one of the simpler silks, but even in this piece the warp has been shaded in gradations of blue which give a rippled effect to the surface. Also, since the pattern has been carried out in metal thread, the effect is subtle rather than simple. This silk also has a self-colored effect in the ground, which increases the illusion. In their Trades Union Agreement with the master weavers in 1769, the journeymen weavers of London listed this effect as a "flush" and charged at least 4d (pence) a yard extra for it.[3] Such effects are colorless but give an additional richness to the texture. They may even carry important parts of the design, as in the cartouches they form in catalogue number 398. The flush may be "made with the ground shuttle,"[4] in which case the weave is broken at these points, or an additional weft may be used, as in catalogue numbers 383 and 398 (plate 25).

There may also be more than one warp, that is, there may be two or three rollers instead of one. In order to get the ribbed, textured *cannelé* effects in silks such as catalogue number 386 (plate 24) or ecclesiastical materials, such a warp had to be used. The looms used to make elaborate silks such as these had shafts which were divided into two series, one lifting and one depressing. With such an arrangement

the weaver could make damask in which the visual effect was achieved by a contrast of light reflecting from the vertical warp and the horizontal weft. The warp effect and the weft effect appear in the same line—a minor mathematical problem when drafting the pattern. A damask could, however, be brocaded like catalogue number 387 so that the polychrome details appeared on top of the damask, an effect that showed itself as the wearer moved or the candle flickered. If the warp and weft of the damask are of different colors, the pattern stands out boldly as in the worsted, catalogue number 396 (fig. 23). This piece, too, has additional brocaded details, but they are subordinate to the damask pattern. It is typical of the glazed worsteds woven in Norwich and in London (as well as the Low Countries) whose patterns echoed those of fashionable silks.

In a tissue or *lampas*[5] the two warps have separate functions. The binding warp in eighteenth-century textiles usually binds the pattern in three-to-one twill, thus permitting large blocks of color. The ground warp made the pattern as dictated by the lashes on the figure harness. In the ground of the textile this warp was also controlled by shafts to make, say, a satin or taffeta ground, to contrast with the twill of the patterned areas. The pattern effects in a tissue could be achieved either by wefts carried from selvage to selvage (cat. no. 391), or by brocaded wefts only (plate 26; cat. no. 400), or by a mixture of the two

PLATE 23
Panel (cat. no. 395).

PLATE 24
Panel (cat. no. 386).

PLATE 25
Panel (cat. no. 398).

PLATE 26
Panel (cat. no. 400).

(cat. no. 381).

In a true velvet, one roller carries the foundation warp which is combined with a ground weft to keep the fabric together, while for the other a set of bobbins is substituted (fig. 17). Each pile warp thread is wound upon its individual bobbin because its journey through the material may vary in length from that of its neighbor. On the shoot which is to make the pile the weaver inserts a wire instead of a weft. This has either a round cross section or a groove, ● or ⊌ . When the weaver has about nine inches or a foot of wires he cuts the pile with a special knife which slides through the groove. Since the cut pile is higher than the uncut, the latter remains undamaged—unless his hand slips! He then slides out the wire for the uncut pile.

Special threads may be used to enhance the texture further. Thus metal threads may be plain (filé),[6] with a silver or gold strip wound on a silk core; frost (frisé), with the silk core overtwisted to produce a sparkling effect; plate (in the terminology of James Leman and Anna Maria Garthwaite), or lamé in French usage, with the metal strip used flat; or a frisé thread may be combined with a lamé strip to produce clinquant. A silk thread may be treated like a frisé, and, if either yellow or pale gray, may deceive the eye into thinking it really is metal. Moreover, using a yellow silk core with a silver strip deceives the beholder into thinking it is at least silver gilt if not pure gold. Chenille ("snail" in eighteenth-century

English), a specially made thread with a pipe cleaner-like appearance, was used to give furry effects. First used in the late seventeenth century, it was also popular in the 1730s and 1760s for special effects, such as the fur in catalogue number 386.

At a time when the raw material was more precious than labor, brocading was a highly desirable technique. This was especially true of silks woven in gold and silver. It was the designer's responsibility "to prevent as much as can be the expense of workmanship, and yet make as great a show for the money as possible."[7] The back of catalogue number 405 shows a very economical use of silver thread.

As if this were not enough, additional details could be embroidered, as in the velvet suiting, catalogue number 378. By the mid-1770s embroidered motifs were as commonly found as woven ones; so catalogue number 404 (plate 27) may be compared with woven silks of about 1776–77.[8]

An edict was even issued in Lyon in 1778[9] to give the same protection to embroidered as to woven designs. It had to be reissued in 1783. Within a few years woven designs were themselves imitating embroidered ones. The silk weavers of Lyon regarded "l'usage de la broderie"[10] as responsible for many of their ills.

All the silks discussed and shown here demonstrate the mastery of texture achieved by the eighteenth-century designer and manufacturer. Such mastery is a third dimension which can hardly be

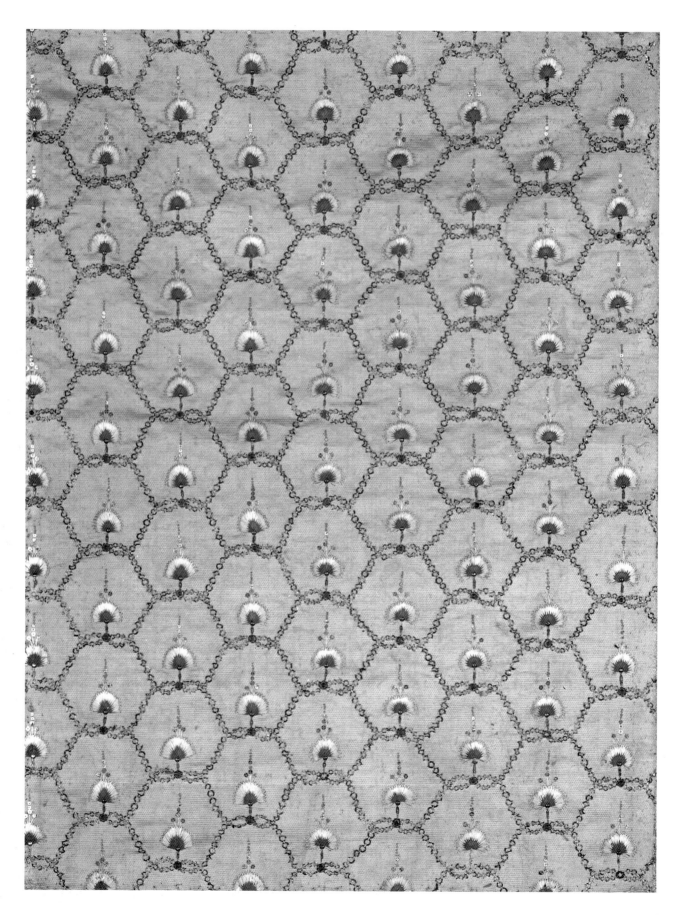

PLATE 27
Panel (cat. no. 404).

appreciated behind museum glass. It was achieved by the designer's study, while he was still an apprentice, of the loom and its possibilities, as well as by artistic ability. The artist then could work in what we today call the applied arts without a loss of caste. His achievements depended in the long run, however, not only upon individual inspiration but upon the pressure of market forces to produce something new for the next season.

FURNISHING SILKS

During the period between 1690 and about 1715 the richest houses had sumptuous interiors. Beds were hung with silk damask —often scarlet, the most expensive color— with enormous patterns carefully matched, the four corner posts surmounted by deeply carved vases with plumes, waiting to gather dust in the ensuing centuries. Walls were hung with matching damask, and there were squabs (ottomanlike pieces of furniture), chairs, and sofas to match. All had extra loose covers[11] en suite for protection—even the curtains. It is not uncommon to find orders for two or three hundred yards in the royal accounts and in those of the greatest nobility. There were also "stained" (i.e., painted or printed) Indian quilts, Turkey carpets, tapestries on the walls, and, for the king, silk sheets.

State rooms in royal palaces retained their silk in the 1720s and so did the richest merchants' parlors, but in other interiors there was an increasing use of worsted upholstery, harrateen, and moreen. The tapestries came down and were rolled up and put into the attics. As the turkeywork upon the chairs wore out it was replaced by leather. Cane chairs began appearing in the more fashionable rooms. The formality of the French court ensured that the richest materials remained in use at Versailles on an extensive scale. While the English court still had its taffeta blinds and silk sheets, orders for wallpaper began superseding those for silk damask, so that, after a time, only the state rooms and the royal barges were invariably decked out in silk. Printed fustians matched the wallpaper when two pavilions were built for George II at Hampton Court in 1747. They contained hundreds of yards of "royal chintz paper" and "fine printed cotton" with "fine festoons of flowers in the cotton" but not a single silk.[12] The chief purveyors of furnishing velvets and silk damasks throughout the century were Italians, while the French and English concentrated their industries upon dress materials. American portraits of the late eighteenth century certainly show silk upholstery, but not used in the lavish way it had been in the early part of the century. By the middle of the century John Singleton Copley's portraits were revealing that prosperous American merchants' homes were furnished as comfortably as those of their counterparts in England. However, it should not be surprising that printed cottons and calicoes enjoyed a wide appeal during most of the century. For as their defenders proclaimed in a campaign of 1719, "nothing else washes near so well."[13]

It is a popular delusion that in the eighteenth century people washed neither themselves nor their fabrics. On the contrary, London supported a good number of "scowerers" and the Lord Chamberlain's office spent large sums each year on cleaning, unripping, and remaking curtains and bedding—as well as getting rid of the bugs and rats!

By the 1760s and 1770s the most fashionable members of society were turning to the painted or papered walls in the Neoclassical taste epitomized by Robert Adam (1728–1792) in England. In France, however, the firm of Camille Pernon was furnishing the courts of Europe, from France to Sweden and Russia, with the grand silks designed by Philippe de Lasalle.[14] Some have been preserved in the Mobilier National in Paris, and there are examples from the period in the Los Angeles collection (cat. nos. 379, 394). Versions of catalogue number 394 have been repeated many times since. Although the name Philippe de Lasalle is associated with such furnishings, he was by no means the only designer working in the period; thus not all of these silks can be attributed to him with any certainty. The grand Neoclassical style was expressed just as well by a Réveillon wallpaper.[15] In the same way, the Gobelins provided tapestries and the

Savonnerie carpets for the same elite clientele. Catalogue number 385 probably dates from the end of the century, its Neoclassical motifs combined with a pair of sphinx-like creatures, which may, perhaps, be an allusion to Napoleon's Egyptian campaign.

SILKS FOR THE CHURCH

A most important customer for fine silks in the seventeenth and eighteenth centuries was the Church, both in Europe and in South America. Although gifts of fine textiles were readily accepted and turned into vestments for high mass, others were woven specifically for the Church. At first in competition with Venice, Lyon came to dominate production. Characteristic *ornements d'église* have heavily diapered gold or silver grounds with point repeats and with elaborate architectural scenes or scrolls—all in the style of about 1736 but probably made from about 1740 to 1765. A type of velvet said to have been made in Lyon for the first time in 1720[16] "à ramages, raz, façonné, figuré ou découpé à l'imitation de ceux de Venise," was made of pure silk, or mixed with gold and silver. This kind of velvet was "propres à des ornements d'église," as well as furniture, suits, and linings of carriages (vehicles that in their time were as much a status symbol as the modern expensive automobile). All the references to *ornements d'église* stress the sizable element of gold and silver, as well as colored silks.

In his treatise on silk designing, the silk designer and author Joubert de L'Hiber-

derie discussed, for instance, "grands desseins, fonds frisés, fonds cannellés, fonds guillochés, fonds argents et or pour ornement d'église."[17] Describing *ras de Sicile,* another rich fabric, he said it was made with two warps and "de tres belle matière & sans aucune économie, elle est d'un si bon usage qu'on voit encore dans vieilles robes, des meubles antiques & d'anciens ornemens d'église..."[18] These silks can be distinguished from normal commercial production for fashionable dress by their over-elaborate grounds, their large quantities of gold and silver thread, their use of too much chenille, a heaviness and lack of spontaneity in their designs, by their point repeats (used especially at times when straight repeats were normally in fashion),[19] and, when made up as vestments, by their total lack of variation from fashionable dress.

Only very occasionally are there any indications in actual eighteenth-century vestments that the material had been woven to fit a vestment. In the seventeenth and in the nineteenth century, on the other hand, orphreys and the like were frequently woven into the designs. The hood of a cope in the Abegg Stiftung in Bern is a rare example of a piece which reveals its purpose.[20] The use of allusive symbols such as ears of corn or vine leaves did not preclude the use of the material for a secular purpose, or indeed for use by Jewish congregations. Occasionally, even, a Christian symbol was omitted from the design by simply not

FIG. 24
Textile Design
France, 1739
Watercolor on paper
Victoria and Albert Museum, London
No. 5974.22

brocading it. There are large collections of such silks in the National Museum in Prague, and in many Italian churches. Occasionally, the material can be dated by some event, but this is rare.

The Church's use of substantial outdated designs, to induce a solemn atmosphere, has meant that many such silks have survived. As Joubert said, they were made of excellent materials and wore very well. Four Los Angeles silks fall into this group and two others may, as well. Of the four, the most obvious are catalogue numbers 392 and 377 (plates 28, 29). Superficially a silk from about 1736–39, the first has several characteristics typical of *ornements d'église*: the point repeat, crosshatched leaves, bunches of grapes, and the central motif, depending on three kinds of fruit. It lacks the spontaneity of French silk designs of 1750–60; the style of the 1730s has fossilized (fig. 24). The second is even more obviously an *ornement d'église* and its design may be compared with those in several other collections.[21] It has a crosshatched silver ground, woven, as Joubert says, "sans aucune économie." The candelabra and three bowls of fruit may be read as allusive symbols but, and this was important to the manufacturer, they did not have to be. Consequently, these panels could line a carriage as well as decorate a set of vestments. Thus the designs could remain in the manufacturer's repertoire from, say, 1740, when this type of design was falling out of fashion, to the mid-1750s or later, a great saving

PLATE 28
Panel (cat. no. 392).

76

PLATE 29
Panel (cat. no. 377, detail).

PLATE 29a
Panel (cat. no. 384).

77

in investment to him. At first sight, there may seem little to distinguish catalogue number 384 (plate 29a) from dress materials of the 1750s, but again we find a point repeat, an elaborately textured *cannelé* ground, and the inevitable use of gold and silver. Point repeats were not normal in the 1750s. There is another in a similar style in Lyon.[22] Catalogue number 389 (plate 29b) may be the back of a chasuble. This in itself would not be enough to distinguish it as an *ornement d'église*. The design, its swags formed by textured oval shapes in gold thread, is reminiscent of those of the 1750s. This is a most attractive silk, its repeat carefully matched at the selvages. Nevertheless, it shares with the others a point repeat and just a little too much detail in the ground.[23]

DRESS MATERIALS
1690–1712

In the first chapter of his book on chinoiserie, Hugh Honour describes more vividly than other art historians the "vision of Cathay," formed by an amalgam of the styles of different countries, media, and periods, which obsessed the West in the seventeenth century.[24] It was not simply China, Japan, or India but Persia and Turkey as well which gave birth to an extraordinary style in silk design, code-named in the twentieth century "the Bizarre."[25] Its characteristics can be seen in modest dimensions in Eastern silks from the late seventeenth century, which were then still

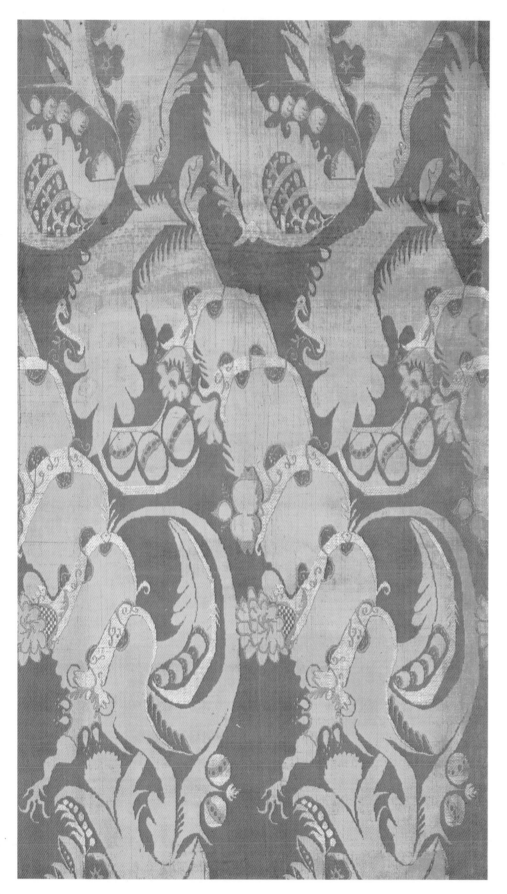

PLATE 30
Panel (cat. no. 393).

being legally and avidly imported into Europe. Catalogue number 391 is typical of the 1690s; its green ground and white pattern with brocaded tan details can be matched by similar silks elsewhere. In a few years, with motifs doubled in size, this design would be the fully fledged Bizarre.

From the same period, or perhaps as late as 1700, but very different in style, is catalogue number 375a, a charming fragment brocaded in silk and chenille, probably woven for the Portuguese market or for Macao. Its lively birds contrast with the formal sprigs, whose ancestry can be traced to the early seventeenth century. The prohibition of oriental silks both in France and in England did not kill the taste for the exotic. On the contrary, since there were no direct models with which to compare European silks legally on sale, designers' imaginations were unlimited. One silk woven in about 1707 even has a false Gujarati mark woven into it.[26]

The fully developed Bizarre, apart from the repertoire of its ornament, combined abstract shapes with very unlikely objects. Such designs were very long. Catalogue number 393 (plate 30), for example, is thirty-eight inches long, but the repeat is incomplete. The piece has the marked diagonal movement which many of these silks share. While the sources of its design are almost impossible to suggest, it has a touch of *japonaiserie* in such details as the belted tennis balls which occur in odd moments in the design. A glimpse at how

FIG. 25
Alexis Simon Belle (pseud.) (English, 1674–1734)
Portrait, 1714
Oil on canvas
54½ x 42½ in.
Victoria and Albert Museum, London

such eccentric designs as this may have been devised can be found in G. Smith's *The Laboratory, or School of Arts*. He remembered a customer telling a pattern-drawer to "draw the gridiron and sprats it will make as odd a pattern as you can think on."[27]

The most extreme form of the Bizarre passed by about 1705, and, from 1706 onward, its later phases can be followed through the designs of James Leman. Catalogue number 397 may be compared with his designs of 1708. This is not to suggest that this silk is English, because by then Fashion was international; silks had to be made to sell. The fence motifs seem to have been current in 1708–09. In Leman's work, too, the line of dots around a larger motif can be found, as can some of the diagonal diapered effects.[28] The disproportion between fences and flowers can be seen in many other silks of the time. The repeat is very long, but the designer has disguised the elongation by introducing two main motifs, the fences at one level and a line of chimney pots at the next.

1712–1731

After 1711–12 bizarre shapes retreated to the damask grounds of textiles, lavishly decorated with gold and silver scrolls, and leaves and flowers in colored silks. Favorite colors for the ground were pale blue or salmon pink. Catalogue number 387 has faded because this shade of pink dye was very fugitive. The original effect, however,

with silver-gilt thread on pink, would have been sumptuous. The vegetation in these designs sprouts delicate semi-naturalistic flowers, often outlined in a paler color, pink with blue or vice versa, for example. The asymmetrical structure was inherited from the Bizarre designs of the previous decade. Although there are few Leman designs from the period 1712–17, there are several dated portraits which show the progress of design. Catalogue number 387 can be compared with Belle's portrait of an unknown man dating from 1714, now in the Victoria and Albert Museum[29] (fig. 25), and with Kneller's signed portrait of Caroline of Ansbach, Princess of Wales, in the Royal Collection, dated 1716. These portraits show that, however stiff the material may seem, it was designed to be worn.

The dominant pattern of the 1720s was the so-called "lace" pattern which, as Miss Santina Levey has shown, influenced the designs of lace rather than the other way around.[30] There are three examples in the Los Angeles collection (cat. nos. 381, 388, 399). The lace pattern owed something to the formal patterns of seventeenth-century furnishing silks, with stylized leaves surrounding a central floral motif. But it owed even more to the designs of the late teens, which were turned to face one another in a point rather than a straight repeat. Lace patterns were woven in France, England, and Holland and, although their subtle texture and coloring make them rather hard to see in portraits, there are

designs by English designers and by a group of French artists in the Cabinet des Estampes of the Bibliothèque Nationale in Paris. Nearly all of these are dated. Through these examples we can follow the pattern from its most abstract form, which appeared about 1720, to designs in which lacy diapered effects predominate, to its final stage, about 1730–31. At that time, the leaves and flowers, which had been growing larger since the mid-1720s, finally broke through the lace framework; only an echo of that framework remains in a few designs of 1732.

The earliest lace pattern silk in this series of Los Angeles examples is probably catalogue number 388, from about 1724–25. Its date may be established by comparison with a design by Christopher Baudouin dated 1724 (fig. 20), as well as with one in Paris inscribed "Nouveau du Printems de l'année 1725."[31] Catalogue number 399 (plate 31) is a much less sophisticated English or Dutch silk, which may, nevertheless, date from the same time. Its narrow width, seventeen and one-half inches (one-half yard wide by silk manufacturers' measurements), simplified treatment of design, and predominance of leaves and flowers over the lightly diapered ground are indications of its origins.[32] In catalogue number 381 (plate 32) little plain ground has been left amid the layers of diapered and floral decoration. The silk can be dated to 1727 or 1728 and shows the lace pattern style at its apogee. The central motif has,

PLATE 31
Panel (cat. no. 399).

PLATE 32
Panel (cat. no. 381).

82

however, begun to push outward the surrounding lace. Significantly, too, the flowers are large and distinct. While the serrated edge of the lace is prominent, it is bordered by a flowering branch, a detail which can also be seen in other silks. The three daughters of George II wore silks like this when Mercier painted their portraits in 1728.[33] The lace patterns, with their use of different metal threads, their subtle command of texture, and their diapered panels apparently on different planes, are the epitome of the eighteenth-century silk designer's art.

1731–1742

Between 1732 and 1735 a total revolution in silk design took place, first described by Peter Thornton in his study of the work of Jean Revel.[34] It is understandable that after ten years of subtly evolving lace patterns, fashion should want something quite new. Moreover, the cut of clothes had changed neither quickly nor radically in the preceding period. Having exploited the surface of the fabric in the 1720s, designers now sought to give three-dimensional effect to their designs. The first to experiment with the idea was a man named Courtois, who laid tones of color side by side in order to produce the effect of rounded forms. His favorite motif was an island in space with a tree and prehistoric-looking flowers, sometimes accompanied by small architectural details in a different scale. Although its aesthetic purpose was

usually misunderstood, this very striking motif was widely copied.

Three-dimensional patterns appear in Anna Maria Garthwaite's work in 1734. It is to this period, too, that catalogue number 390 (plate 34) belongs.[35] Though point repeats do not really suit this type of design, they have been incorporated here. This feature, together with the narrow width, slightly livid coloring, and flat treatment of the design, which totally misses the effect for which the original was aiming, suggests a center far from Lyon—perhaps Holland. The quality of the silk is excellent and the dyes are rich. Catalogue number 407 is a total contrast. This is one of the finest silks in the Los Angeles collection, showing as it does the astonishing degree to which rounded form could be simulated through use of the *points rentrés* technique invented by Jean Revel. By this method, adjacent colors were dovetailed as in tapestry weaving.

Since silk designers had by this part of the century learned to handle perspective, it was an easy step to decorate a dress silk with a landscape, or with a ship at sea glimpsed through a grotto (a favorite motif), or, perhaps, with a fountain playing in a distant garden. One of Joubert's critics recalled in 1763 some of the types of designs that had come and gone "...tantôt il faut des figures, des châteaux, des ornements, des guirlandes..."[36] While not granted everlasting life, such patterns were given at least a very long run as *ornements*

d'église, which is why so many have survived. Catalogue number 376 (fig. 26), which falls into this group, may be dated to about 1737–39.

As designers sought to exploit three-dimensional effects still further, the scale of their patterns grew ever larger and bolder. It was a time when, as Smith said, it was fashionable to give the size of a pumpkin to an olive.[37] To this order belongs catalogue number 401. It is almost certainly French, but there are English silks on an even more massive scale.

1742–1765

The reaction to the three-dimensional style came about 1742–43. Although no French designs of the time appear to have survived, Garthwaite turned to a lighter style halfway through 1742 and to the Rococo in the autumn of 1743. There is only one silk from the 1740s in the Los Angeles collection, catalogue number 398, which may be dated to the mid-1740s. It is probably English rather than French. The open ground, with its self-colored pattern forming asymmetrical cartouches, is a complete contrast to that of catalogue number 401 (plate 33). Whereas Garthwaite was interested in botanical naturalism, the designer of this silk was still using the "Indian" flowers of earlier years. Garthwaite had at least one major rival, John Vansommer, whose work is known from only one dated silk. Catalogue number 401 could be his, or it could, of course,

Fig. 26
Panel (cat. no. 376).

be French.

An increasing stylization came into silk design in the early 1750s. By the end of the decade it had developed characteristics that can be found in catalogue number 383; this may be compared with some of the samples in an English pattern book dating from about 1755–65.[38] The double trail of flowers seems to have been a fashionable device, as well as the flowers tied in a bunch with a ribbon.

The early 1760s saw the last flourish of the silk designer's art, with the exception of the important furnishings of Philippe de Lasalle. Although floral motifs had by then been restricted virtually to roses, carnations, pinks, and little trees not unlike bonsai in scale, these were combined with gold and silver ribbons, feathers, simulated fur, and even simulated billowing silks (on silks!) to create rich and exuberant effects. Grounds were frequently ribbed and coloring daring, with green roses and purple chenille. There are three excellent examples in the Los Angeles collection (cat. nos. 380, 386, 403), which may all be dated to about 1762–66. They can be compared with the designs by Gallien of Lyon, of which there are a substantial number in the Victoria and Albert Museum, as well as some in Paris and a few in The Metropolitan Museum of Art. An order book from a Lyon *négociant* which is now in the Victoria and Albert Museum contains many examples of such materials. Additionally, there are some excellent portraits in which

they are depicted, notably that of Marie Caroline, Queen of Naples, by Raphael Mengs, now in the Prado.

By the late 1760s designs were becoming less elaborate and smaller in scale. Thus much more plain ground began to appear. The general outline of the dresses worn by the most fashionable was also changing. Although there had been some striped designs in the early 1760s, there was, by the last part of the decade, hardly a design without them. (The width and distribution of the stripes was, however, carefully varied, so there is no danger of mistaking a stripe of 1769–70 for one of the mid-1780s.[39])

1765–1800
The collapse of silk design for fashionable dress can be seen between the years 1770 and 1775, when designs diminished until their repeats were seldom more than an inch long. This decline can be followed year by year in one of the pattern books of Batchelor, Ham and Perigal.[40] Thus it is that the embroidered dress material (cat. no. 404) can be dated to about 1776. Apart from the worsted (cat. no. 396), which can be dated to the 1760s by comparison with the pattern books of John Kelly of Norwich,[41] this is almost the end of the story. Dress silks were eclipsed as works of art by printed cottons. The softer, more flowing, Neoclassical outline of the 1770s and 1780s required fine lawn, and perhaps a few ribbons and stripes (fig. 16). When silks were

used at all they were mostly plain or gauze, often enriched with silver or gold thread.

When N. Heideloff's *Gallery of Fashion* first appeared in 1794, he illustrated court dresses with decorated flounces, but these were usually embroidered. There are patterns for English woven silk flounces of the period,[42] but though they are pleasant enough in themselves, they lack the dramatic effects which could be achieved with embroidery. Catalogue number 378, the panel of velvet for a man's suiting, is difficult to date more precisely than about 1755–65, for such materials, unlike men's waistcoats, did not respond so readily to changes in fashion. Waistcoats continued to be very important, but, again, after the early 1790s it is difficult to find any with woven patterns; the magnificently decorated affairs of the late eighteenth century are embroidered. It was a bad time for both the French and the English silk industries. The magnificent furnishings commissioned by Napoleon did much to carry into the next century the tradition of silk designing in France when it had all but died in the rest of Europe.

PLATE 34
Panel (cat. no. 390).

PLATE 33
Panel (cat. no. 401).

NOTES

1
J. Godart, *L'ouvrier en soie*, Lyon, 1899.

2
Victoria and Albert Museum, T.374–1972 to T.385–1972.

3
A List of Prices in the Foot-Figured and Flowered Branch, London, 1769, no. 2, ¾ plain and foot-figured mantuas, p. 8 (photocopy in library of Victoria and Albert Museum).

4
List of Prices, no. 8, single tissues, p. 14.

5
Lampas, the French term, has been adopted by CIETA (Centre International d'Étude des Textiles Anciens). The writer prefers to use the English term current in the period under discussion.

6
A. Joubert de L'Hiberderie, *Le Dessinateur pour les fabriques d'étoffes, d'or, d'argent et de soie....*new ed., Paris, 1774, p. 51. He lists the metal threads available to the designer, and he refers to *filé* as *glacé*.

7
G. Smith, *The Laboratory, or School of Arts*, London, 1756, vol. 2, p. 41, under *lutestring brocades*.

8
D. King, ed., *British Textile Design in the Victoria and Albert Museum*, Tokyo, 1980, vol. 2; cf. illus. 65, 66, for example, dated 1776.

9
Lyon, Archives Municipales, HH 135, 652, and 656.

10
Lyon, Chambre de Commerce Lettres, tome 2, p. 279v, August 19, 1780.

11
The best silk could be itself in the form of a loose cover, as in Count Valetti's portrait.

12
London, Public Record Office, LC 9 290, fol. 192.

13
London, Goldsmith's Library, *A further examination of the Weavers Pretences being...an Answer to a late pamphlet of theirs...the Just Complaints & a review of two others lately written on the same side...by the author.*

14
The best recent work on Philippe de Lasalle is D. M. Hafter, "Philippe de Lasalle from mise-en-carte to Industrial Design," *Winterthur Portfolio*, 1978, pp. 139–64.

15
J. B. Réveillon, active 1752 onward; set up own factory 1765; died 1811.

16
P. Bertholon, *Du Commerce et des Manufactures de Lyon*, Montpellier, 1787, p. 41.

17
Joubert, *Le Dessinateur* p. 26.

18
Joubert, *Le Dessinateur* p. 10.

19
Joubert, *Le Dessinateur* p. 44. He refers to their point repeats when "*étoffes de goût*" have straight repeats.

20
Abegg Stiftung, Bern, 1835. I am very grateful to Frau Flury for sending me detailed photographs of this cope.

21
Victoria and Albert Museum, 1341–1871, T.451–1977; Hamburg Kunstindustriemuseum 188–37; Vienna, Museum für Angewandte Kunst, T.7048.

22
Musée des Tissus, Lyon, 25644. I am very grateful to Monsieur Tuchscherer for giving me permission to search his collection for these silks.

23
Cat. no. 384 may belong to this group. I had some doubts about cat. no. 401.

24
H. Honour, *Chinoiserie: The Vision of Cathay*, London, 1961, paperback reprint 1973, pp. 1–29.

25
P. Thornton, *Baroque and Rococo Silks*, London, 1965, p. 95, n. 1. Vilhelm Slomann coined the term in 1953.

26
English private collection, Victoria and Albert Museum, negative number FD682.

27
Smith, *The Laboratory*, p. 43.

28
Vanners Silks, 33, 77 (1708), and 86 (1709).

29
Inv. no. P. 12–1978.

30
S. Levey, "Lace and Lace Patterned Silks: Some Comparative Illustrations," *Studies in Textile History*, ed. V. Gervers, Toronto, 1977, pp. 184–202.

31
Paris, Bibliothèque Nationale, Cabinet des Estampes, vol. Lh44.

32
The evidence was set out by the author, "Dutch Silks: An Important but Forgotten Industry of the 18th Century or a Hypothesis?" *Oud Holland*, 3:79, 1964, pp. 152–72.

33
All are illustrated in the exhibition catalogue *Ph. Mercier*, City Art Gallery, York, June–July 1969, and Iveagh Bequest Kenwood, July–September 1969, pp. 28–29.

34
P. Thornton, "Jean Revel: Dessinateur de la Grand Fabrique," *Gazette des Beaux Arts*, July 1960, pp. 71–86.

35
There is another piece of the same silk in the Victoria and Albert Museum, T.239–1965.

36
Lyon, Archives Municipales, Inventaire Chappe, T.7, 229–31 (HH 158). He also made the point that perhaps one day fashion would return to designs "à la pointe."

37
Smith, *The Laboratory*, p. 39.

38
Victoria and Albert Museum, T.375–1972.

39
The portrait of Mrs. Siddons may be compared with that of Lady Sefton, painted in 1769, illustrated in A. Buck, *Dress in 18th-Century England*, London, 1979, p. 28.

40
Victoria and Albert Museum, T.374–1972.

41
Victoria and Albert Museum, 67 and 68–1885.

42
Two dating from 1792–94 are illustrated in D. King, ed., *British Textile Design*, 11: 218 and 219.

NIKKI SCHEUER

THE ELEGANT ART OF EMBROIDERY

"Sumptuary Laws, for differing reasons, were passed in vain forbidding the usage of embroidery. Luxury and its industry have always spread and reappeared in a thousand different forms."

CHARLES GERMAIN DE SAINT-AUBIN,
L'ART DU BRODEUR, 1770

As a reflection of eighteenth-century taste, embroidery was the embodiment of elegance and sophistication in form and texture. It was not only appreciated as a status symbol in the world of the fashionable—at times reserved only for the nobility—but was also an important part of the decorative arts.

The emphasis on charm, subtlety, fluidity, and grace in this period, following the reign of Louis XIV, was partially responsible for the small scale of designs, which complemented the intimate life-style of the eighteenth century. The embroiderer had to master remarkable skills in order to execute the varied stitches and complex patterns created by special designers. Both design and execution achieved aesthetic merit that has not since been equalled in the field of embroidery (plates 35, 36; cat. nos. 221, 316).

In France, embroidery designers were often people of great renown. One group worked exclusively for the king and his court; another worked for the great textile and embroidery manufactories. France's leading eighteenth-century embroiderer, who was also official designer to Louis XV, was Charles Germain de Saint-Aubin. He recorded his theories and techniques in a superb book, *L'Art du Brodeur* (*Art of the Embroiderer*).[1] In it he tells us that other nations competed to obtain French embroidery because, as he wrote, "they are seduced apparently by the novelty of the materials, the variety of the designs, and

the beauty of their execution." Saint-Aubin maintains that it would not be difficult to prove "that Design is the base and foundation of embroidery," and he regards as a necessity "that embroiderers understand at least the primary elements of Design." At the same time he acknowledges that designers need some technical expertise to understand what is required for the execution of their designs.

The largest and most famous textile workshops were located in Lyon (fig. 27), where Philippe de Lasalle's designs for embroideries and woven silks were *le dernier cri* before the Revolution. Among his important works were those created for Catherine the Great, Empress of Russia (cat. no. 379b). In addition to the widely recognized Philippe de Lasalle, many other designers and embroiderers were employed by the various workshops. Roland de la Platière, Inspector of Manufactories for Louis XVI, wrote in 1785 in the *Encyclopédie méthodique* that on visiting Lyon in 1778 he found twenty thousand people employed in the textile industry, six thousand of whom were embroideresses. This great industry competitively marketed its fabric and embroidery all over Europe by making samples available. A customer could order, among many other items, an uncut embroidered suit chosen from the latest embroidery model. In fact, it was the foreign orders that prevented the Lyon industry's collapse at the time of the French Revolution.

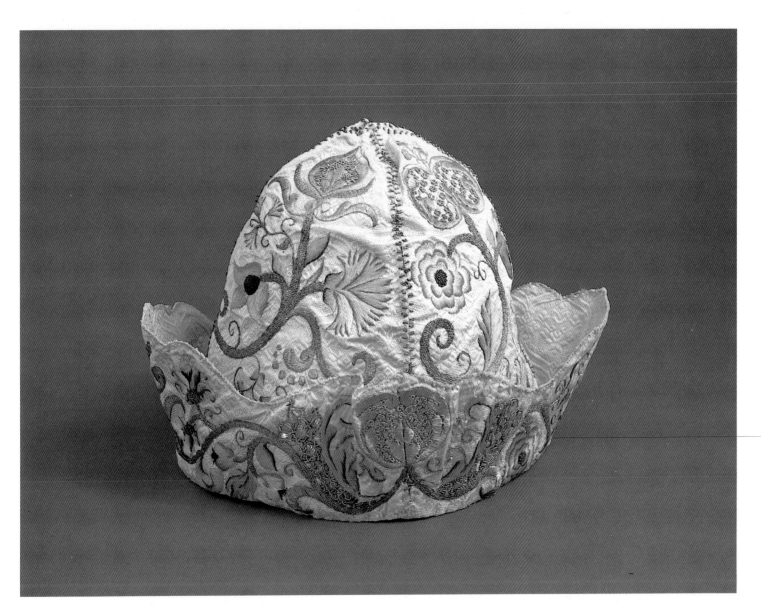

PLATE 36
At-Home Cap (cat. no. 316).

PLATE 35
Banyan and Waistcoat (sleeved; cat. no. 221).

Fig. 27
Charles Germain de Saint-Aubin (French,
1721–1786)
Embroidery Workshop, 1770
(from *L'Art du Brodeur*)
Engraving on paper
13⅝ x 8¹³⁄₁₆ in.
Los Angeles County Museum of Art,
Annis Van Nuys Schweppe Endowment

Embroiderers also worked in other cities, such as Paris and London, though they did so on a much smaller scale. In 1748 in Paris, the Embroiderers' Guild had won the right for its members to buy any kind of fabric to use for their productions and to sell their own work. However, in practice, these functions were usually served by the silk merchant, as the procuring of fabric and embroidery supplies entailed a financial burden. Robert Campbell, in his 1747 survey of the *London Tradesman*, details this as follows:

Embroiderers may be reckoned among the descendants of the lace man; as in his shop the greatest part of their richwork is vended, and he furnishes them with all materials for their business. It is chiefly performed by women...[2]

By modern standards the professional embroiderer's life was a harsh one. Saint-Aubin wrote that the French embroiderer worked from six in the morning until eight in the evening. According to the 1757 *Universal Dictionary of Trade and Commerce*, his English counterpart also put in a fourteen-hour day.[3] However, Saint-Aubin assures his readers that female embroiderers earned better wages than women in other crafts, though these wages were less than those paid to men: embroideresses ordinarily earned 24 sols per day, or four francs, for working embroidery that used "passing" (a thread used for satin stitch). A comparison of these wages with the actual prices paid for embroidered dresses is revealing. As described in the Paris fashion journal *Galerie des Modes*, published from 1778 to 1787, simply embroidered dresses cost between 150 and 600 livres, while a dress embroidered with precious metals, silk, and stones cost from 3000 to 3500 livres (the terms franc and livre were then used interchangeably). In her correspondence about her visit to Lyon in 1784, a Mrs. Berz states:

We saw the pattern of one velvet [suit], with false stones set in silver, like diamonds, disposed upon it like embroidery, which they had made for Prince Potemkin and had cost 10,000 louis; it must have been frightfully heavy.[4]

Obviously the high cost of material rather than labor was responsible for the excessive prices quoted, and was among the principal reasons why this luxury trade almost disappeared with the Revolution. In 1779 there were 262 master embroiderers registered with the Paris guild; by 1789, when the Revolution took place, only 11 remained.[5] Before the upheaval and especially during the first half of the century, professional embroiderers were kept very busy, not only for court wear but for less formal wear as well.

Pattern books of embroidery were published in all European countries during the eighteenth century, showing the popular design styles. These volumes were created for the use of the amateur and the edification of the professional. Though some of them served design needs in various other fields, many were created for the exclusive use of the embroiderer.

Embroidery as an avocation of the amateur was fashionable during the entire eighteenth century. To be an accomplished embroiderer was synonymous with being educated. There was even some suggestion that the importance given to needlework in a lady's education was won at the expense of literacy. In a satirical essay in *The Idler* (1758), Dr. Samuel Johnson attacks the practice:

My wife's notions of education differ widely from mine...She calls up her daughters and appoints them a task of needlework to be performed before breakfast...Their mother sits with them the whole afternoon, to direct their operations, and to draw patterns...by this continual exercise of their diligence...we have twice as many fire screens as chimneys, and three flourished [flowered] quilts for every bed...In the meantime the girls grow up in total ignorance of everything past, present and future...[6]

Nonetheless, for aristocratic and wealthy women creating embroidered objects served their aesthetic sense. It also gave them a feeling of accomplishment and diminished the tedium of the long, monotonous days. In fact, this particular labor was one of the very few permitted the rich.

THE NOMENCLATURE OF SAINT-AUBIN

It was also this very same class of aristocrats who, while competing for social prominence by means of opulent clothing, fostered the use of sumptuous gold and silver embroidery. The complexity and difficulty of the techniques involved removed these

PLATE 38
Coat and Waistcoat (cat. no. 237, detail).

PLATE 37
Suit (coat, waistcoat, and breeches; cat. no. 237).

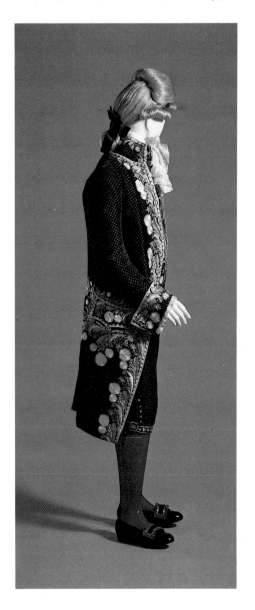

garments from amateur spheres, requiring the expertise of the professional embroiderer. Gold embroidery, which used thread that was actually gilded silver wrapped around a core of silk, was made in various ways. Saint-Aubin in *Art of the Embroiderer* discusses the various types of embroidery and their nomenclature, for which there are no modern-day equivalents.

GOLD AND SILVER EMBROIDERY

The style of raised gold embroidery resembling a waffle made of gold was known as *gaufrure embroidery.* It decorated the French royal carpet and was more durable than brilliant. Built up of heavy waxed thread, the padding was completely covered by rows of double gold strands. These were held in place by the underside couching of equally spaced sets of four stitches.

Another type of gold work in relief was *guipure embroidery,* which embellished ecclesiastical furnishings, men's suits, and horse and carriage trappings. This form of embroidery made use of vellum cut in the shapes of different design motifs to create the raised effect. Smoothly laid gold thread covered these vellum cutouts, held in place by stitches along the edges of each motif. This embroidery was further decorated with gold strips, drawn gold wire, and other metal trimmings.

According to Saint-Aubin, *couching work* was the most popular kind of embroidery, though the least durable. It too was made with gold thread, and might be either raised or flat. The placement of the securing stitches often created patterns, and the name of each variety of couching was taken from the design it formed, such as shell, lozenge, or serpentine. This embroidery often was decorated further with a variety of gold trimmings.

A popular type of gold embroidery used on clothing was that known as *embroidery in paillettes* (sequins). It was sometimes added to heavy padded gold thread embroidery. When made reversible, it was a time-consuming process with unique results (plates 37, 38; cat. no. 237).[7]

Embroidery in high relief existed in several forms; a most impressive form consisted of magnificent life-size figures of humans and animals that decorated the king's throne as well as his apartments. These rare embroidered figures were considered great works of art.

On the other hand, *embroidery in low relief* was almost common, being found on such diverse objects as altar frontals, church vestments, court costumes, masks, horse trappings, and saddlecloths. The relief was built up of two types of waxed thread, molded to form the desired shape of each motif. The padding was then covered with gold thread that was sewn fast by underside couching. Various types of gold trim and silk cord further embellished the surface (plate 39; cat. no. 340, detail).

Both *satin stitch* and *modified satin stitch* were executed with gold, silver, or colored threads. A very skilled and steady hand

PLATE 40
Altar Frontal (cat. no. 340, detail).

was needed to achieve the precision required. Lending a luminous quality to both fashionable and ecclesiastical dress, satin stitch in its various forms had universal appeal (plates 41–43; cat. nos. 260, 321). Embroidery of this type was often further enriched with gold and silver paillettes and crimped gold wire.

Rapport work made use of net, satin stitch, spangles, and a multitude of gold trimmings. It was worked in separate parts, which were sold ready-made at embroidery or silk merchant shops. These appliqués were then used for the borders of men's suits, embroidered sections of ladies' skirts, and Brandenburgs (a form of frog-closing), enabling the customer to "have in twenty-four hours that which would have taken a month to embroider."

Chain stitch and *tambour embroidery* were related kinds of another desirable embroidery style, executed in gold and colors. *Art of the Embroiderer* notes that this was a work popular with ladies of leisure, and was made until about 1760 with a needle. At that time a new method was imported ·"which is just as accurate and six times more expeditious. Now the other manners of working have been abandoned." This new method from the Orient utilized a circular tambour frame and a tiny crochet hook. It allowed the embroideress to create delicate patterns in colored silks and metallic thread with a minimum of effort. Needle chain stitch required the drawing through the fabric of the entire thread with each

stitch, and most metallic threads could not withstand this continual abrasion.

COLORED EMBROIDERY

Embroidery in colors was also much in demand, and Saint-Aubin describes *shaded embroidery* (satin stitch, split stitch, and laid work in silk, wool, or chenille) as "the art of blending shades, to make light and shape emerge, it is not an easy art." This embroidery composed pictures of historic events and personages and was also used to decorate upholstery and clothing, often with floral designs (cat. no. 299). Saint-Aubin states that "a number of fastidious people have had their clothing embroidered [in shaded work] by the Chinese with the greatest regularity. Merchants carry an assortment of these embroideries."

Other varieties of embroidery in colors include *chenille embroidery*, which used a fuzzy, caterpillarlike thread that was couched down. It was also sewn either in satin stitch or in long and short stitches. This impractical material was popular, as it could create shaded motifs or be used to fill large embroidered sections in but one color (plate 40; cat. no. 340, detail).

Wool embroidery was made with threads whose colors could be brighter and stronger than silk. It was worked in split and satin stitch and decorated women's dresses, church ornaments, and military accoutrements.

Taillure embroidery was a classic form of applied work, using fabric cut into the

PLATE 39
Altar Frontal (cat. no. 340, detail).

PLATE 41
Waistcoat (cat. no. 260).

PLATE 42
Waistcoat (cat. no. 260, detail).

PLATE 44
Fire Screen (cat. no. 423, detail).

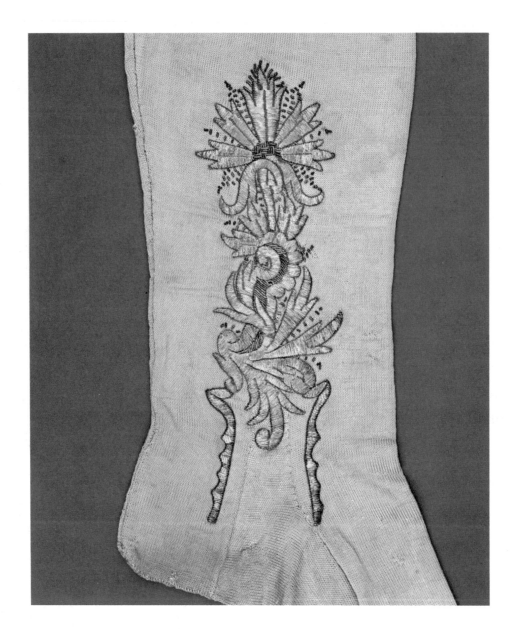

PLATE 43
Stockings (cat. no. 321, detail).

FIG. 28
Horse Trapping (cat. no. 422).

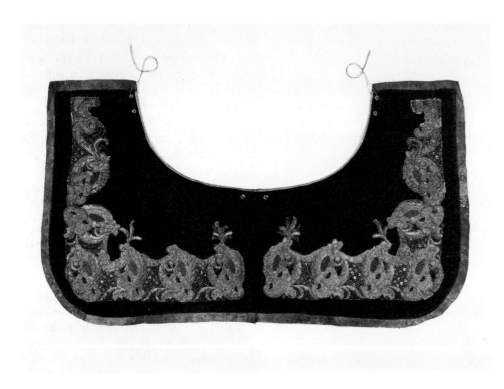

shapes of the various motifs found in the design. It was used on coverings of rich furniture, carriages, military equipage, and horse trappings (fig. 28; cat. no. 422).[8]

NOVELTY EMBROIDERIES

Embroidery in jais (a type of tiny glass tube) we are told "can readily scratch the user; it is generally not suitable for wearing apparel" (plate 44; cat. no. 423), while *embroidery in fur* was made either with dyed ermine or Astrakhan lamb, or alternatively might be worked with chenille and silk merely to imitate fur. Saint-Aubin notes that bird feathers and insect wings were also in use, and adds that "these are among the thousands of inventive notions which emerge from time to time." Ribbons and straw were also most appreciated in embroidered form.

Embroidery with knots (cat. no. 345) was another type of ladies' pastime. Made with a shuttle, it consisted of tying knots in a strong silk, cotton, or linen thread, creating a kind of textured cord. This cord was either made into looped fringe or couched into naturalistic patterns, and was added to dresses, accessories, draperies, and furnishings.

The *embroidery of Marseille* (quilting) employed two different techniques. In the first style, which was sometimes used to decorate furniture coverings for the dressing room, designs of flowers and other motifs were raised with stuffing, while the background was covered with tiny knots (fig. 29; cat. no. 78). The second type, worked on bed coverlets and clothing, outlined the design motifs of fish scales, squares, and mosaics with fine stitches that were sewn through three layers of fabric. Quilting took other forms as well.

White embroidery (white work), made on fine cotton muslin in various stitches, was particularly appreciated in the latter part of the eighteenth century and was stitched on sleeve ruffles and clothing by women workers. This type of embroidery was scorned by Saint-Aubin, since he considered it to require little skill, and its producers were poorly paid. These *brodeuses en blanc* (white workers) were never part of the Embroiderers' Guild; they worked mainly in linen and mercers' shops.

The most refined white work was called Dresden work and was made in Saxony (fig. 30; cat. no. 94). It beautifully imitated lace work, and was so admired that white-work clothing industries sprang up in France copying the Dresden work.

We know that during this period silk thread embroidery replaced wool as a favorite for elegant costumes and even furnishings. Embroidery with chenille thread grew more common as the century progressed, and cotton, the staple of white-work embroidery, reached new heights of popularity.

Naturalism and delicacy dominated design considerations, and the ubiquitous floral motif admirably fulfilled aesthetic requirements during most of the century. Flowers were represented in a wide spectrum of styles. In the first third of the eighteenth century, overly large flowers in full bloom, symmetrically balanced and covering most of the surface, were in favor. By the 1730s the floral motifs appear to be life-size, fresh-cut blossoms, and are often shown on a geometric background. In the final third of the century, only narrow, elegant borders of delicate floral patterns and some tiny scattered buds are found filling the expanse.

When toward the end of the century naturalism and asymmetry had been pushed to their limits, they were eclipsed by the Neoclassic decoration that then reigned supreme. This decoration, based on symmetry and order, retained the era's love of small-scale ornamentation.

This design progression was accompanied by changing taste in color as well. During the early part of the eighteenth century, the importation of Chinese and Indian goods brought about an appreciation of the clear, natural colors they introduced. These colors superseded those of somber richness so popular during the Baroque period. Much silver and gold was used, along with garden shades, and by the 1730s "natural" colors were used alone.

White and cream remained favorite background colors for women's costume and men's waistcoats, and served as a great foil for the colored silk and metallic thread used in embroidery. By the mid-century, however, the range of pastel colors increased to include the bright, rather acid colors found on the porcelain of the time. By the last quarter of the century, colors clouded as muted earth tones became the rage. Discoveries made while excavating classical sites influenced color tastes, as did the new and eccentric colors made possible by experimentation with dyes and bleaches.

A visitor to England in 1722 wrote:

The dress of the English is like the French but not so gaudy; they generally go plain but in the best cloths and stuffs...Not but they wear embroidery and laces on their cloathes on solemn days, but they don't make it their daily wear, as the French do.[9]

By the 1780s a mania developed for men's embroidered waistcoats. It was common for a man of fashion in Paris to own as many as three hundred of these embroidered masterpieces. Yet the 1790s saw the use of embroidery pass from fashion, with the exception of women's clothes decorated with white work (fig. 31; cat. no. 107). Though Napoleon and his court resurrected the art some years later, the breadth and artistry which embroidery attained in the eighteenth century remain unique in our historical perspective.

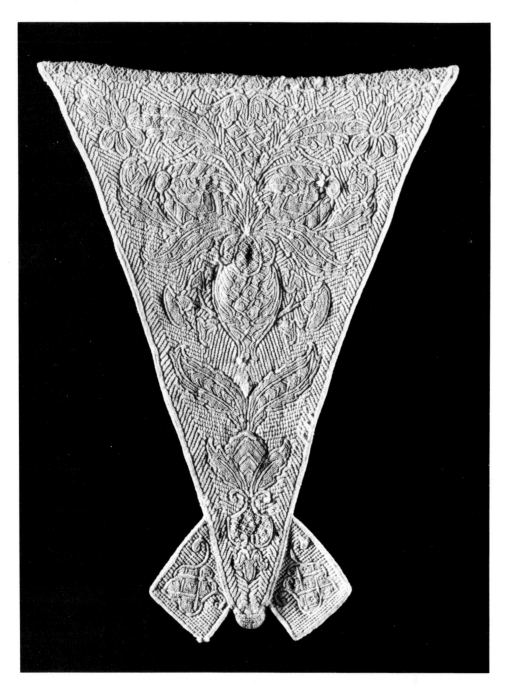

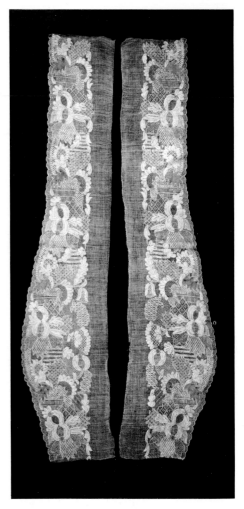

Fig. 30
Engageantes (cat. no. 94).

Fig. 29
Stomacher (cat. no. 78).

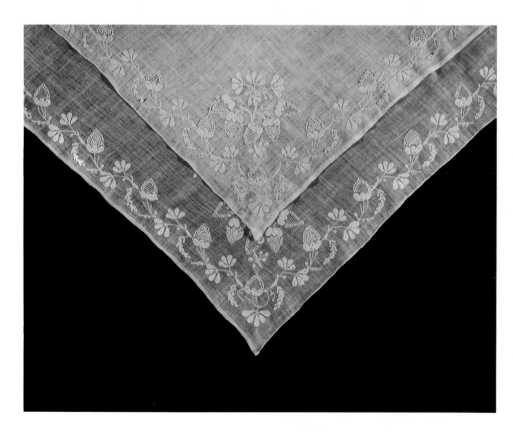

FIG. 31
Fichu (cat. no. 107, detail).

NOTES

1
C. de Saint-Aubin, *L'Art du Brodeur*, Paris, 1770.
[Ed. note: The quotations and information in this
essay are from Nikki Scheuer's translation from
the French, *Art of the Embroiderer*, in press from the
Los Angeles County Museum of Art, 1983. Notes
giving specific page references are not possible,
as no pagination is available at this time.]

2
R. Campbell, "Survey of the London Trades," *London Tradesman*, 1747, p. 153.

3
J. Savary des Bruslons, *The Universal Dictionary of
Trade and Commerce*, London, 1757, p. 7.

4
Berz, *Journal and Correspondence*, London, 1865,
1:135:

5
H. Havard, *Dictionnaire de l'ameublement de la décoration, depuis le XIIIe siècle jusqu'à nos jours*, Paris,
1887, p. 438.

6
S. Johnson, *The Idler*, London, 1758.

7
[Note: The exact definition of this embroidery is
controversial. A type of *embroidery in paillettes* could
be found as ornamentation on patterned cut velvet
and on ribbon appliqué with satin stitch.—Edward
Maeder]

8
One type of embroidery not in the province of the
professional was *canvas work,* both petit and gros
point, because it was an "easy work." Used for the
upholstery of furniture, some merchants sold canvas whose motifs were already embroidered but
whose background was to be filled in by someone
looking for work without much bother.

9
J. Macky, *A Journey Through England*, London,
1722.

ANNE RATZKI-KRAATZ
LACE CONSULTANT,
MUSÉE DES ARTS DÉCORATIFS, PARIS

THE ELEGANT ART OF LACE

"She has new bodices made, cloaks, daycaps and nightcaps, a quantity of lace trimmings, of ribbons and flowers, all manner of things! And all this to go to the country!"

CARLO GOLDONI,
LA VILLEGIATURA, 1761

Lace was so indispensable in the eighteenth century that it was as commonly found as the poorest of stuffs, yet costlier than silks and satins. Lace was so intricately woven into the fabric of everyday life that no garment, no elegant accessory was without it, yet the narrowest strip took months to make. So exclusive and elegant was lace that only nobles and high-ranking clergymen could afford it, yet servant girls and burgers' wives saved and scraped to buy it. To the twentieth-century imagination, lace is primarily an erotic accessory; considerable exploration is required to comprehend the role of lace as status symbol in the elaborate dress of the eighteenth century. The following pages may serve in this capacity, beginning with an introduction to lace-making on the Continent and continuing with an evaluation of lace's aesthetic contributions to the era's attire, illustrated by representative examples from the Los Angeles County Museum of Art's collection. An inquiry into the quantitative and financial importance of lace in the elegant man's or woman's wardrobe is then conducted through the examination of various records, inventories, and bills of the period, some of which have been kept or incurred in relation to gala occasions such as weddings and coronations. Our investigation culminates in the transformation of lace from social marker to feminine trimming, a transition that had occurred by the close of the century.[1]

LACE-MAKING ON THE CONTINENT IN THE EIGHTEENTH CENTURY

Although in the seventeenth century Jean-Baptiste Colbert, Louis XIV's Minister of Finance from 1661 to 1683, succeeded in establishing lace-making on a large scale in France, the only royal manufactory to survive after the heavy flow of government subsidy had stopped (c. 1675) was that of Alençon in Normandy. Its production, however, was always relatively small; perhaps that is why the laces of Alençon and of neighboring Argentan held their place as the aristocratic laces par excellence throughout the eighteenth and into the nineteenth century. Until around 1740 these laces were made into large, made-to-order items of costume and decoration, such as aprons, alb flounces, or covers for dressing tables, while subsequently they made up only fairly narrow trimming widths.

Out of the other French centers of production came both bobbin and needle laces that were largely mediocre. They did not often make their way into court circles, being destined either for export or local use. The gold and silver laces of Aurillac were a possible exception, as were the laces of Valenciennes (plate 45; cat. no. 339). Yet the latter city fell to France only by conquest and treaty in 1678. It was not until the 1740s that its lace industry rid itself of the aesthetic influence of the Low Countries, and attained its definitive style and square

PLATE 45
Chasuble (cat. no. 339).

mesh ground.

Belgium (Flanders) even before Louis XIV's death in 1715 had become the most important producer of bobbin laces, with Brussels lace (*point d'Angleterre*) in particular being universally in demand. During the eighteenth century, Belgium produced significant quantities of needle laces as well, and her designs, initially awkward imitations of French classical style, grew to brilliantly interpret French taste. This development, in combination with the quality of Belgium's remarkably tenuous flax thread, made her lace industry the leading one in Europe.

By the beginning of the eighteenth century, Venice was moribund as a lace-producing center, although the last manifestations of its elegant art of lace constitute a show of bravura (fig. 34; cat. no. 348, detail).

Throughout the first half of the century Brussels lace was in great demand, as were the laces of Mechlin and Binche. When in the latter half of the 1750s Valenciennes lace became most fashionable, Belgium still maintained a quantitative edge over France, for the same type of lace was manufactured in Antwerp and in other Belgian locales.

In the second half of the eighteenth century blond lace (plate 46; cat. no. 195) became popular, and it was made in large quantities. The slightly golden color of this silk bobbin lace is responsible for its name. Blonds could be produced quickly, and

France, Italy, and Spain manufactured them extensively. Even the Venetian lace industry revived somewhat at this time, largely because of its ability to copy French Alençon and blond laces. Often blond silk laces had little or no design, consisting primarily of a large-mesh ground with scalloped edges. The frequency of the mention of "blond lace" in the records of this period, along with other indications, suggests that the term "blond" became a generic, indiscriminate one for all bobbin laces, whether black or white (cat. no. 195).

The number of persons involved in the lace-making industry fluctuated widely, at least in France, during the eighteenth century. Low since the 1690s, a period of general economic malaise, it increased during the reign of Louis XV, when demand for lace was at its highest point. Lacemakers then numbered in the hundreds of thousands, decreasing again as early as the 1770s, and steadily dwindling until the French Revolution in 1789. The lace industry did not disappear along with the Ancien Régime, however. Lace continued to be manufactured for export purposes, as well as for a greater local demand brought about by a new clientele of villagers and farmers. An aesthetic explosion in peasant costumes occurred late in the century, and lacemakers, often from peasant stock themselves, began to wear their own productions. The democratization of lace contributed more than any other factor to the fall of lace from its pedestal; it was no

longer the symbol of aristocratic prestige.

THE AESTHETIC CONTRIBUTION OF LACE TO ELEGANCE IN THE EIGHTEENTH CENTURY

It is said that the eighteenth century did not begin until after Louis XIV's death in 1715. Certainly prior to that time, elegance was linked more closely with status than with glamour, and wearing expensive laces was a way to display one's fame and fortune, rather than one's taste. Until the young Louis XV (1710–1774) came of age, Philippe, the Duke of Orléans (1674–1723) served as Regent, ushering in a new concept of elegance. To be elegant became synonymous with looking uncontrived, however many intellectual or physical contortions one had to go through to achieve this appearance. Lace designs of the most sophisticated "naturalness" reflect this aspect of the period extending from the second decade of the century until Madame de Pompadour's death in 1764; designers improved upon nature by redistributing its elements into the most pleasing man-made combinations. This aesthetic philosophy continued until the great romantic reversal of the 1780s, which decreed that man must on no account interfere with nature.

From 1720 to 1770 lace was of unparalleled importance as the finishing touch without which there could be no talk of elegant dressing. Its function on clothes was akin to that of gilded bronze ornaments on furniture or the carving on wood panels:

it underscored the elegance of the whole. Sociologically, lace for the most part retained its status-symbol value, being still very expensive, as we shall see later on. However, in contrast to the seventeenth century, all strata of society (excepting farmers) now felt worthy enough to wear it, so long as they could afford to purchase it. Wealthy people simply bought the best and others contented themselves with the rest, but lace was demanded if the occasion were to be an elegant one.

The grandeur that lace brought to costume may be best appreciated within the three-dimensional, living setting of the century it so generously embellished. While the past may not be wholly regained, paintings and engravings from the era provide some perspective and illuminate the impact of the lace ensemble, as in figure 32, the *Portrait of Mademoiselle de Beaujolais,* of about 1745. The young girl in the picture wears a set of matching laces known, and henceforward referred to, as a parure. It includes a neckline ruffle worn gathered around the décolletage, another flounce of larger width worn flat around the shoulders, arm flounces composed of two rows of straight laces, triple elbow frills, a stomacher, and an apron gathered into a point at the waist and finished off with a ruffled flounce forming three scallops. The lace is *point d'Argentan,* as may be seen from the large-mesh ground and the terse, perfectly balanced design of classically arranged flowers. With the exception of the apron,

reserved for young ladies, this parure, worn more or less as it is here, remained standard for formal wear throughout the century.

In figure 33, an engraving from the same period entitled *La Folie pare la Décrépitude des ajustemens de la Jeunesse (Folly Adorns Decrepitude with the Attire of Youth),* the prominent dressing-table cover is made out of a tall flounce of *point de France;* similar lace trims the "decrepit" old lady's dressing gown and cap. Such heavy needle laces with thickly padded contours were very popular in the late seventeenth and early eighteenth century. The clearly delineated design is typical of the late Louis XIV period, that is, 1700–1715, and it is recorded that the king himself liked to present his court ladies with just such lace dressing-table covers as a gallant promotion of the industry. Since the engraving is dated 1745, at least thirty years after such lace designs had gone out of style, along with the high relief that gave them body, it may be inferred that the artist intentionally used "old-fashioned" lace, the better to underscore the hopelessness of the old lady's attempts at being "in." It should be noted, however, that alb flounces of similar *point de France* continued to be worn until the 1750s by well-dressed ecclesiastics—churchmen being notoriously conservative, if expensive, dressers.

Turning to the more isolated but no less splendid laces of this exhibition and catalogue, we find an item suitable for the most

fastidious ecclesiastical dandy. This alb flounce of what is most probably Brussels lace (c. 1720, fig. 36; cat. no. 362) is a beautiful example of the "improvement upon nature" so characteristic of the Louis XV years. The rendering of the flowers within an overall rigorous composition announces the tendency to circumscribe loose designs within compartments or medallions, juxtaposing them with free-floating elements. By contrast, another flounce of Brussels lace (fig. 35; cat. no. 364)—datable to approximately twenty years earlier—imitates *point de France* needle laces: flowers are summarily drawn within a formal composition in which Baroque volutes add to the general impression of heaviness.

Elegance as deliverance from the gilded caparison of the Louis XIV period is exemplified by the introduction, about 1720, of the *robe volante,* referred to elsewhere in this catalogue as the sack-back gown, a dress with a fitted bodice and a back whose box pleats were sewn down to just below the shoulders, at which point they hung loose. Lace too became a floating object; it hung in oval-shaped engageantes, fluttered around ladies' bosoms, and frothed up gentlemen's cravats. Belgian bobbin lace, made of thread gossamer-fine and light as a butterfly wing, was naturally better suited to this vaporous role than needle lace whose technique, primarily based on the buttonhole stitch, rendered it much stiffer. However, when needle lace does succeed

PLATE 46
Indispensable (cat. no. 195).

FIG. 33
Louis de Surugue de Surgis (French, 1686–1762)
Folly Adorns Decrepitude with the Attire of Youth,
1745 (detail)
Engraving on paper after a pastel painting by
Charles Coypel (1694–1752)
11¾ x 9⅞ in.
Courtesy Bibliothèque Nationale, Paris

FIG. 32
Attributed to Jean Marc Nattier (French,
1685–1766)
Portrait of Mademoiselle de Beaujolais, c. 1745
Oil on canvas
54 x 41 in.
Courtesy La Réunion des Musées Nationaux, Paris

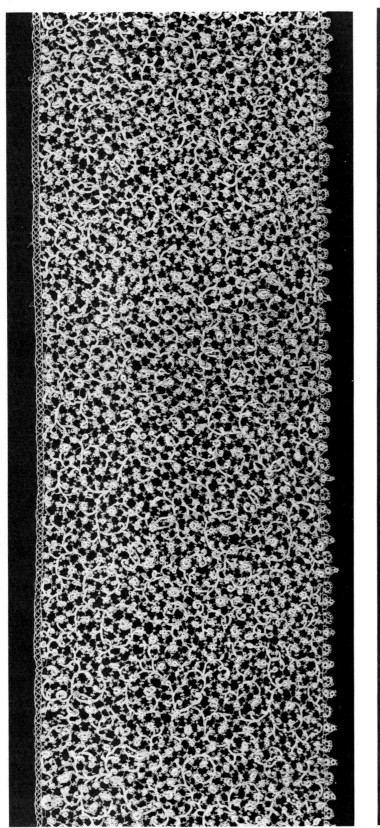

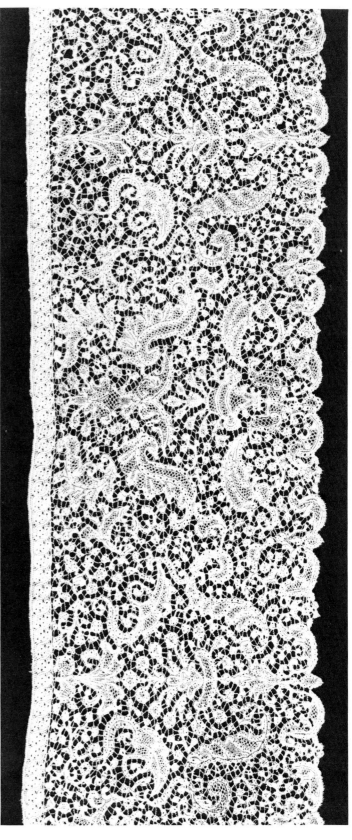

FIG. 34
Lace (flounce; cat. no. 348, detail).

FIG. 35
Lace (alb flounce; cat. no. 364, detail).

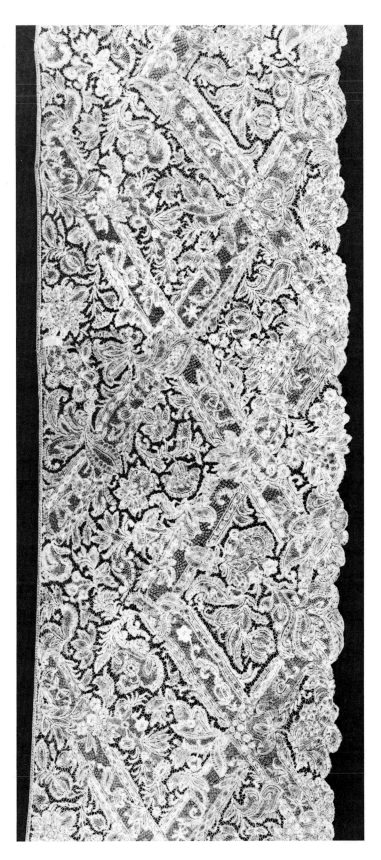

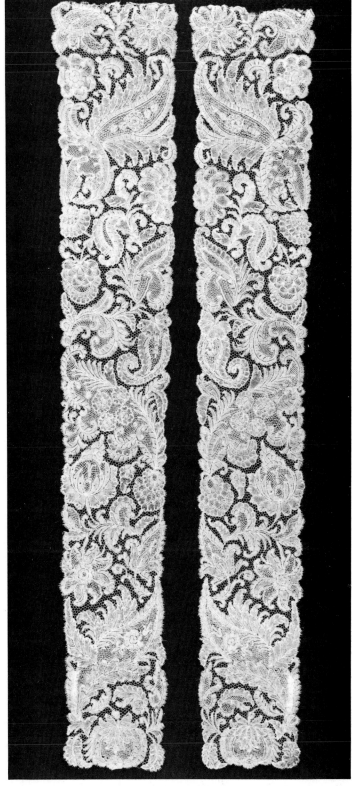

FIG. 36
Lace (alb flounce; cat. no. 362).

FIG. 37
Lace (pair of lappets; cat. no. 367, detail).

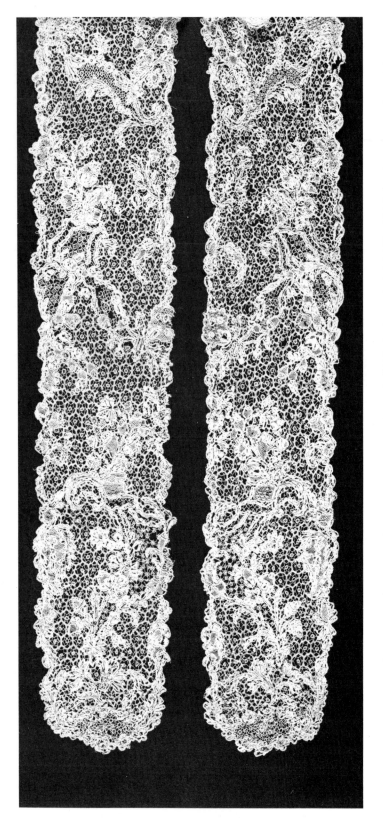

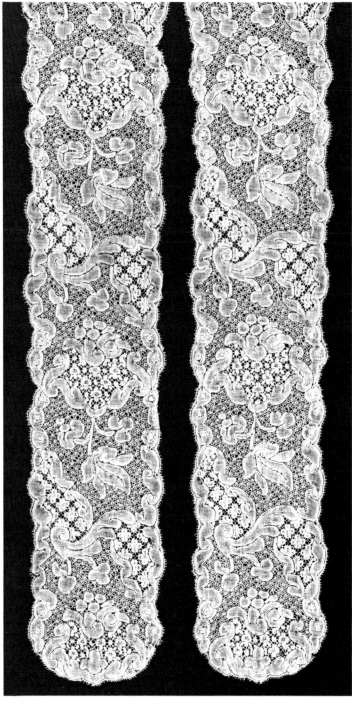

Fig. 38
Lace (pair of lappets; cat. no. 352, detail).

Fig. 39
Lace (pair of lappets; cat. no. 360, detail).

in combining the freedom of design that its technique allows with bobbinlike fineness of thread, it constitutes perhaps the most splendid manifestation of the elegant art of lace. Catalogue number 373 is one such specimen made about 1700–1710, when the trend toward lighter laces was already well established. It was probably used as a bodice trimming.

Ladies' lappets were very much in evidence in the eighteenth century. During the Regency (1715–23) they were worn flat, hanging loose from the cap crown; after that time they were either folded into *coques* (loops) or were gathered in the middle and pinned back up on the cap itself. In England such a head covering was referred to as a pinner. Catalogue number 367 (fig. 37) shows one such pair of Brussels bobbin-lace Regency lappets (about 1720).

In the 30s and 40s, the *réseau* or ground of laces took on greater importance, with expanses being used to separate the elements of the design. The tendency was to use the ground rather than the design itself to display the lacemaker's virtuosity. Alençon lace particularly developed its series of variegated fillings, known as *modes*. Catalogue number 352 (fig. 38) is a pair of Alençon/Argentan lappets with a partridge eye (*oeil-de-perdrix*) ground motif. The design, which includes acorns as well as flowers, could not be easily distinguished were it not for the stiff raised *brode* underscoring its contours. Also datable to the same period (about 1738) is a beautiful pair

of bobbin-lace lappets (fig. 39; cat. no. 360) from Mechlin. The *réseau* is *fond de neige*, so called because it resembles falling snow.

Catalogue number 372 represents a narrow flounce of Valenciennes lace used for trimming. Datable to the late 40s, it has the characteristic square Valenciennes mesh, the final shape of which was then being defined. On this particular piece of lace the background is plain; elaborate fillings are confined to the *rocaille* elements separating the flowers, which play a supportive rather than major role in the design composition. This tendency will go on accentuating itself throughout the 50s and 60s, when grounds became all-important in terms of expanse and completely plain in terms of technique.

If in 1715 the Sun King's death released the eighteenth century from its gilded prison, in 1764 Mme de Pompadour's own departure from the scene signaled another ending. From the day in 1745 when she was installed at Versailles as the mistress and thereafter political adviser of Louis XV, she reigned as unofficial queen of elegance, and she and her peers made the word *France* synonymous with elegance. But a few years later when Marie-Antoinette—a foreigner after all—was crowned queen of France, extravagance of dress became the norm. As parodied by many caricatures of the time, elegance gave way to the excesses of fashion. The queen did not adopt her famous milkmaid country look until the 1780s, when the state of the

country's economy practically demanded a "poor" appearance.

But by 1770 lace had already lost its critical significance. It continued to be used in profusion, but became a support for various other decorations: ribbons were threaded through its ever-larger meshes, and artificial flowers and feathers practically hid it from view. Under the circumstances, design obviously lost its importance; it now relied chiefly on rather boring variations on the theme of flowering branches and dots interspersed with minute medallions. Gone are the carnations, peonies, butterflies, and bees; they have all migrated to the embroidery field that has stolen the limelight. By the time the economic crunch came and simplicity ruled the day, lace was still used in quantity but no longer deserved the name. It had become a fabric, bought almost exclusively by the yard.

The Museum's pair of triple Alençon/Argentan engageantes (c. 1770, fig. 40, cat. no. 97; cf. fig. 41 and plate 47; cat. nos. 89, 41) is a representative example of the last manifestations of the art of lace-making in the eighteenth century. Although graphic invention and originality have gone out of the design, a certain air of brittle elegance is retained, with spare Japanese-like plum or cherry boughs finely traced against the large mesh Argentan ground.

During the last three decades of the century, lace designs continued to decline in sophistication. Catalogue number 374, an

FIG. 40
Engageantes (pair; cat. no. 97).

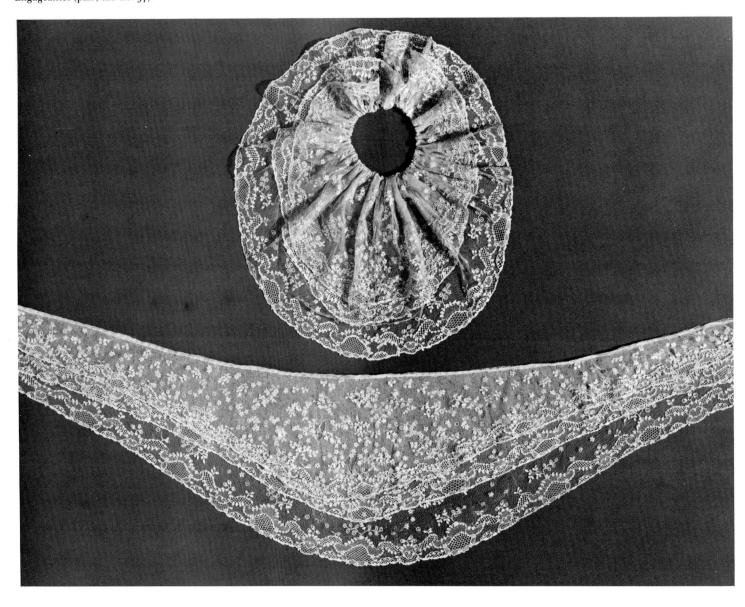

FIG. 41
Engageantes (pair; cat. no. 89).

Alençon lace cravat datable to the middle 90s, is representative of the comparative simplicity of the final years. Elongated border medallions, frankly shapeless, and stiffly aligned strings of pearls provide the only decoration.

QUANTITATIVE AND FINANCIAL IMPORTANCE OF LACE

Louis XV was crowned king on October 25, 1722. On that occasion much lace was worn by the participants in the ceremony. Exactly what kind and how much was strictly regulated. The Grand Master of Ceremonies was entitled to wear

…an open doublet of silver cloth adorned with silver laces and ribbons, slashed black velvet, puffed-up breeches with lace-lined slashes and silver ribbons, a hooded cloak of black velvet with silver toile lining, the outer side trimmed with black laces and the underside with silver ones…[2]

Marie Leszczynska (1703–1768) married Louis XV at the age of twenty-two, when the groom was only fourteen. The future queen was provided with a wedding allowance of 200,000 livres for the purchase of her "habits, linen and laces, both bobbin and needle,"[3] a sum equal to the total amount of revenue produced by the Valenciennes lace industry for the same year, 1725.[4]

Other countries, such as Italy, never lagged behind France in adopting the latest fashions. Lace in particular was an important item in noble ladies' trousseaus, as numerous inventories testify. One such inventory has come down to us from the Dogal House of Tron in Venice, and includes twenty-one complete parures.[5] The entries include the value of the laces, as well as indications of their fates: some were sold, others were soiled or torn, and some can no longer be found. An entry dated April 23, 1747, is entitled "Casket with Laces of the First Gift," presumably referring to a wedding gift. It details an ensemble of bobbin laces valued at 4,433 lire: a bonnet with lappets, matching triple sleeve flounces ornamented with "rich silver braids," a small lace scarf (stoletta), a lace bosom kerchief (pettorina), and lace trimmings for the bodice. In another "Casket of the Second Gift," the assortment is valued at 5,285 lire and composed of similar items, but this time of needle lace, referred to as punto in aria ("point in air"), a very archaic term by then.

Turning our attention to France once more, in 1765 a few months after Mme de Pompadour's death, we find the king's wardrobe accounts of January alone indicating that 16,250 livres were paid Monsieur Vanot, Marchand de Dentelles du Roy ("Lace Merchant to the King"). Here is the bill for one day's purchases:

On January 7:

1 and ¼ aune [or ell] collet [a measure of width] of Argentan point for a pair of sleeve ruffles, at 190 livres the ell = 237 livres 10 sols

5 aunes collet of Valenciennes lace for 8 nightcaps, at 190 livres the ell = 950 livres

15 aunes collet of Valenciennes lace for 12 pairs of nightcuffs at 110 livres the ell = 1,650 livres

18 aunes Mechlin cuffs for 12 pairs of nightcuffs at 54 livres the ell = 972 livres

2 and ½ aunes collet of superfine needle point for two pairs of cuffs at 480 livres the ell = 1,200 livres

1 aune ¼ collet of Brussels lace for a pair of cuffs at 230 livres the ell = 287 livres 10 sols.[6]

Since M. Vanot submits a similar bill every month, we must assume that Louis XV almost never went to bed twice wearing the same lace cap! A method of comparing the sums expended on lace relative to other items of the king's wardrobe is provided to us by a bill from M. Balzac, the king's embroiderer, for the delivery in April 1765 of a richly worked coat of silver watered silk, charging 233 livres 55 sols, or almost exactly the price of one ell of Brussels lace.[7] Amounts paid to those servicing the king's laces appear to range widely. We note that M. Vanot charges only 24 livres to assemble and mount the 24 pairs of cuffs included here, yet the king's lace mender, Anne Catherine Baritauld, widow Pipart, receives 300 livres for the "mending and general care of the points and laces of the King" for the sole month of September 1765.[8] The income of the actual creator of the lace provides the most vivid contrast: the average yearly wage of a Valenciennes lace-worker for the period 1748 to 1774 was 156.6 livres, or less than the cost of one ell of her own lace.[9]

In 1769, the noble Venetian lady Elisabetta Grimani prepared for her marriage to

PLATE 47
Dress (cat. no. 41).

Don Cesare Caetini, Prince del Cayer, by ordering 2,024 livres 14 soldi worth of laces, mostly Brussels or blond, to use as engageantes, trimming flounces, or *baute,* the typical black lace capelets worn by men and women alike in Venice.[10] In contrast, the sixteen pairs of shoes purchased for the wedding cost only 162 livres 40 soldi, and the bride's portrait sent to the groom fetched a mere 187 livres! It is interesting to compare the price of lace with that of fabrics so late in the century, for clearly a length of lace was still as much as twenty times as expensive as a length of fashionable, imported silk.

As mentioned previously, by the 1770s the quality of lace experienced a decline, and its price likewise dropped. Yet quantities did not decrease until after the French Revolution of 1789; indeed, because the lace industry now produced less elaborate pieces which could be executed with much greater speed, the volume of business remained more or less at the same level, at least for the bobbin-lace industry, as during the heyday of lace consumption.[11] Marie-Antoinette (1755–1793), her daughters, and the ladies of her court remained to the last great consumers of lace. The diary of Mme Éloffe, the favorite *Marchande de Modes* ("Fashion Merchant") of the queen, shows us that even between 1787 and 1793, the last years of her existence, she spent an average of 14,500 livres a year on ribbons and blond and Alençon lace trimmings, camisoles, bonnets, lappets, and

other frippery.[12] On December 30, 1790, for example, when the royal family had already been forced to move from Versailles and take up residence in Paris at the Tuileries Palace, Mme Éloffe provided the queen with a bill for a variety of blond laces, as well as a number of other kerchiefs and trimmings, and several lengths of fabric on which to mount the lace.[13] The bill reflects prices that have obviously plummeted since the time of the bill previously quoted: included is a length of white silk taffeta, on which the sleeve ruffles were mounted, that cost 5 livres the ell, as much as did the same amount of medium-width blond lace with Alençon ground! That particular day's charges amounted to 101 livres, 3 sols 6 sous. Such amounts occur almost daily in Mme Éloffe's diary. By contrast, a loaf of bread was then worth 3 sols.[14]

Marie-Antoinette's daughters, Marie-Thérèse Charlotte and Sophie Hélène Beatrice, were equally well supplied. In a register for the accounting of the items in the Royal Wardrobe "in the chambers of the princes of the blood," we find an entry dated November 3, 1789, which indicates that Mme Vanot, *Marchande de Toiles, Mousselines, Linons* ("Merchant of Linens, Muslins, Lawns"— of the same firm that supplied laces to Louis xv in 1765, as we mentioned earlier?) furnished a considerable amount of laces, including among other items nine parures of *point d'Alençon* lace, three of Valenciennes, and four of Mech-

lin.[15] In terms of working hours, the day's total represented several years of a lace-maker's life. The last entry on these accounts is dated April 12, 1792, four months before the queen's imprisonment on August 10. By then there were no more laces. Marie-Antoinette died on the scaffold October 16, 1793, nine months after the execution of her husband, Louis XVI.

LACE, FROM STATUS SYMBOL TO EROTIC ACCESSORY

When Venetian gros point reigned supreme in the second half of the seventeenth century, lace was a heavy and opaque affair. It was meant to be worn flat, in such a way as to display its design to full advantage. Compositions often included a number of symbols alluding to the wearer's rank, marital status, ancestry, or specific events in his or her life: coats of arms, the sun for the king's laces, the torch of hymen for married ladies, dolphins for royal births, and so forth. Lace had to be read and not just seen. Nevertheless, its function was not terribly different from that of other trimmings—that is, lace served as a very expensive form of decoration. Later in the century, when fashions became less rigidly gilded, laces were used as frosting on a cake: they gave any ensemble the touch of fluffiness which the garment by itself lacked. New techniques had made lace considerably lighter and more transparent, enabling its fine tracery to detach itself with a frosty exactness on the deep colors then preferred.

During the Louis XV period, the word "glamorous" best defines the social function of lace; wearing it automatically gave one a touch of class—the reverse of how lace functioned in the Louis XIV years, when one had to have class to wear it! Lace did not take on an exclusively feminine quality, though; for the time being it remained an indispensable element of men's wardrobes. Masculine cuffs, cravats, or jabots were still ones of lace which, as it was not reserved for the fair sex, had yet to acquire the erotic value ascribed to it later on. In fact, a certain amount of "undress" was considered the height of eroticism. Prints of the period, which abound in representations of *scènes galantes*, picnic parties, and other pleasure expeditions, show that the proper outfit for such occasions usually did not include lace. It was at night during elegant dinner parties or at gaming tables that lace was *de rigueur*. The fine flax thread out of which it was made had a soft natural sheen, to which candlelight added a marvelous glow. What could set off to greater advantage the pastel silks of that era than those ivory-colored, elegantly patined laces?

As mentioned earlier, in the 1730s and 40s the *réseau* became progressively more important as motifs were reduced in size. This had the effect of introducing the idea of complete transparency that has remained attached to lace ever since. In the 70s, along with English fashion, the romantic look was in vogue. Perhaps because this trend constituted a puritanical reaction to the excessive libertinage and indiscriminate spending of the previous decades, it called for less superfluous ornaments. Lace went underground as a result; as early as 1785, it had practically disappeared from all but the most formal court dresses. For the first time in its history, more of it was used for at-home wear, mostly on undergarments, than for show.

These years also signaled the end of lace-wearing for men. It is true that George Washington did pose for his 1797 portrait by Adolph Wertmuller (c. 1750–1811), still wearing a full jabot of Alençon lace. But from then on, both in America and on the Continent, no personage of note will ever be represented wearing lace again. Even during the Napoleonic years, when lace cravats and cuffs for men were a mandatory part of formal court attire, the femininity of lace as a concept went unquestioned. Napoleon's generals hardly went to battle with a fresh set of laces, as did their counterparts fifty years before them.

By the end of the eighteenth century, lace was an exclusively feminine affair, the very mention of which connoted erotic-romantic visions. The specificity of this sensual purpose definitely removed lace from the higher spheres of elegance and transformed it into one of the most successful items ever to be included in the panoply of erotic accessories around the feminine mystique. That is still its main role today.

NOTES

1
[Ed. note: The French monetary unit of the livre is mentioned throughout this essay, particularly in the section on the "Quantitative and Financial Importance of Lace." In 1795 the use of this Continental accounting unit ceased in France, which converted to the franc. During the eighteenth century, rates were of course subject to fluctuation, and it is difficult to give a modern equivalent of the livre. However, between three and ten dollars in current purchasing power serves as a very rough estimate.]

2
Paris, Archives Nationales, 013259, "Habillement des différentes personnes qui ont assisté aux cérémonies du sacre en 1722." [Ed. note: This translation and all others in this essay are by the author.]

3
Paris, Archives Nationales, 011043, "Papiers du Grand Maître des Ceremonies."

4
A. Malotet, *La dentelle à Valenciennes*, Paris, 1927, p. 21.

5
Venice, Museo Correr, 2254/2, "Inventario generale di casa Tron."

6
Paris, Archives Nationales, 01830/176, "Garde-robe du roy, maison du roi."

7
Ibid., 01830/114.

8
Ibid., 01830/18.

9
P. Guignet, "The Lacemakers of Valenciennes in the 18th Century, an Economic and Social Study of a Group of Female Workers under the Ancient Regime," *Textile History*, 1979, 10:96–113.

10
Baute were not used during carnival only but were worn "for six months of the year," P. Molmenti, *La Storia di Venezia nella vita privata*, 1929, vol. 2, *Lo Splendore*, p. 167.

11
Malotet, Paris, 1927, p. 34.

12
G. A. H. de Reisert, *Modes et usages au temps de Marie Antoinette: livre-journal de Mme. Éloffe, marchande de modes, couturière lingère ordinaire de la reine et des dames de sa cour*, Paris, 1855.

13
Ibid., 1790–93, 2:182.

14
Paris, Archives Nationales, KK523, "Journal des dépenses d'une dame de la cour, 1783–1792."

15
Paris, Archives Nationales, KK378, "registre pour la tenue journalière des atours de la garde-robe et autres détails des chambres des enfants de France."

ANNA G. BENNETT
CURATOR OF TEXTILES,
THE FINE ARTS MUSEUMS
OF SAN FRANCISCO

THE ELEGANT ART OF TAPESTRY

"Tapestry in its eighteenth-century form answered the needs of that escapist society, serving as a screen for privacy, a shield from reality, and a magic carpet to carry the observer to amorous adventure and fantasy land."

ANNA G. BENNETT,
LETTER TO EDWARD MAEDER, NOVEMBER 1981

When Louis XIV died in 1715 after a reign of seventy-two years, the event was generally felt to be overdue. His courtiers were free at last to leave magnificent, uncomfortable Versailles, where the king's presence pervaded every golden room. As Mars, his image confronted them in the Salon de la Guerre; his sunburst symbol challenged them at the doors of the Salon d'Apollon. The very walls, hung with tapestry series, reiterated his martial victories and the events of his personal life.

Turning their backs on these persistent reminders, the courtiers left behind not only the king, but also the grand manner he had invented. This had, in fact, begun to erode during Louis' lifetime, and the old king had perceived it. He, too, felt the need to leaven the heavy, official style. "Il faut qu'il y ait de la jeunesse mêlée dans ce que l'on fera." (A little youth must be mixed into what is undertaken.)[1] Heroics were going out of fashion. The courtiers set their faces toward Paris and a new life of privacy and pleasure.

FUNCTION AND FORM

The shift in focus, lowering of sights, and diminution of scale following Louis' death made changes that were felt in all the arts but especially in tapestry, which served as a backdrop for living. These new surroundings called for a pretty, protective shell. Artists were no longer commanded to create godlike images of the monarch, but were asked instead to fashion designs showing gods with all-too-human frailties. Woven in simulated gold frames or fixed, borderless, into carved paneling, the new tapestries of the post-Louis era helped set a tone of airy elegance and careless extravagance. Although light years removed from the free-hanging, majestic tapestries of Medieval times, they served the needs of the new age with equal success.

Tracing the origins of tapestry weaving as we know it is a difficult business, since examples from its formative period in the Middle Ages have virtually disappeared. But a brief review of how its form and social function evolved from Medieval times should show what tapestry became in the eighteenth century, and why.

However different in form eighteenth-century tapestries were from those of earlier eras, one aspect stayed the same: in the eighteenth-century salon, as in the baronial castle, tapestry was the hallmark of wealth. Whatever the era, tapestries were tailored to the high-style living of their patrons. In general, architectural setting as well as specific purpose determined the dimensions and forms of the weavings.

The fortified homes of the Medieval age were cavernous structures with windowless stone walls. The tapestries of the time, brightly and perhaps—to our eyes—garishly colored in their original state, modified these grim settings, providing comfort, insulation, and decoration. Their narrative mode offered entertainment as well. Separate episodes, linked side by side in the manner of a comic strip, or combined within a single panel, depicted stories from the Bible, romances, or scenes from everyday life. Hunting scenes, in which the chase and the kill appeared together, also exemplified Medieval tapestries' narrative mode. So did morality plays, in which the sinner fell from grace and was saved in the same design. The flattened figures of this two-dimensional style emphasized the castle wall beneath. With the advent of the Italian Renaissance, changing social conditions made this style obsolete. A new architecture crept northward from Italy, demanding a fresh kind of tapestry.

By the sixteenth century, life had shed some of the old Medieval harshness and hostility. Due to the development of firearms, armor was now more for show than for protection. Landowners were leaving their strongholds to build palaces in the Italian manner with open loggias, windows, and gardens. In these new-style buildings, tapestries were no longer essential as insulators. Surprisingly, as they became functionally obsolescent, their owners valued them even more highly, collecting and hoarding them with rapacious energy. Designed in vast series to line interior rooms, sixteenth-century tapestries had borders filled with flowers or grotesque ornament. Hanging, they produced the effect of multiple window openings, each framing a deep picture space in which stirring events took place. Full-bodied figures in tumultuous motion enacted key histori-

cal moments. The weaver now had access to a wider range of color, and used highlights of silk and touches of silver and gold to create lavish effects. Consistent with the Renaissance ethos, tapestries of this period were often exercises in splendor.

Generally speaking, the artistic goals of the sixteenth century were over-realized in the seventeenth. In the visual arts, the creation of an illusion of depth became an end in itself. Excesses are particularly evident in tapestry borders of this period, some of which imitate stucco work with three-dimensional forms thrusting outward toward the viewer. The central picture panel, on the other hand, imitates an oil painting, with deep vistas and perspective effects. Inflated figures and over-dramatic gestures further contributed to the creation of a grandiose style of art, perfectly suited to public spaces.

Engravings of interiors by Abraham Bosse (1602–1676) reveal the role played by tapestry in Northern European homes of the seventeenth century. These engravings show tapestries fitted around windows and doors and pierced with holes to accommodate wall sconces, much as wallpaper would come to be used later on.[2] The need for insulation may in part have dictated this new application. However, the high regard accorded oil painting in this, the age of Rubens and Rembrandt, may also have contributed to tapestry's devaluation. Thus, paintings took pride of place and were hung on top of tapestries, with

total disregard for the works of art underneath.

Toward the end of the seventeenth century the figures depicted on tapestries grew smaller, and the dramatic action they displayed grew calmer. Conservative French influence may have encouraged this trend, for at this time leadership in tapestry production passed from the Netherlands to France. Louis XIV's minister Colbert (1619–1683) established the Gobelins Manufactory in Paris in 1663 to supply the royal residences; the factory in Beauvais, just northwest of Paris, was opened the following year to execute private commissions. Financially, Beauvais was on its own, and insolvency dogged its early years. Its output, dependent on individual orders, reflects the taste of the times more accurately than that of the Gobelins, where subjects were often chosen for political reasons.

The great talent of Charles Lebrun (1619–1690) brought Gobelins tapestry design to a high level. He achieved grandeur without baroque excess, and his designs, circulated as prints through the *Cabinet du Roi* of 1697 were widely copied.[3] One might suspect that, whatever the title of the tapestry, Lebrun's subject was always the king. Louis' martial aspirations, for example, may be seen in the *Story of Alexander* (fig. 42; cat. no. 417), which was copied in Brussels, Aubusson, Oudenaarde, and Munich. Royal patronage did not, however, bring the Gobelins complete security. Louis' excursions into the field of Mars

FIG. 42
The Triumph of Alexander (cat. no. 417).

FIG. 43
Psyche Carried on the Mountain
France (Paris, Rue de la Chaise), 1660–70
Wool and silk
155⅔ x 238¾ in.
Cliché des Musées Nationaux, Paris

FIG. 44
Psyche Carried on the Mountain
France (Paris, Atelier du Louvre), 1658–70
Wool and silk
119 x 204 in.
Courtesy Wadsworth Atheneum, Hartford
Gift of Mrs. N. Clarkson Earl

emptied the royal coffers and brought France to the brink of bankruptcy. The silver plate disappeared from Versailles. Commissions for the royal manufactories dried up. The Gobelins closed its doors in 1694 and stood idle until 1699, its unemployed workers migrating to the Netherlands or to Beauvais. The great period of Beauvais lay ahead, in the eighteenth century, when a combination of artistic and managerial ability brought it a success that was envied by its sister manufactory. Its production supplied the leaders of fashion with the backdrop of elegant fantasy that they required. Beauvais tapestries splendidly illuminate the self-absorption and escapism that dominated French taste in the years following its release from interminable orbit around the Sun King.

THE WEB AND THE WEAVERS

Present-day tapestries are often designed and woven by the same artist. Traditionally, however (from the first evolutionary steps of the art in the fourteenth century), tapestries were the work of many specialists. A literary person was usually responsible for the scenario, an artist for the small model, a cartoon-maker for the full-size pattern made for the weavers.[4] Finally, the weavers, who followed the cartoon, actually produced the weaving. When the first tapestry had been taken from the loom, the cartoon usually became the property of the master weaver, who could have duplicate tapestries woven from the same design

(figs. 43–45; cat. no. 416).

The early cartoons seem to have been summary guides, with only bare indications of color. Much was left to the weavers' artistic judgment. Whether working on a vertical (high warp) loom or on a horizontal (low warp) loom, the weavers had to realize the artist's concept in a far less flexible medium. Cartoons became increasingly detailed and specific as time went on, finally becoming, in the eighteenth century, finished oil paintings that left no decisions to the weaver.

The principle of simple weaving is generally understood as the interlacing of two elements, as in darning or basket work. When the same material is used for both elements, the result is a checkerboard effect. In tapestry weaving the warp threads, held taut in the loom, are completely covered by interlacing and packing the finer, colored weft. The picture is built up by the weft alone, the buried warp being detected only by surface ridges.

The work does not proceed evenly, as it does when the weft is carried from one selvage to the other. The weft travels only to the limit of the color area being worked, then doubles back to its starting point. This interruption of the interlacing grid results in the formation of slits, a normal feature of tapestry weaving which can be, and often was in the eighteenth century, used for expressive effect.

Present-day visitors to the Gobelins can still see the magnificent vertical high warp

Fig. 46
High Warp Looms at the Gobelins, c. 1751–72 (detail)
Engraving on paper
13 x 16⅞ in.
from Diderot, *Encyclopedia or Dictionary of Sciences,
Arts, and Trades*

looms in operation (fig. 46). The weaver
sits behind the warp on which he has traced
the design. He may refer to a small pattern
posted behind him or above his head, but
he must walk around the loom to check the
front face of the tapestry. Traditionally,
the high warp weavers possessed superior
skill and earned about double the pay of
their low warp counterparts. Low warp
weaving was perfected in the Netherlands
in the early sixteenth century (fig. 47). It
was faster and more mechanical than the
high warp technique. The warp threads
were stretched horizontally between two
rollers. Two harnesses suspended above the
warp controlled the odd and even threads
attached to them. The harnesses were
raised and lowered by foot pedals, opening
a passage or "shed" for the weft to travel
between warp groups. The foot control
freed both of the weaver's hands for
manipulating the weft, while the high warp
weaver had to change the shed with one
hand and simultaneously pass the bobbin
through the other (fig. 48). The high warp
weaver's bobbin, known as a "broach," was
longer and more pointed than that used
in the low warp technique.

The weaving of large tapestries was done
by a team of weavers, sitting side by side,
each one controlling about twenty inches.
The cartoon-maker reversed the artist's
design in preparation for low warp weaving. It was then cut into strips which were
laid one at a time beneath the warp. The
weaver peered down through the warp to

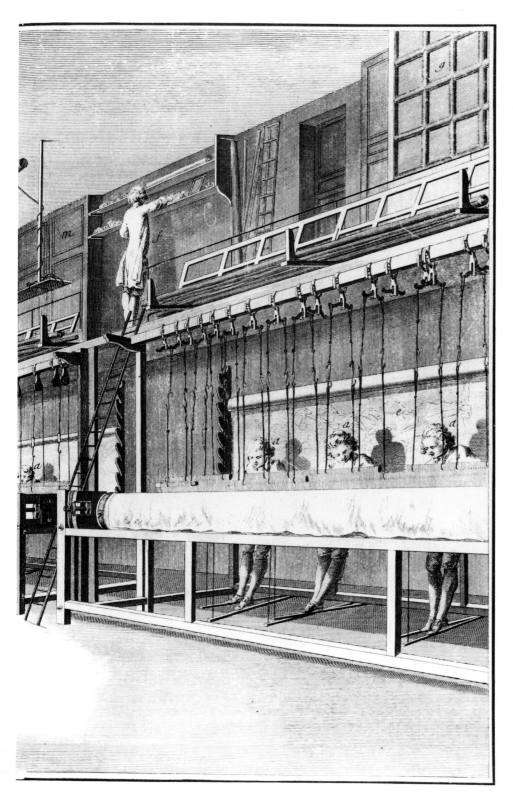

FIG. 47
Low Warp Loom at the Gobelins, c. 1751–72 (detail)
Engraving on paper
12½ x 8¼ in.
from Diderot, *Encyclopedia or Dictionary of Sciences, Arts, and Trades*

follow the design (fig. 49). He worked from the back also and could not see the entire front face until the tapestry was cut from the loom. The finished low warp tapestry was a mirror image of the (reversed) cartoon. This double negative brought the end product into agreement with the artist's original concept and model.

The weaver had to deal with one further complication: the design was placed sideways on the warp threads. In this way, a tapestry like *Venus and Vulcan* (fig. 50; cat. no. 419), twenty-four feet in width, could be woven on a twelve-foot loom, only slightly wider than the height of the tapestry itself.

The publication, beginning in 1751, of Diderot's *Encyclopedia or Dictionary of Sciences, Arts, and Trades,* the first work of its kind, attests to the universal fascination of mechanical advances and scientific investigation in the second half of the eighteenth century. Jacques Germain Soufflot (1709–1780), architect of the Panthéon and longtime director of the Gobelins and the Savonnerie, applied this scientific curiosity to tapestry manufacture. Letters he wrote to his superiors between 1756 and 1780 describe not only his continuous administrative problems, but also his interest in chemical experiments with dyestuffs, his concern with the control of insect infestation, and, especially, his efforts to improve the low warp loom. He addressed the low warp weaver's most serious handicap by initiating the development of a horizontal

FIG. 48
High Warp Weaver Changing the Shed, c. 1751–72
(detail)
Engraving on paper
12½ x 8¼ in.
from Diderot, *Encyclopedia or Dictionary of Sciences,
Arts, and Trades*

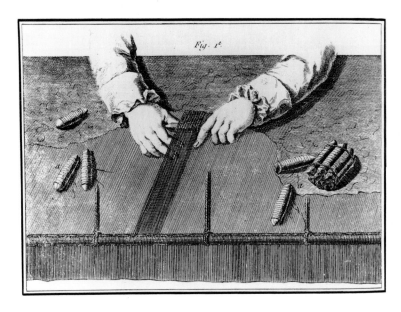

FIG. 49
Low Warp Weaver Passing Bobbin through Shed,
c. 1751–72 (detail)
Engraving on paper
12½ x 8¼ in.
from Diderot, *Encyclopedia or Dictionary of Sciences, Arts, and Trades*

loom that could be tipped up to allow the weaver to check his work. This innovation, realized by the engineer Jacques de Vaucanson (1709–1782) in 1757, speeded up the work, encouraged greater accuracy, and doubtless spared the poor weavers continuous frustration.

The technical problems of their difficult art, however, were not the most immediate ones facing the Gobelins weavers of the eighteenth century. Apprentices entered training at twelve or fourteen years of age and worked for six years from five in the morning to eight at night during the summer months, and from six to nine in winter. As full-fledged weavers they were paid so irregularly and so poorly that many died of malnutrition. Conditions grew continually worse. In 1770 Soufflot wrote to the Abbé Terray that he lacked the "funds necessary to prevent two hundred workers from starving to death." His efforts did not stave off anarchy. In 1771 he recognized the desperate straits of the manufactories… "*tous sont aux abois.*" Unfortunately, he failed to reverse this downward trend.

Soufflot's scientific experiments with color, intended as improvements, actually contributed to the later color losses that diminish the beauty of many surviving eighteenth-century tapestries. He set aside the dyers' traditional restrictions that had been observed for centuries and developed the procedures for making all the colors and halftones needed to reproduce the painted cartoons exactly.[5] Certain Boucher

tapestries go as far as to reproduce the artist's brushstrokes (plate 48; cat. no. 419, detail). The accuracy of reproduction was facilitated by the use of more silk and an increased fineness in the weaving. The artist's control of the weaving was extended by his supervision of the painting of the cartoon, and sometimes by his actual painting of the cartoon himself.[6] These changes in technique were strengthened by administrative changes first effected at Beauvais under the directorship of Jean-Baptiste Oudry (1686–1775), and later at the Gobelins.

THE ASCENDANCY OF THE PAINTER

Like the Gobelins, Beauvais found itself in the fiscal doldrums at the end of the seventeenth century, but, unlike the latter, it did not close down. Established by Colbert to compete with Flemish imports and satisfy private patrons, Beauvais of necessity stayed in the mainstream of popular taste. Under Philippe Behagle's directorship, which began in 1684, two brilliantly successful series rescued Beauvais at the turn of the century: the *Bérain Grotesques*, by Jean-Baptiste Monnoyer, and *The Audience of the Emperor of China* by Louis-Guy de Vernansal and Belin de Fontenay (fig. 51). These two series established themes that proved influential during the first half of the eighteenth century. The *Grotesques* satisfied popular tastes with its playfulness and love of ornament, as did *The Audience*

of the Emperor series, with its exoticism, nurtured by the tales of missionaries, explorers, and merchants of the Dutch East India Company. This wave of Beauvais' success was nearly expended when it was again rescued, this time by Oudry, who became its director in 1733. A nature painter and an uncompromising organizer, he demanded from the weavers a new respect for the cartoon. They were not to make color choices or to interpret the cartoon in matters of light or shadow. They felt downgraded and complained, but Oudry held firm. Having established the cartoon's supremacy, he brought in the foremost painters to supply the best possible images.

The most talented of these new men was the young François Boucher (1703–1770), who produced forty-five designs for Beauvais between 1736 and 1753. These designs continued to be woven into the 1770s. Boucher's contribution, surpassing that of Oudry, can scarcely be overstated. Though his name became an anathema in the period of the French Revolution because he symbolized all the values then under fire, subsequent generations of critics have reinstated his style without necessarily upholding the politics or morals it reflects. The de Goncourt brothers, nineteenth-century historians of French art, identified him as "one of those men who announce the taste of a century, who explain, personify and embody it." The present-day art historian Alexandre Ananoff wonders what the eighteenth century

would have been like if Boucher had never existed. With an apologetic nod in the direction of Diderot, Boucher's most ardent detractor, Ananoff calls Boucher "the benevolent genius of eternal youth, the magician who fashioned the marvelous French eighteenth century, filling it with lovely pastorals, nudes, and cherubs, bringing to each the imprint of his smile."[7] Mythological subjects comprise the lion's share of Boucher's oeuvre. They provided the best opportunity for exploiting his specialty, the female nude. Lightly draped nymphs and goddesses, cushioned on clouds or floating on waves, imparted a gentle seductive glow to such Ovidian tales as Zeus and Europa, Bacchus and Ariadne, and to reenactments of the domestic struggles of Venus and her husband, Vulcan.

When Boucher took a studio at the Gobelins in 1749 and succeeded Oudry as director in 1755, the delighted *chefs d'ateliers* expected him to produce the kind of cartoon that had been so successful at Beauvais. In this respect they were somewhat disappointed, for Boucher's main contribution to the Gobelins was medallion designs incorporated into the ornate scheme of *alentours*, or bordered tapestries. His rectangular or oval vignettes, framed like easel paintings and draped with floral garlands, appeared to hang against backgrounds of figured damask. The simulated carved and gilded frame surrounding this ensemble was often piled with assorted ornamental objects. Louis Tessier and Maurice Jacques were specialists in this genre. They orchestrated the various forms of exquisite deception into masterpieces of *trompe l'oeil* decorative art. *Alentour* tapestries provided a total textile environment that covered all four walls and was often accompanied by furniture designed to match. A splendid example in this style hangs in the Croome Court of The Metropolitan Museum of Art (fig. 52).

Six tapestries (cat. nos. 416–21) have been selected from the permanent collection of the Los Angeles County Museum of Art for inclusion in this catalogue to illustrate the elegance of tapestry in the eighteenth century. They represent precursors of eighteenth-century forms and themes, its mid-century triumphs, and its final curtain calls. Detailed listings on these tapestries, including information on artists, materials, dimensions, donors, and relevant literature, may be found in the catalogue checklist.

FIG. 51
The Audience of the Emperor of China
France (Beauvais), before 1732; after a design by
Louis-Guy de Vernansal (1648–1729) and Belin
de Fontenay (1653–1729)
Wool and silk
125 x 198 in.
The Fine Arts Museums of San Francisco,
Gift of the Roscoe and Margaret Oakes
Foundation
59.49.1

FIG. 52
Overdoor Panel from Croome Court
France (Gobelins), c. 1764–71; after a design by
Louis Tessier (active 1749–84)
Wool and silk
61½ x 52 in.
The Metropolitan Museum of Art, Gift of the
Samuel H. Kress Foundation, 1958
58.75.6

PLATE 48
Venus and Vulcan (cat. no. 419, detail).

NOTES

1
F. Kimball, *The Creation of the Rococo*, New York, 1943, p. 58.

2
E. A. Standen, "I. Tapestries in Use: Indoors," *Apollo*, 113: 233, July 1981, p. 8, fig. 6.

3
E. A. Standen, letter to the author, Nov. 30, 1981.

4
Cartoon, from It. *cartone*, pasteboard. A preparatory drawing or painting in full size, usually on paper, to be used for the final work in another medium.

5
J. Mondain-Monval, ed., *Correspondance de Soufflot (1756–1780)*, Paris, 1918, Introduction, p. 19.

6
E. A. Standen, "Some Notes on the Cartoons Used at the Gobelins and Beauvais Manufactories in the Eighteenth Century," *The J. Paul Getty Museum Journal*, 4: 1977, p. 25.

7
A. Ananoff and D. Wildenstein, *François Boucher*, vol. 2, Lausanne, 1976.

AILEEN RIBEIRO
DEPARTMENT HEAD,
HISTORY OF DRESS,
COURTAULD INSTITUTE OF ART
UNIVERSITY OF LONDON

THE ELEGANT ART OF FANCY DRESS

"O Jesu—Coz—why this fantastick dress?
I fear some Frenzy does your Head possess;
That thus you sweep along a Turkish Tail,
And let that Robe o'er Modesty prevail…
Why in this naughty Vestment are you seen?
Dress'd up for Love, with such an Air and Mien,
As if you wou'd commence Sultana Queen."

J. ARBUTHNOT,
"THE BALL, STATED IN A DIALOGUE
BETWIXT A PRUDE AND A COQUET," 1724

Among the other art forms that reached a peak of excellence in the eighteenth century can be counted the elegant art of fancy dress. "Avant tout," writes one authority, "le dix-huitième siècle est un siècle de masques."[1] This refers not only to the popularity of masquerades but also to the period's fascination with fancy dress in portraiture. In both arenas, there was a particularly absorbing interest in the dress of the exotic present and the historic past, which was encouraged by attendance at masquerades and was perpetuated through the creative imagination of the artist. It is often difficult, when looking at the vanished world of the *fêtes galantes* depicted by Watteau, or at the romantic portraits by Gainsborough that hark back to an idealized historic past, to disentangle fantasy from reality. To some extent the two coincided in the 1770s and 1780s, decades during which fashionable female dress was infiltrated by elements of the historic and the exotic; "Vandyke" costume could be *de rigueur* at a formal function (fig. 53) or, according to the *Magazine à la Mode* (1777), an English lady "taken from one of our polite assemblies and conducted to Constantinople, would be properly dressed to appear before the Grand Signior."[2]

This vast and complex subject can only be roughly sketched within the limits of this necessarily brief essay. So, although the story of masking and dressing up can be traced back to antiquity, we begin with the Italian carnival as the source for the masquerade, which spread throughout Europe in the eighteenth century. The carnival began after Christmas and extended through Ash Wednesday. It took place in many Italian cities and was marked by an explosion of revelry that included horse races, street theater performances, pageants, and processions. An English tutor in Rome in 1780 found all the citizens

appearing in the streets, masked, in the characters of Harlequins, Pantaloons, Punchinellos, and all the fantastic variety of a masquerade. This humour spreads to men, women and children; descends to the lowest ranks and becomes universal. Even those who have no mask…reject their usual clothes and assume some whimsical dress. The coachmen generally affect some ridiculous disguise—many of them chuse a woman's dress and have their faces painted and adorned with patches.[3]

Dressing in the clothes of the opposite sex was universally popular, and attracted much criticism from moralists. One visitor to the Roman carnival in 1741 found that the favorite dress of women maskers was "breeches with gold clock'd stockings, shoes buckled to the toes, a laced coat and a hat cocked à la mode de Paris."[4]

Pageant cars enacting themes from classical history or depicting the exotic inhabitants of faraway lands made their way through the streets. In Rome some of the most popular and lavish of these carnival processions were organized by the students of the French Academy. In 1735, for example, they put on a *mascarade chinoise*, parading in Chinese costumes through the Corso.

FIG. 53
Thomas Hudson (English, 1701–1779)
Mary, Duchess of Ancaster, 1757
Oil on canvas
94 x 54 in.
By courtesy of Grimsthorpe and Drummond
Castle Trustees

FIG. 54
L. Boquet (French, active second half of
18th century)
Madame Favart as a Sultana, 1760
Oil on canvas
Bibliothèque de l'Opera, Paris

The 1748 carnival found them dressed as members of the court of the sultan in Constantinople on their way to Mecca (fig. 54). The latter masquerade was deemed to be particularly inventive, though in true theatrical style, cheap materials were painted to represent rich damasks and brocades. A number of the artists taking part in the masquerade recorded these costumes, finding them useful for creating portraits that employed the ever-popular Turkish costume.[5]

It was in Venice that the most characteristic costume of the masquerade, adapted from the habits [dress] of the patrician Venetians, developed. It consisted of an all-enveloping black cloak or domino (fig. 55), a mask (either the *gnaga*, made of grotesquely shaped white waxed material, or the *moreta*, made of black velvet), a frill covering the lower jaw, a black silk or lace mantle, and a three-cornered black hat. An alternative to the domino was the *tabarro* (a short cloak) or the even shorter *mantellina*, which covered only the shoulders. But everyone wore the mask and hat, and absolute incognito was the rule.

Venetians wore this distinctive masquerade costume not only at the carnival but at other times of the year, including during the numerous public holidays. At the carnival in Florence in 1740, Horace Walpole joyously catalogued his day: "I have done nothing but slip out of my domino into bed, and out of bed into my domino; all the morn one makes parties in masque to the shops and coffeehouses, and all the evening to operas and balls."[6] Very few domino gowns survived. One famous exception is the domino worn by Gustavus III of Sweden when he was fatally shot at a masquerade in the Royal Opera House in Stockholm in 1792, his identity made plain by the decorations he wore on the beige silk doublet of his Vandyke suit. Outside Venice, the city in which black was the rule, colored dominos were popular, and were often elaborately trimmed with capes, frills, and ribbons.

By the early eighteenth century the masquerade was an essential part of court and carnival entertainment in most European countries. Masquerades were organized at courts to celebrate events of national rejoicing such as royal marriages or peace treaties. In Catholic countries, where there was a long tradition of carnival, masquerades were held in the streets and in theaters. In addition, many large cities had pleasure gardens, based on the French and English models, where alfresco masquerades could take place all year around.

Theaters were obvious places in which to hold masquerades, for they had orchestras for dancing and space for hundreds of maskers to walk and to dine. At these masquerades theatrical costumiers provided many of the costumes, and, at least at English masquerades, professional actors and actresses were paid to encourage a more sophisticated repartee.

In France the first *bals masqués* were held

FIG. 55
Couple in Masquerade Dress
France (?), c. 1750
Engraving on paper
3⅝ x 3 in.
Los Angeles County Museum of Art,
Mrs. Irene Salinger in Memory of Her Mother
54.89.149

at the Opéra in 1715, the year Louis XIV died. A new atmosphere of indulgence allowed for the spread of this novel entertainment, with its opportunities for adventure and intrigue; the court of Louis XV adopted the masquerade with enthusiasm. *Fêtes galantes*, rural masquerades immortalized by artists such as Watteau, Lancret, and Boucher, were occasions when courtly love and social graces were displayed, when courtiers dressed as shepherds and shepherdesses, as Harlequin and Columbine— for the Italian players were allowed to return to France in 1716, after a long banishment. They proved a perennially inspired source of costume for masquerade, and created a vogue for fashionable sitters to be portrayed as sophisticated inhabitants of an idyllic Arcadian countryside.

The absolutism of the French court ensured that a license for wealth would be displayed in dazzling masquerades. When the dauphin was married to a Spanish infanta in 1745, the Galerie des Glaces at Versailles provided a spectacular venue for a masked ball. The French queen appeared in a dress covered with pearls and wearing the two Crown diamonds, the Regent and the Sancy. The dauphin and his new wife came as a shepherd and shepherdess. But all were eclipsed by Louis XV and seven of his courtiers, who came as yew trees clipped to the shape of pillars, each with a vase on top. It was at this masquerade that the king met Madame le Normand d'É-toiles, later the Marquise de Pompadour, who came as the goddess Diana. They were publicly seen together, disguised in light silk dominos, at a masked ball held a few days later at the Hôtel de Ville in Paris. The court, led by Madame de Pompadour, performed in plays put on in her private theater, the Théâtre des Petits Cabinets, which was decorated by Boucher, who also helped design the costumes.

Some masquerades derived more or less directly from the staged *tableaux vivants* of the Renaissance, merged with the later Baroque courtly opera-ballets. Elaborate carousels or equestrian displays, in which the exotically dressed participants performed quadrilles on horseback, were popular at the Austrian court. Turkish costumes and the many handsome uniforms of regiments from the far-flung Holy Roman Empire clothed those taking part in such entertainments, favored by the Empress Maria Theresa for the celebration of military victories. The German courts were fond of mock tournaments as occasions on which to simultaneously display military skills and splendid costumes. In 1722, for example, the Bavarian court celebrated the marriage of the electoral prince with a tournament in which the court dressed as Greeks and Romans, in gold-embroidered costumes studded with diamonds.[7] An even more lavish fête was held in Potsdam in 1750, when the Prussian princes of the blood led opposing teams of courtiers dressed as Romans, Greeks, Carthaginians, and Persians. Their costumes

were copied from those worn in the theater—light, glittering fabrics with stiffened skirts, helmets, immense amounts of feathers and jeweled ornamentation—and they were worn also at the masked ball which followed.[8] It seems likely that actual theatrical costumes were used by Gustavus III and his court for the pageants and tournaments, some of which the king himself devised, which took place at the royal palaces of Drottningholm and Gripsholm in the 1770s and 1780s. Popular themes for the Swedish court were the mythological and historical, the latter including Medieval *chansons de geste*, and more recent periods of Swedish history, such as the reign of Gustavus Adolphus in the early seventeenth century.[9]

Masquerades were particularly popular at the German courts because they were "so much harassed with ceremony and form…[and] are glad to seize every opportunity of assuming the masque and domino, that they may taste the pleasures of familiar conversation and social mirth."[10] A visitor to Hanover in 1740 found that the tedium of life there was only ameliorated by the winter masked balls held at the opera house, and the summer masquerades at Herrenhausen, where the white dominos in the lamp-lit gardens gave them "the appearance of the Elysian fields." White or light-colored dominos were the customary wear at masquerades in Vienna. Four thousand people attended a masquerade at the royal summer palace of Schoenbrunn in

1775, and watched a ballet danced by members of the imperial family and the nobility, "all of them dressed in white silk fancy dresses trimmed with pink ribbons and blazing with diamonds."[11]

In England the financial restrictions placed on the Hanoverian kings meant that there could be no lavish court masquerades as in other European capitals. In the words of a German visitor, the English court was "the residence of dullness," and only with the Prince Regent (later George IV) was there any real leader of fashion. Though averse to paying for them, the English kings of the early eighteenth century were keen to attend masquerades. George II in particular was very fond of this form of entertainment; as Prince of Wales, he is to be seen in Hogarth's engraving *Masquerades and Operas* (fig. 56) helping to push people into a colonnade entitled MASQUERADE, while Heidegger looks out of a window above. It was Heidegger, a Swiss who arrived in England in 1708, who had first established masquerades at the opera house in the Haymarket. He set down the rules of masquerade etiquette (rather like Beau Nash in Bath), instructing people how to conduct themselves and when to unmask. He laid on refreshments and dancing, and soon the masquerade became the most popular entertainment in town, impressive both in scale and splendor (plate 54 and figs. 56, 61).

Hogarth's implied comment, in the engraving mentioned above, that people of

could new dumb Faustus, to reform the Age,
Conjure up Shakespear's or Ben Johnson's Ghost,
They'd blush for shame, to see the English Stage
Debauch'd by fool'ries, at so great a cost.

What would their Manes say? should they behold
Monsters and Masquerades, where usefull Plays
Adorn'd the fruitfull Theatre of old.
And Rival Wits contended for the Bays.

Price 1 Shilling. 1724

FIG. 56
William Hogarth (English, 1697–1764)
Masquerades and Operas, 1724
Engraving on paper
5 x 6¹¹⁄₁₆ in.
British Museum, London

FIG. 57
Giovanni Antonio Canal, called Canaletto
(Italian, 1697–1768)
The Interior of the Rotunda at Ranelagh, 1754
Oil on canvas
18½ x 29¾ in.
National Gallery, London

FIG. 58
Thomas Bowles (English, 1712–?)
A View of the Chinese Pavilions and Boxes in
Vauxhall Gardens
Engraving on paper; after a painting by S. Wale
(?–1786)
7⅞ x 12½ in.
British Library, London

PLATE 49
Petticoat (cat. no. 67)

PLATE 50
Petticoat (cat. no. 67, detail)

PLATE 51
Dress (cat. no. 28).

FIG. 59
Nicolaus von Heideloff (German, 1761–1837)
Afternoon Dresses, 1795
Colored engraving on paper
11½ x 8¾ in.
from Heideloff's *Gallery of Fashion*, vol. 1, January
1795

PLATE 52
Shoe (cat. no. 180).

FIG. 60
Afternoon Dresses (detail)

PLATE 53
Dress (cat. no. 35).

fashion were being overwhelmed by the popularity of such foreign and decadent pursuits as the masquerade, which was flourishing at the expense of native theater and literature, was typical of the concern felt about this new entertainment, with its potential for subverting morals. By the early eighteenth century it was the custom for groups of young people to dress up and disport themselves in the shady walks of Vauxhall Gardens in Lambeth, south London (fig. 58). "There is not a Girl in the Town but let her have her Will in going to a Masque and she shall dress as a Shepherdess," was the comment in the *Spectator* of 1711. Due to their dubious reputation, the gardens closed shortly after this, only to reopen in 1732, extended and improved, with long vistas, lawns, fountains, and supper boxes in the Chinese taste, decorated inside with scenes of contemporary life.

Vauxhall's popularity for concerts and masquerades was only eclipsed by the opening, in 1742, of Ranelagh Gardens in Chelsea, with its famous rotunda (fig. 57), formal walks, and canal, one of whose islands had a Chinese house on it. In 1749 a famous series of masquerades was held in Ranelagh to celebrate the Peace of Aix-la-Chapelle, which had ended the War of the Austrian Succession the year before. One of the masked balls was described by that indefatigable partygoer Horace Walpole, who found the grounds full of

masks and spread with tents....In one quarter was a Maypole dressed with garlands and people dancing round it to a tabor and pipe and rustic music, all masked as were all the various bands of music that were disposed in different parts of the garden; some like huntsmen with French horns, some like peasants and a troop of harlequins and scaramouches in the little open temple on the mount....All round the outside of the amphitheatre were shops filled with Dresden china, japan, &c, and all the shopkeepers in mask.[12]

The English propensity for masquerades *en plein air* (all the more startling in view of the uncertain climate) was encouraged by the great popularity of the pleasure gardens, where the entertainments were open to all on payment of a relatively small sum. Even indoors, the rooms of such fashionable abodes as Carlisle House in Soho, a favorite place for masquerades in the 1760s and 1770s, were decorated to resemble the countryside, with flowers, shrubs, and even trees. In the second half of the century, the vogue for the "picturesque" and the "wild simplicities" of nature, as revealed particularly in the English landscaped garden, gave a new lease of life to Arcadia, a favorite theme. In 1774 a *fête champêtre* was held by Lord Stanley on the grounds of his house The Oaks near Epsom in Surrey to celebrate his engagement to Lady Betty Hamilton. A temporary amphitheater, designed by Robert Adam, housed the guests, and dances and songs were performed by professional artists dressed as shepherds and sylvans, druids and wood nymphs. Though Lord Stanley and his fiancée chose to appear as Rubens and his wife, the theme of the masquerade was the

FIG. 61
A Masquerade Scene at the Pantheon
England, 1772
Engraving on paper; after a painting by
S. Wale (?–1786)
4¼ x 5⅜ in.
British Museum, London

pastoral, whose rustic costumes were popular because they were easily concocted and did not involve any of the character acting that such familiar parts as, for example, Punch, the fool, or the witch did.

Fancy dress in the eighteenth century meant fashionable dress accompanied by some elements of theatrical costume, such as floating scarves, sequins, braid, puffs of gauze, and bunches of flowers. These adornments were flattering (often incorporating a tight-fitting bodice or riding jacket) and at the same time conformed to the conventions of disguise, however slight. It was thus that Harriet Byron, the heroine of Richardson's novel *Sir Charles Grandison* (1753–54), went to a masquerade as an Arcadian princess wearing a blue satin bodice and skirt trimmed with silver braid and fringe, a scarf floating from her shoulders, a cap of white net with spangles, artificial flowers, and a white feather. It was the custom at many of the German courts to provide rural entertainments or *Wirtschaften*, in which guests dressed in the romanticized costumes of peasants, shepherds, and shepherdesses to act out the verses and plays of the court poet set to music.

One of the most popular themes for fancy dress in the eighteenth century was the oriental. Chinese styles had the most influence on the applied arts[13] and the Turkish on costume and portraiture. One famous "Chinese regatta" was given in Venice for the Elector of Saxony in 1716,

which possibly inspired those on the Thames in 1749 and 1775 in which the watermen raced for prizes wearing "very well fancied loose Chinese dresses." *Fêtes chinoises* were common occurrences in the pleasure gardens of cities and on the grounds of royal palaces, and those wishing to wear the correct costume could consult Sir William Chambers' *Designs of Chinese Buildings, Furniture, Dresses, Machines and Utensils* of 1757 (fig. 61).

In the eighteenth century Turkey was opened up to trade and travel, and accounts of its fabled splendors were revealed to the fascinated European eye. A number of Western artists were more or less permanently settled in Turkey at this time. They helped support themselves by painting some of the increasing number of travelers who were extending their Grand Tour to include Constantinople. They also illustrated travel books and collections of engravings depicting the richness and variety of costume within the Turkish empire. The most influential collection of such engravings, entitled *Recueil de Cent Estampes représentant différentes Nations du Levant*, was published in Paris in 1714, after paintings by J.B. Vanmour, an artist who settled in Turkey at the end of the seventeenth century. The beauty and accuracy of detail revealed in its plates inspired a number of artists who had never been to the East to paint sitters dressed *à la turque*. Thomas Jefferys, in *A Collection of the Dresses of Different Nations…*(1757), found them useful

as sources for masquerade costumes, as he also found himself indebted to the illustrations of the *1748 Caravanne du Sultan à la Mecque*, which had been performed by the students of the French Academy in Rome.

Turkey—or European perceptions of it—inspired a number of masquerades. At the fairy-tale court of Dresden in the early part of the century, the Elector Augustus II appeared as the Grand Sultan among a seraglio of court beauties in Turkish costume. At the other end of the century, in 1781, to celebrate the coming-of-age of William Beckford, Fonthill was transformed by the stage designer de Loutherbourg into a Turkish palace for three days of oriental entertainments.

For men, Turkish costume consisted of a long, fur-trimmed robe worn over baggy trousers, sashed at the waist, and a turban—the Europeanized version of Turkish clothing worn by travelers and merchants there. The loose gown was familiar to many fashionable men through the long-established popularity of the "Indian" or "Turkish" dressing gowns, worn as undress before the formal dressing for the day; the shorter, fitted banyans with frogged fastening were also a familiar morning negligee, as were the turbans, worn over shorn heads.

It was largely due to the fame of Lady Mary Wortley Montagu (1689–1762), through her travels and letters, that the vogue for Turkish costume became well

PLATE 54
Jean Baptiste Greuze (French, 1725–1805)
Portrait of an Actress in Oriental Dress, c. 1790
Oil on canvas
46 x 35¾ in.
Los Angeles County Museum of Art, William
Randolph Hearst Collection
47.29.6

established in England. Accompanying her husband on an ambassadorial visit to Turkey (1716–18), she noted in great detail every aspect of the life led by noble Turkish ladies, including their form of dress, a copy of which she had made for herself. The dress, as described in a letter to her sister in Paris, consisted of full gathered drawers of rose-colored damask; a fine smock of almost transparent silk gauze which revealed the whiteness of the bosom and which fastened at the neck with a diamond button; a tight-fitting waistcoat with long-fringed sleeves; and a caftan or "robe exactly fitted to my shape, and reaching to my feet, with very long strait falling sleeves."[14] This type of caftan, very often of the richest materials, was frequently caught up at one side and sometimes fastened under a jeweled girdle—a feature that was adopted by the theater and by fashionable ladies, linking the modish love of asymmetry in dress with the novelty of the recognizably oriental. With the dress of noble Turkish ladies, Lady Mary found that on the head was worn either a small cap trimmed with pearls or diamonds, or an embroidered silk scarf, both in conjunction, very often, with an aigrette of feathers or jeweled flowers. In cold weather ladies wore a *curdee*, a short-sleeved robe lined either with ermine or sable. In the Western interpretation of Turkish dress some fur trimming was an essential element. Greuze's *Portrait of an Actress in Oriental Dress* (plate 54) displays most of these elements of

Turkish masquerade costume: the sitter wears (over a modesty piece) a low-cut dress in European style with an embroidered "oriental" gown with characteristic central front opening, hitched up to one side, and with a wide-fringed sash.

Plays with oriental themes were all the rage, particularly in France, where in 1721 a Turkish embassy from the court of the Grand Sultan helped to encourage a vogue for *turquerie* in interior design and theatrical productions. Some actresses wore real Turkish dress, as Madame Favart did for her role in *Soliman* in 1767 (fig. 54). Others used the services of the fashionable portrait painter Jean-Étienne Liotard (1702–1789), who designed costumes both for the stage[15] and for a whole range of sitters, from the crowned heads of Europe to the ladies of the demimonde. Liotard, who dressed like a Turk and wore a long beard, lived for many years in Turkey. So popular was the fashion for being painted *à la turque* that many artists who had never been to Turkey were forced to paint their sitters in this style of dress. None, however, achieved the delicacy and detail which was Liotard's forte.

In high fashion, too, the influence of Turkey was particularly important; turbans, fur-lined gowns and trimmings, hanging sleeves and fringed sashes were a kind of easily recognized shorthand for oriental dress. (Only a few daring women, and some actresses, actually wore the voluminous silk trousers which were part of

FIG. 62
Johan Zoffany (German, 1733–1810)
The Family of Sir William Young, c. 1766
Oil on canvas
45⅛ x 66 in.
Walker Art Gallery, Liverpool

real Turkish costume.) A look at the well-known collection of fashion plates, the *Galerie des Modes* (1778–87), reveals the popularity of such gowns as *sultanes* and *circassiennes*.

From the 1760s onward many artists preferred the "oriental" deshabille, with its supposed simplicity of style in cut and fabric, to the minutiae of high fashion, with its stiffness and elaborate trimming. A popular informal dress at this time was a cross-over gown which tied at the waist with a sash; it was often made of light muslin embroidered with tambour work. This style of dress made it easier for artists like Reynolds and Angelica Kauffmann to give their sitters both a fashionable exoticism and, at the same time, a timeless flavor. Reynolds wrote in his *Seventh Discourse* (1776) that "the modern dress is sufficient to destroy all dignity." So he argued for a dress combining "the general air of the antique" with "something of the modern for the sake of likeness."

Yet for most of the century this classical ideal was appreciated more by artists than by sitters, and was difficult to achieve. It could lead to manifest absurdities such as the "large historical family piece" which Goldsmith's *Vicar of Wakefield* (1766), in his desire to be in fashion, orders. The vicar's wife was to be Venus "and the painter was requested not to be too frugal of his diamonds in her stomacher." The two smallest children were to be Cupids, Olivia was an Amazon in her green riding jacket, Sophia was to be a shepherdess, and the vicar himself "in my gown and band" was to present his wife with "my books on the Whistonian controversy."

The first stirrings of classical influences in dress did not come until the 1780s. This was a period when the simple white chemise gown popularized by Marie-Antoinette could be seen to resemble the chiton of Greek antiquity, and when artists such as Romney in England and Vigée-Lebrun in France were persuading some of their sitters to adopt a plain, unadorned gown without stays or hoops. It was, however, in the 1790s in France, when revolutionary political developments caused parallels to be drawn between contemporary events and those of ancient Greece and Rome, that the Neoclassical style caught the imagination. It was then that the figure-revealing muslin gowns with high waist and short sleeves, sandals and flowing shawls, and closely curled hairstyles, made the ideal a figure from a Greek vase or from a wall painting in Herculaneum.

To most people who attended masquerades or who were painted in fancy dress, the costume of more recent historical periods was preferred. The dress of the late sixteenth and early seventeenth centuries was particularly popular, for it was not too far away in time to be impossibly remote, nor too close to be subject to ridicule (fig. 62). For many of the countries instrumental in popularizing this taste, such as France and England, the late six-teenth and early seventeenth centuries were believed to be periods of political and cultural supremacy. In France, it was the period of Henri IV which caught the imagination, and the costume of that time was adopted by Marie Antoinette and other leaders of fashion for court balls in the 1770s. For men, trunk hose, slashed doublets, lace collars, short cloaks, and black hats with white feathers were worn. For women, raised collars—often with Vandyked lace edging, slashed sleeves, looped-up overskirts, and feathered hats, were prominent features.

Walpole was one of those who had helped to make popular a taste for antiquarianism. His influence, and the growing interest in historical accuracy which was slowly making headway in the costuming of historical plays on the stage, coupled with a new school of history painting glorifying the English past, encouraged the publication of such books as Thomas Jefferys' *A Collection of the Dresses of Different Nations both Ancient and Modern, and more particularly Old English Dresses after the designs of Holbein, Vandyke, Hollar and others*, first mentioned above. This collection was of immense importance in disseminating the taste for historical fancy dress, not just for the masquerader but also for the artist and drapery painters (figs. 63–66). The popularity of the sixteenth and early seventeenth centuries referred to in the title of Jefferys' work was noted by Walpole at a Vauxhall masquerade in 1742. There he saw "dozens

Habit of the Sultaness Queen in 1749.

La Sultane Reine.

FIG. 63
Habit of the Sultaness Queen (of 1748)
Engraving on paper
10¼ x 8 in.
from Thomas Jefferys' *A Collection of the Dresses of Different Nations...*, 1757 and 1772
(vol. 1, pl. 3)

FIG. 64
A Gentleman of Persia in 1568
Engraving on paper
10¼ x 8 in.
from Thomas Jefferys' *A Collection of the Dresses of Different Nations...*, 1757 and 1772
(vol. 1, pl. 82)

Habit of a Gentleman of Persia, in 1568.

Gentilhomme Persan.

FIG. 65
Habit of Mary Queen of Scots in 1570
Engraving on paper
10¼ x 8 in.
from Thomas Jefferys' *A Collection of the Dresses of Different Nations...*, 1757 and 1772
(vol. 2, pl. 204)

Habit of an English Lady of Quality, in 1640.

Dame Anglisede Qualité.

FIG. 66
Habit of an English Lady of Quality in 1640
Engraving on paper
10¼ x 8 in.
from Thomas Jefferys' *A Collection of the Dresses of Different Nations...*, 1757 and 1772
(vol. 2, pl. 216)

Fɪɢ. 66a
Artist's Lay Figure and Wardrobe (cat. no. 331)

of ugly Queens of Scotts...the Princess of Wales was one, covered with diamonds.... The finest and most charming masks were their Graces of Richmond like Harry the Eighth and Jane Seymour, excessively rich and both so handsome. There were quantities of pretty Vandykes and all kinds of pictures walked out of their frames."[16]

The vogue for Vandyke dress extended in England from the 1730s through the early 1790s. It was widely worn for plays with historical themes. It may be seen in Reynolds' portrait of *Sir Watkin Williams Wynn and His First Wife, Lady Henrietta Wynn* of 1769–70 (Collection of Sir H.L. Watkin Williams Wynn, Bart.) Sir Watkin owned a private theater; the inventory of its costumes includes many Vandyke suits in bright colors with much trimming of braid and metal lace. The Vandyke suits ordered in 1781 by the Prince of Wales for his brother including one made of "white sattin with pink puffs and knots" and another of "lylach silk...with pale buff puffs and knots,"[17] sound similar in fussiness of detail to surviving Vandyke suits, such as the pair from about 1780 recently acquired by the Royal Scottish Museum. One of these is of ruched ivory satin trimmed with silver lace, tinsel tassels, and sequins; the other is of pink satin, slashed to reveal puffs of ivory satin, edged with black linen, silver lace, and sequins.[18] Similar slashes of cream satin trim the pink suit worn by *Master Nicholls* in the Gainsborough painting of 1782 (Waddesdon Manor). Pink was

a popular color for Vandyke costume. One of the best-preserved suits in this style, of salmon-pink damask with matching short cloak, is in the collection of the Rijksmuseum in Amsterdam.[19] Many young men and boys wore Vandyke suits for sport, especially archery.[20]

Any artist who wished to be thought a fashionable portraitist needed to paint sitters in this kind of dress. His studio would either contain costume drawings or engravings from which sitters could make a choice, or lay figures with miniature clothes. A unique example of a lay figure with a complete wardrobe of male and female clothing is included in this exhibition and catalogue (fig. 66a; cat. no. 331). It was once the property of Ann Whytell (an artist about whom virtually nothing is known), is dated 1769, and includes a Vandyke costume comprised of slashed breeches, a sleeveless slashed doublet with shoulder wings, and separate slashed sleeves. The piece adds considerably to our information about the widespread use of Vandyke costume as an accepted element of eighteenth-century portraiture.

Such androgynous lay figures were necessary equipment for artists of the period, since a fashionable sitter sat only long enough to have his or her face painted, and the pose and dress roughly sketched out. The artist Arthur Devis (1711–1787), for example, probably used the small model hussar costumes in blue and pink satin trimmed with gold braid and tassels which

are in the collection of the Harris Museum and Art Gallery in Preston, Lancashire.[21] Hungarian hussar uniform, consisting of a dolman with slanting triangular flap and frogged fastening, trousers, and fur-lined pelisse, was a popular masquerade costume. It is featured in a number of fancy dress portraits, notably by Devis, such as his painting of *Mr. and Mrs. William Ricketts at a Masquerade at Ranelagh* (private collection).

Mrs. Ricketts wears a version of the popular Rubens' wife costume. This mode of dress was named after Rubens' portrait of *Helena Fourment* of the early 1630s, which for most of the eighteenth century was in the collection of Sir Robert Walpole; it is now in the Gulbenkian Museum in Lisbon. In the early part of the century the work was attributed to Vandyke, but it was correctly identified by Jefferys in his 1757 *Collection of Dresses*. The sitter in Rubens' work wears a silk dress with a bunched-up overskirt edged with pearls, chemise sleeves tied with ribbon, a jeweled chain looping over the shoulder from a central brooch, a falling collar, and a hat fastened up at one side and adorned with white feathers (fig. 53). Some or all of these features were copied from the original portrait for masquerade costumes. In addition, this costume was a conventional stock dress for portraiture, an idea first introduced by the artist Johan van der Bank (1686–1739) in 1732.[22] It enjoyed its greatest popularity in this regard in the middle years of the century.

By the 1770s many elements of this kind of fancy dress had been incorporated into the general romantic flavor of the dress of this period, typified perhaps best of all in such Gainsborough portraits as the *Hon. Mrs. Graham* of 1777 (National Gallery of Scotland) or the *Hon. Frances Duncombe* (The Frick Collection, New York) of about the same date. Fashion and the dress of the past are mingled in these paintings: the bunched-up drapery of the Rubens original becomes the fashionable polonaise of the 1770s, and the Rubens feathered hat turns into the "picture" hat familiar through the portraits of Gainsborough and his contemporaries.

There were, of course, many other kinds of Vandyke dress for women that contained more or less accurate elements of this costume—rounded or paned sleeves, lace collars, and decorative rosettes at bosom and waist—cut in the style of the eighteenth century, with long, pointed waist and hooped skirt. The search for accuracy did not usually extend to copying early Stuart hairstyles, unless one was highly educated like Elizabeth Montagu, the famous bluestocking who attended the 1749 Ranelagh masquerade dressed after a portrait of Queen Henrietta Maria, wife of Charles I, in white satin and pearls "and my hair curled after the Vandyke picture."[23] An element of fancy dress can also be discerned in the fondness for soft satin "nightgowns," some of which can be seen to derive from paintings by Lely and Kneller in which the sitters wear a simple form of "undress" over a plain linen chemise.[24]

The masquerade helped to popularize fancy dress, whether revealed in the dreamlike Arcadian *fêtes galantes* of the French Rococo painters, or in the more prosaic English interpretation of the past set firmly in the present. Its importance was reflected in the way that masking and dressing up were not confined to a very limited section of society, as in previous centuries, but were open to anyone with imagination. Sir Charles Grandison, in Richardson's eponymous novel, rejoiced "when I see advertised an eighteen-penny masquerade, for all the pretty 'prentice souls who will that evening be Arcadian Shepherdesses, Goddesses and Queens." Particularly in the first half of the century, the fondness for fancy dress reflected a general desire to escape from the conventions of formal dress. But much more, it evinced a mood of optimistic romanticism and a love of fantasy which were typical of the period and which were swept away forever by the French Revolution and the wars that succeeded it. The ponderous nineteenth-century fancy dress revivals failed to capture the spirit of wit and elegance which was such an integral part of the eighteenth century's world of masquerade.

NOTES

1
É. Pilon and F. Saisset, *Les Fêtes en Europe au XVIIIe siècle*, Saint-Gratien, 1943, p. 2.

2
Magazine à la Mode, London 1777, p. 367.

3
J. Moore, *A View of Society and Manners in Italy*, 2 vols., London, 1781, 2:84. There is a useful chapter on the carnival in Venice in A. Lowe, *La Serenissima: The Last Flowering of the Venetian Republic*, London, 1974.

4
J. Russel, *Letters from a Young Painter abroad to his Friends in England*, 2 vols., London, 1750, 1:44. Dressing up in the clothes of the opposite sex at masquerades was universal. In the 1740s the Empress Elizabeth of Russia established masked balls, called Metamorphoses, to which the men wore the wide-hooped skirted dresses of current fashion and the women wore men's suits. The empress herself liked to dress either as a cossack or as a Dutch sailor, the latter being a costume particularly favored by her father, Peter the Great.

5
See F. Boucher, "An Episode in the Life of the Académie de France à Rome," *Connoisseur*, Oct. 1961.

6
H. Walpole, *Letters*, ed. P. Toynbee, 16 vols., Oxford, 1903–05, 1:48.

7
P. de Bretagne, *Réjouissances et fêtes magnifiques qui se sont faites en Bavière l'an 1722...*Munich, 1723.

8
*Journal Historique des Fêtes que le Roi a données à Potsdam...*Berlin, 1750.

9
The Drottningholms Teatermuseum in Stockholm has a collection of carousel costumes worn by Gustavus III. The national dress Gustavus established in 1778 was based on the costume of the early seventeenth century and was probably inspired by the Henri IV styles at the French court. The everyday dress was red and black with slashed sleeves and rosettes, and there was a gala dress of blue and white trimmed with braid.

10
J. Moore, *A View of Society and Manners in France, Switzerland and Germany*, 2 vols., London, 1779, 2:80.

11
Ibid., 2:379.

12
Walpole, *Letters*, 2:369. Vauxhall and Ranelagh Gardens were only two of the pleasure gardens in London providing masquerades and other entertainments. The most comprehensive account of them is still W. Wroth, *The London Pleasure Gardens of the Eighteenth Century*, London, 1896; it has recently been reissued in facsimile.

13
For a discussion of the taste for chinoiserie in the eighteenth century, see O. Impey, *Chinoiserie: The Impact of Oriental Styles on Western Art and Decoration*, Oxford, 1977.

14
Lady Mary Wortley Montagu's letters circulated in manuscript before being published in 1763. The best edition of them is *The Complete Letters of Lady Mary Wortley Montagu*, ed. R. Halsband, 3 vols., Oxford, 1965–67. Lady Mary's descriptions of clothing, though occasionally in error about the correct words for certain types of dress, are lively and full of information; it is not surprising that, along with the many portraits painted of her in Turkish dress, they should have contributed to the popularity of this fancy dress.

15
J. L. Vaudoyer, "L'Orientalisme en Europe au XVIIIe siècle," *Gazette des beaux-arts*, 1911, p. 98.

16
Walpole, *Letters*, 1:82.

17
The Correspondence of George, Prince of Wales, 1770–1812, ed. A. Aspinall, 8 vols., London, 1963–71, 1:62.

18
Royal Scottish Museum, Edinburgh, inv. nos. 1980.157 and 1980.158.

19
Rijksmuseum, Amsterdam, no. KOG 2611.

20
Ipswich Museum has a green Vandyke suit (a doublet of green satin trimmed with white gimp and matching breeches), a doublet of green satin decorated with green and cream silk ribbon with white silk imitating a slashed sleeve, and a semicircular cloak. J.L. Nevinson, "The Vogue of the Vandyke Dress," *Country Life Annual*, 1959, believes these items may have been worn by young archers.

21
See A. Ribeiro, "Hussars in Masquerade," *Apollo*, Feb. 1977.

22
Vertue Notebooks, 3, Walpole Society, London, 1933–34, p. 57. J. Steegman, "A Drapery Painter of the Eighteenth Century," *Connoisseur*, June 1936, puts forward the theory that it was the drapery painter Joseph van Aken, who assisted many important artists in the 1730s and 1740s with their draperies, who was instrumental in popularizing the Rubens' wife costume.

23
E. Montagu, *The Queen of the Blue-Stockings: Correspondence 1720–1761*, ed. E. J. Climenson, 2 vols., London, 1906, 1:264. It is not known which portrait of Henrietta Maria was copied, for the painting of Mrs. Montagu which was to be done by Hoare (if it was ever attempted) has not been identified. On the subject of Vandyke dress in general, see J. L. Nevinson, "Vandyke Dress," *Connoisseur*, Nov. 1964.

24
See A. Ribeiro, "Some Evidence of the Influence of the Dress of the Seventeenth Century on Costume in Eighteenth-Century Female Portraiture," *Burlington Magazine*, Dec. 1978.

CATALOGUE

Measuring eighteenth-century apparel is a prodigious task. Modern terminology and technique, though adaptable, are not meant to describe a fichu, a pair of engageantes, or many other articles of clothing commonly worn during the Age of Elegance. In this catalogue, the dimension measured within each category is the same, but there is, necessarily, a wide diversity between categories. Height precedes width unless otherwise specified. A listing of the most commonly used abbreviations follows:

cb	Center back measurement, from top edge to bottom edge
cf	Center front measurement, from top edge to bottom edge
circum	Circumference
d	Depth
diam	Diameter

Some objects could only be measured in a manner that matched their unique construction. These methods are described the first time an object belonging to a particular category appears; an asterisk placed after the catalogue number calls the reader's attention to the description provided in a footnote.

All relevant bibliographic references and exhibitions are presented in abbreviated form, consisting simply of a capital letter for exhibitions and a number for publications. These are keyed to a full listing of citations, to be found at the back of the catalogue.

Catalogue illustrations are always above their captions.

1

DRESS (open robe)
England, c. 1735; altered 1770
Multicolored brocaded floral pattern in orange,
pink, brown, tan, and blue on dark green twill
silk ground; linen-lined bodice; Spitalfields.
cb: 52¾ in. (134 cm.)
Gift of Mrs. Henry Salvatori
M.80.70.4

2

DRESS (closed robe)
England, c. 1735
Multicolored floral brocade, drizzled, all metallic
threads removed from motifs, on red silk
ground; linen-lined bodice; silk-lined skirt;
Spitalfields.
cb: 52⅜ in. (133 cm.)
Mrs. Alice F. Schott Bequest
M.67.8.72
Exh: R
See plate 10

3

DRESS (robe with petticoat)
England, c. 1730
Multicolored brocade, of restrained branch and
floral design, on ribbed beige silk ground;
quilted taupe silk petticoat; linen-lined bodice;
Spitalfields.
cb of dress: 56½ in. (143.5 cm.)
cf of petticoat: 36½ in. (92.7 cm.)
Mrs. Alice F. Schott Bequest
M.67.8.73a,b

4

DRESS (gown and petticoat)
England, c. 1730–40
Metallic gold geometric and floral design
brocaded on cream patterned silk ground; linen-
lined bodice.
cb of dress: 48¼ in. (122.6 cm.)
cf of petticoat: 39⅛ in. (99.4 cm.)
Costume Council Fund
M.57.24.2a,b; ex-coll. Doris Langley Moore
Exh: C, J
Pub: 14, p. 4 (ill.); 37, p. 184, pl. 89b (ill.)
See plate 21

5

DRESS (open court robe and petticoat)
England, c. 1750–60
Silver floral brocade on yellow and white silk
diapered ground; silver bobbin lace trim; linen-
lined bodice.
cb of dress: 57½ in. (144.5 cm.)
cf of petticoat: 34 in. (86.4 cm.)
Gift of Mrs. Henry Salvatori
M.79.118a,b
See plate 5

6

DRESS (open robe and petticoat)
England, c. 1750–75
Green ombré and multicolored vertical woven
stripes on peach silk taffeta ground; petticoat
and dress robings of pinked and punched self-
fabric; linen-lined bodice; silk-lined petticoat.
cb of dress: 58⅜ in. (148 cm.)
cf of petticoat: 34⅜ in. (87.4 cm.)
Costume Council Fund
M.57.24.4a,b; ex-coll. Doris Langley Moore
Exh: C
Pub: 14, p. 5 (ill.)

7

DRESS (closed robe)
England, c. 1750–75
Shaded silk polychrome floral embroidery on
cream silk satin with linen weft; sleeve trimmed
with dark green passementerie; linen-lined
bodice.
cb: 50¼ in. (128.5 cm.)
Costume Council Fund
M.57.23; ex-coll. Mrs. R. Skinner
Exh: C, Q
Pub: 14, p. 9 (ill.)

8

DRESS (closed robe)
England, c. 1750–60
White floral design on gray and tan shaded,
vertical striped, figured silk ground; matching
attached and buttoned stomacher; linen-lined
bodice and stomacher.
cb: 54¼ in. (137.5 cm.)
Costume Council Fund
M.59.24.3; ex-coll. Doris Langley Moore
Exh: D
Pub: 12, p. 5 (ill.)

9

DRESS (polonaise and petticoat)
England, c. 1750–65
Multicolored floral design on yellow patterned
silk ground; trimmed with brown silk, cording,
and tassels; matching petticoat; linen-lined
bodice.
cb of dress: 47½ in. (120.5 cm.)
cf of petticoat: 36⅛ in. (91.8 cm.)
Gift of Mr. and Mrs. Joseph Cotten
M.59.17a,b
Exh: D, Q
Pub: 12, p. 6 (ill.); 26, pp. 8–9 (ill.)

10

DRESS (open robe and petticoat)
England or France, c. 1750–75
Brilliantly colored, richly brocaded floral design
with black chenille on white silk satin ground;
appliquéd bows, ruching, and ribbon flowers;
matching petticoat with elaborate trim; linen-
lined bodice.
cb of dress: 67¼ in. (171.5 cm.)
cf of petticoat: 38¼ in. (97.1 cm.)
Costume Council Fund
M.57.24.5a,b; ex-coll. Doris Langley Moore
Exh: C, D, J, R
Pub: 14, p. 6 (ill.); 26, p. 9 (ill.)

11

DRESS (sack-back open robe and petticoat)
England, c. 1760
Olive green and pale blue vertical stripes on a
light tan silk taffeta ground; matching petticoat
and buttoned stomacher; linen-lined bodice.
cb of dress: 58¼ in. (148 cm.)
cf of petticoat: 36⅜ in. (92.5 cm.)
Gift of Loewi-Robertson
M.80.14a,b

12
DRESS (open robe and petticoat)
England, c. 1760–70
Shaded colors of amaranth, red, green, and blue silk, in chain stitch embroidered design of flowers, on white cotton twill ground; embroidered in India, probably Kashmir; fashioned from a large panel; linen-lined bodice.
cb of dress: 55¾ in. (141.5 cm.)
cf of petticoat: 39⅛ in. (99.4 cm.)
Gift of Mrs. William Clayton
M.66.31a,b
Exh: N
Pub: 30, p. 17 (ill.); 31, p. 91 (ill.)

13
DRESS (open robe and petticoat)
England, c. 1770
Pale blue, white, and narrow black stripes, with superimposed garlands of white flowers, on silk satin ground; petticoat of pale blue and cream shot-silk taffeta; robe skirt lined with cream China silk; linen-lined bodice.
cb of dress: 57¼ in. (145.5 cm.)
cf of petticoat: 39⅜ in. (100.1 cm.)
Costume Council Fund
M.64.83.2a,b

14
DRESS (open robe and petticoat)
England, c. 1770
Multicolored small sprigs of wool crewel embroidered flowers on white linen; diamond-patterned quilted petticoat of dark green silk lined with glazed wool; linen-lined bodice.
cb of dress: 59½ in. (151 cm.)
cf of petticoat: 34 in. (86.4 cm.)
Costume Council Fund
M.59.25a–d
Exh: D
Pub: 26, p. 9 (ill.)
See plate 16, fig. 6

15
DRESS (sack-back closed robe)
England, c. 1770–80
Multicolored flowers in vertical design on mauve striped silk taffeta ground; adjustable, to be worn over large side hoops; linen-lined throughout.
cb: 61¼ in. (155.5 cm.)
Purchased with Funds Provided by John Jewett Garland
M.56.1.1
Exh: D, K
Pub: 12, p. 9 (ill.); 26, p. 9 (ill.)
See plate 13

16
DRESS (open robe)
England: fabric, after 1774; dress, c. 1780–90
Multicolored floral print, with stems and flowers in imitation of Indian design, on cotton ground; selvage contains blue threads required by law on all domestically produced printed cottons between 1774 and 1811; linen-lined bodice.
cb: 52¾ in. (134 cm.)
Costume Council Fund
M.81.135.2

17
DRESS (open robe)
England, c. 1785
Blue and brown toned tendrils and scattered delicate floral pattern of wild flowers printed on white cotton ground; linen-lined bodice.
cb: 60¼ in. (153.5 cm.)
Costume Council Fund
M.80.138

18
DRESS (sack-back open court robe and petticoat)
England, c. 1760–70
Large stylized silver floral motif, connected with silver ribbonlike forms, on patterned cream silk ground; ruchings and trim edged with silver bobbin lace; matching petticoat lined with China silk; linen-lined bodice.
cb of dress: 63 in. (155.5 cm.)
cf of petticoat: 40 in. (101.6 cm.)
Costume Council Fund
M.57.24.7a,b; ex-coll. Doris Langley Moore
Exh: C, J
Pub: 14, p. 8 (ill.)

19
DRESS (polonaise)
England, c. 1785
Multicolored ombré, vertical floral, warp-float patterned silk on cream silk ground; pinked trim; wool-lined skirt; linen-lined bodice.
cb: 52¼ in. (133 cm.)
Purchased with Funds Provided by Nancy Yewell
M.82.22

20
DRESS (sack-back open robe and petticoat)
England, c. 1765–70
Multicolored vertical floral and ombré stripes on pale yellow and cream striped silk ground; elaborate flounces and puffs, passementerie, and chenille flowers on front of robe and petticoat; linen-lined bodice.
cb of dress: 65 in. (157.5 cm.)
cf of petticoat: 40⅝ in. (103.2 cm.)
Gift of Mrs. Delmer Lawrence Davis
M.64.66.1a,b
Exh: P
Pub: 29, pp. 83, 190 (ill.)

21
DRESS (open robe)
England, c. 1780
Aubergine silk taffeta (lustring); trimmed with pinked and pleated white silk; linen-lined bodice.
cb: 59¾ in. (152 cm.)
Gift of Mrs. Murray Ward
M.72.48.1

22
DRESS (open robe or polonaise)
England, c. 1785
Multicolored vertical floral ribbon stripes and scattered bows on diapered cream silk ground; linen-lined bodice.
cb: 54¼ in. (137.5 cm.)
Gift of Derek A. Colls in Memory of Mrs. Joanna Christie Crawford
M.70.85

23
DRESS (trained open robe)
England, c. 1790; altered, after 1795
Metallic chain stitch and silk floral embroidery scattered on fine cream-colored Indian cotton mull; cream silk fly fringe edging with tassels; finely pleated and starched cotton elbow cuffs; linen-lined bodice.
cb: 62⅝ in. (158.9 cm.)
Costume Council Fund
M.80.190.1a,b

24
DRESS
England, c. 1790–95
Pink and brown flowers embroidered in silk, with strip-silver metal crescents, on fine white cotton ground; probably embroidered in India for the English market; under bodice of linen; cream silk satin sleeves.
cb: 59 in. (150 cm.)
Costume Council Fund
M.57.24.11; ex-coll. Doris Langley Moore
Exh: C
Pub: 14, p. 13 (ill.)

25
DRESS
England, c. 1795
Red, green, blue, tan, and lavender hand-painted designs of plants, animals, and architecture on glazed natural linen ground; made in South India for English market.
cb: 71¾ in. (181.4 cm.)
Gift of Mrs. Henry Salvatori
M.79.84.2
Exh: S
See plate 1

26

DRESS (open robe)
England, 1794
Multicolored vertical satin stripes on solid and *chiné* horizontal stripes of silk; military-style with triple-cape collar and large revers; shaped sleeves; frock buttons at center back of skirt; linen-lined under bodice; Directoire style.
cb: 58¼ in. (148 cm.)
Promised Gift of the Costume Council
TR.3630.1
See plate 19

27

COAT (redingote)
England, c. 1790–97
Blue gray silk moiré; long, close-fitting sleeves, large lapels, stand-up and cape collars; buttons down front to floor; linen-lined bodice; Directoire style.
cb: 59 in. (150 cm.)
Costume Council Fund
M.57.24.9; ex-coll. Doris Langley Moore
Exh: C, K
Pub: 14, p. 11 (ill.)
See plate 2

28

DRESS
England, c. 1800
Gold embroidered bows and garlands, made with thin strips of silver gilt, on white cotton muslin; probably manufactured in India for English market; gold fringe and white loop fringe at hem; sleeves shaped over the elbow and finished with self-ruffle.
cb: 64½ in. (163.9 cm.)
Costume Council Fund
M.57.24.12; ex-coll. Doris Langley Moore
Exh: C
Pub: 14, p. 14 (ill.)
See plate 51

29

DRESS (sack-back open robe)
England, c. 1750–60
Patterned cream silk satin trimmed with cream silk braid; fabric made in China for European market; skirt adjustable for side hoops; linen-lined bodice.
cb: 50¼ in. (127.7 cm.)
Gift of Mrs. Henry Salvatori
M.79.19.1
Exh: S

30

DRESS
England, c. 1801
Cerise ribbed silk; black stamped silk velvet trim; apron front; train.
cb: 64½ in. (161.3 cm.)
Costume Council Fund
M.57.24.13; ex-coll. Doris Langley Moore
Exh: C, R
Pub: 14, p. 15 (ill.); 33, p. 35, pl. 2

31

DRESS (open robe, petticoat, and stomacher)
England, c. 1760–80
Multicolored painted floral designs on cream silk satin fabric; painted in China for European market; stuffed robing; linen-lined bodice.
cb of dress: 54¼ in. (137.8 cm.)
cf of petticoat: 39 in. (99.1 cm.)
Costume Council Fund
M.55.24.3
Exh: B, D, E, M
Pub: 12, p. 9 (ill.)

32

DRESS
England, c. 1798–1802
Pastel embroidered appliquéd scenes, in silk and spot motif with sequins, on aubergine and puce vertical striped silk satin; short puffed sleeves; Directoire style.
cb: 50⅛ in. (127.2 cm.)
Costume Council Fund
M.59.28.1
Exh: N
Pub: 30, pl. 28

33

DRESS (sack-back open robe)
England, c. 1760
Lilac and blue brocaded floral designs on pale yellow figured silk ground; stuffed robings edged with black lace; linen-lined bodice.
cb of dress: 59½ in. (151.2 cm.)
cf of petticoat: 34 in. (86.4 cm.)
Costume Council Fund
M.63.52.4a,b

34

DRESS (open robe and petticoat)
England, c. 1770–80
Polychrome silk floral bouquet designs, in shades of red, green, and yellow, brocaded on pink and tan shot-silk ground; box-pleated robings; shaped sleeves; linen-lined bodice.
cb of dress: 62½ in. (158.8 cm.)
cf of petticoat: 37½ in. (95.3 cm.)
Costume Council Fund
M.57.24.8a,b; ex-coll. Doris Langley Moore
Exh: C, D, L
Pub: 14, p. 10 (ill.); 26, p. 9 (ill.)
See plate 20

35

DRESS
England, c. 1790–95
Small gold, green, and red brocaded flowers on diamond-figured buff silk ground; long shaped sleeves; skirt with lace flounce and train; linen-lined bodice; Directoire style.
cb of dress: 64 in. (162.6 cm.)
Costume Council Fund
M.57.24.10; ex-coll. Doris Langley Moore
Exh: C
Pub: 14, p. 12 (ill.)
See plate 53

36

DRESS
England, c. 1800
Coarse white cotton embroidery on fine white cotton; apron front, long sleeves, and train; unlined; Empire style.
cb: 93 in. (236.2 cm.)
Gift of Mrs. Henry Salvatori
M.79.19.5
Exh: S

37
DRESS
England, c. 1807–10
White cotton floral embroidery in vertical bands
with sprigs on fine white cotton; short puffed
sleeves; drawstring closures on bodice back.
cb: 52¾ in. (134 cm.)
Gift of Mrs. Henry Salvatori
M.79.19.4
Exh: S

38
DRESS
England, c. 1804
Fine gold and cream vertical striped silk taffeta;
apron front closing; long sleeves; inverted
double pleat at center back; train; linen-lined
bodice; Empire style.
cb: 57 in. (144.8 cm.)
Costume Council Fund
M.57.24.14; ex-coll. Doris Langley Moore
Exh: C, K
Pub: 14, p. 16 (ill.)

39
DRESS (sack-back open robe and petticoat)
France, c. 1750–60
Lavender, red, and green meandering floral
pattern brocaded on silver and cream silk
ground; gold metallic orris bobbin lace trim;
linen-lined bodice.
cb: 62½ in. (158.8 cm.)
Gift of Mrs. Aldrich Peck
M.56.6a,b; ex-coll. Princess Lubomirski
Exh: D, J
Pub: 12, p. 8 (ill.)

40
DRESS (sack-back open robe)
France, c. 1750–60
Rose, lilac, and green warp-printed silk taffeta,
in floral pattern, on pale peach ground;
attached stomacher of pinked and gathered self-
fabric; pinked and punched box-pleated robings
and sleeve ruffles; unlined bodice.
cb: 66¼ in. (168 cm.)
Gift of Mrs. Frederick Kingston
M.60.36.1
Exh: D, E, N
Pub: 26, p. 9 (ill.); 30, pl. 19

41
DRESS
France, c. 1750–60
Blue silk moiré; padded and puckered robings
with fly fringe trim; double sleeve ruffles; linen-
lined bodice.
cb: 65⅜ in. (165.5 cm.)
Mrs. Alice F. Schott Bequest
M.67.8.71
See plate 47

42
DRESS (sack-back open robe)
France, c. 1760
Brown pinstripes on rust silk; gathered robings
and sleeve ruffles edged with metallic silver lace;
linen-lined bodice.
cb: 59 in. (150 cm.)
Mrs. Alice F. Schott Bequest
CR.448.67.49

43
DRESS (sack-back open robe and petticoat)
England or France, c. 1770–80
Narrow reddish brown and cream spotted
vertical stripes; thread buttons; stomacher tabs
for fichu; striped linen-lined bodice and
petticoat.
cb of dress: 58 in. (148.5 cm.)
cb of petticoat: 39 in. (99.1 cm.)
Costume Council Fund
M.59.12a,b
Exh: D, H, K, R
Pub: 12, p. 7 (ill.); 26, p. 9 (ill.)

44
DRESS (sack-back gown and petticoat)
France, c. 1760–75
Silver brocaded design of flowers and leaves, on
pale yellow silk taffeta, pin-striped with
horizontal metallic silver thread; edged with
metallic silver orris bobbin lace.
cb: 53 in. (134.5 cm.)
Costume Council Fund
M.59.24.1a,b
Exh: D
Pub: 26, p. 9 (ill.)
See figs. 67–69

45
DRESS (caraco jacket and petticoat)
France, c. 1760–80
Blue and red wool floral brocade on natural
linen ground (*toile de Normandie*); petticoat on
drawstring; linen-lined bodice.
cb of jacket: 25 in. (63.5 cm.)
cb of petticoat: 37 in. (94 cm.)
Mrs. Alice F. Schott Bequest
M.67.8.74a,b
See plate 9

46
CAPE WITH HOOD
France, c. 1780–90
Multicolored delicate leaf, stem, and flower
pattern overprinted on brown cotton resist;
fabric printed at Hausmann Factory in Colmar,
Alsace; elaborate finely pleated trim around
entire edge of cape and hood.
cf: 60 in. (152.3 cm.)
Mrs. Alice F. Schott Bequest
M.67.8.29
Exh: Q

47
DRESS (sack-back open robe)
Italy (?), c. 1740–55
Pale gold stylized floral twill pattern on red
damask patterned silk ground; pinked and
gathered robings; linen-lined bodice.
cb: 53 in. (134.5 cm.)
Costume Council Fund
M.64.83.1
Exh: L

48
RIDING HABIT
Italy (Venice), c. 1780
Yellow green and cerise watered silk with silver
basket buttons and trim; skirt opens at front and
back; drawstrings in side seams; waistcoat, coat
cuffs, and lapels of cerise watered silk; waistcoat
and coat lined with pale blue linen.
cb of coat: 24½ in. (62.2 cm.)
cb of vest: 25 in. (63.5 cm.)
cb of skirt: 35 in. (90.2 cm.)
Purchased with Funds Provided by
Mr. and Mrs. Dennis C. Stanfill
M.82.162a–c
See plate 22

49
FOLK DRESS
Italy, late 18th century
Indigo blue cotton and natural linen pleated
skirt; wine wool broadcloth bodice boned with
reeds; side-back seams open with metal rings
and linen tape lacing; pairs of dull-red natural
silk ribbons stitched to back edge of armscye;
coarse linen-lined bodice.
cb: 56½ in. (143.5 cm.)
Purchased with Funds Provided by
Mr. and Mrs. Grant Theis
M.82.16.1

50
DRESS (open robe and petticoat)
Colonial America, c. 1750–60
Shaded red, pink, brown, yellow, and green
floral brocade on sprigged cream silk damask
ground; linen-lined bodice.
cb of dress: 66 in. (167.7 cm.)
cb of petticoat: 35½ in. (90.1 cm.)
Gift of Mrs. James Stoddard and
Mrs. Walter E. Stewart
M.71.60.1a,b

51
DRESS
United States, c. 1800–1810
White cotton embroidered meandering vertical
motif on fine Indian cotton; apron-front bodice;
thread buttons; linen-lined bodice.
cb: 55 in. (141 cm.)
Gift of Mrs. Charles D. Grace
M.60.12.9
Exh: I

52
DRESS
United States, c. 1800
White raised cotton embroidered dot pattern on
fine white cotton; long sleeves gathered in three
rows at wrists; center-back opening; linen-lined
bodice.
cb: 54 in. (137.2 cm.)
Promised Gift of Phoebe Waln
L.982.25.51
Exh: I

53
CAPE (cardinal)
United States, 1780–1800
Red wool broadcloth gathered at neckline;
unlined; rayonne hood lined and edged with
black silk; center-front opening edged with
black silk; ankle-length.
cb: 48¾ in. (123.8 cm.)
Mrs. Alice F. Schott Bequest
CR.448.67.48

54
BODICE
France, c. 1790–1800
Multicolored striped, warp-patterned cut silk
velvet, with miniature floral design, on cream
silk satin ground; boned back; linen lined;
Directoire style. (See also cat. no. 279.)
cb: 13½ in. (34.3 cm.)
Promised Gift of Dr. and Mrs. Pratapaditya Pal
L.80.37.2

55
BODICE
France, c. 1790
Blue warp-patterned *droguet* silk; silk and linen
lining; attached lower sleeves of similar blue
patterned silk.
cb: 18 in. (45.5 cm.)
Gift of Mrs. Aldrich Peck
M.54.18.5

56
BODICE
Italy, c. 1720–30
Yellow, rose, and white brocaded silk floral
design on green silk ground; linen lined.
cb: 18¼ in. (46.5 cm.)
Gift of Mr. Jack Cole
63.24.2

57
BODICE
Italy, c. 1725–30
Yellow, cream, pink silk, and metallic floral
design on blue patterned damask ground; linen
lined.
cb: 20⅜ in. (51.5 cm.)
Gift of Mr. Jack Cole
63.24.3

58
BODICE (short gown)
France, c. 1795
White linen edged with scalloped striped white
cotton frill; double drawstring front closing,
shaped back, and long sleeves; fine cotton ruffle
at wrist and neck openings; possibly a maternity
garment.
cb: 16¾ in. (43 cm.)
cf: 19½ in. (49.5 cm.)
Purchased with Funds Provided by
Phoebe and John Dillon
M.82.26.3

59
BODICE (pair of jumps)
Italy (?), mid-18th century
White silk and silver metallic floral design on
blue and white patterned silk ground; linen
lined.
cb: 14¾ in. (37.5 cm.)
Mrs. Alice F. Schott Bequest
M.67.8.84a,b

60
BODICE
England (?), second quarter of 18th century
Polychrome silk and gold metallic floral motif
brocaded on coral silk damask ground; sleeves
with fan cuffs; partially boned; linen lined.
cb: 14⅜ in. (36.5 cm.)
Costume Council Fund
M.58.27

61
BODICE (spencer)
England, c. 1797–1805
Gold sequin embroidery on patterned striped
ivory silk; boned back; linen lined.
cb: 11¾ in. (30.2 cm.)
Mrs. Alice F. Schott Bequest
CR.448.67.230

62
WAISTCOAT
England, c. 1700–1710
White linen with corded quilting in floral and
leaf design; worn for undress over corset.
cb: 20¼ in. (51.4 cm.)
Costume Council Fund
M.80.70.1

63
POWDERING JACKET
England, mid-18th century
Fine white linen, quilted with silk, in geometric
and leaf patterns.
cb: 30¾ in. (78.2 cm.)
Gift of I. Arditti
M.63.44.2

64
BODICE (fancy dress)
France or England, second half of 18th century
Pale turquoise silk velvet with gold metallic braid
trim; linen lined.
cb: 22¼ in. (55.5 cm.)
Gift of Edward Maeder
M.81.331

65
CHILD'S BODICE
England, c. 1745
Multicolored silk brocading on cream silk
ground; Spitalfields.
cb: 11 in. (28 cm.)
Costume Council Fund
M.81.242.2

66
PETTICOAT
England, c. 1760 (detail)
Pink puckered silk; wool lined.
cf: 37 in. (94 cm.)
circum: 106 in. (265.2 cm.)
Costume Council Fund
M.57.24.6; ex-coll. Doris Langley Moore
Exh: C
Pub: 14, p. 3 (ill.)

67
PETTICOAT
Italy, mid-18th century
Multicolored silk and metallic thread
embroidery, in chinoiserie design,
on yellow silk satin; quilted; linen lined.
cf: 42½ in. (109 cm.)
circum: 148½ in. (376 cm.)
Costume Council Fund
M.59.27.1a
Exh: D
Pub: 12, p. 10 (ill.); 26, p. 9 (ill.)
See plates 49, 50

68
PETTICOAT
Colonial America, mid-18th century
Blue silk satin; quilted; wool lined.
cf: 39 in. (99 cm.)
circum: 123½ in. (313 cm.)
Gift of Mrs. H. B. Padelford and Mrs.
G. S. Housh
M.82.67

69
PETTICOAT
Portugal, c. 1700
Multicolored silk and gold metallic thread
embroidery on cream patterned silk; silver
bobbin lace trim; unlined.
cf: 38¼ in. (96.9 cm.)
circum: 117 in. (297.2 cm.)
Costume Council Fund
M.63.55.3

70
PETTICOAT
England, c. 1760
White silk satin; quilted; silk lined.
cf: 39 in. (99 cm.)
circum: 122 in. (306 cm.)
Gift of Mrs. Henry Salvatori
M.79.19.2
Exh: S

71
PETTICOAT
Colonial America, mid-18th century
Pink silk satin; quilted; linen lined.
cf: 38¾ in. (98.4 cm.)
circum: 113 in. (287 cm.)
Gift of Mrs. John Mage
M.57.29
Exh: N
Pub: 30, p. 19 (ill.)

72
PETTICOAT
England, c. 1750
Pink silk satin; quilted; wool lined.
cf: 37 in. (94 cm.)
circum: 113 in. (287 cm.)
Mrs. Alice F. Schott Bequest
CR.448.67.231

73*
STOMACHER
England, mid-18th century
Shaded red and brown silk and metallic thread
embroidery, in a floral bouquet design, on white
linen; yellow silk embroidered trellis pattern;
metallic and yellow silk ribbon edging.
h: 10⅝ in. (27 cm.)
Gift of Dr. Alessandro Morandotti
M.59.21.2
Exh: J, L

74
STOMACHER
Italy, mid-18th century
Polychrome silk and metallic thread embroidery,
in stylized floral motif, on white linen; edge
bound with yellow silk ribbon.
h: 10¾ in. (27.3 cm.)
Gift of Dr. Alessandro Morandotti
M.59.21.3
Exh: D
Pub: 12, p. 8 (ill.)

*Stomachers are measured from the apex of the
triangle to the center point of the top edge.

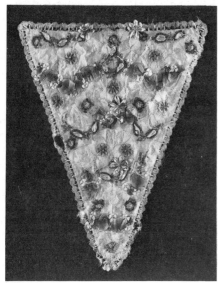

75
STOMACHER
France or Italy, c. 1750
Shaded blue and pink silk ribbon, blue silk
thread rosettes, fly fringe, and horizontal bands
of blond lace on white patterned silk; blond lace
edging; paper backing.
h: 13½ in. (34.5 cm.)
Costume Council Fund
M.80.27.1
Exh: T

76
STOMACHER
France or Italy, c. 1750
Shaded pink, blue, and green silk fly fringe;
metal ribbon rosettes on bands of silk gauze
ribbon, trimmed with silver orris lace; green
silk tufted braid; on cream silk satin.
h: 16⅛ in. (41 cm.)
Costume Council Fund
M.80.27.2
Exh: T

77
STOMACHER
France, 18th century
Polychrome silk brocaded floral bouquet and
diaper motif on beige patterned silk ground;
linen lined; fully boned.
h: 13 in. (33 cm.)
Mrs. Alice F. Schott Bequest
M.67.8.97

78
STOMACHER
Holland, c. 1740–50
White linen corded quilting and knotted
embroidery on white linen; tabbed lower edge.
h: 14¼ in. (36.2 cm.)
Mrs. Alice F. Schott Bequest
M.67.8.98
Exh: S
See fig. 29

79
STOMACHER
France, first half of 18th century
Gold orris lace and metallic passementerie on
cream silk satin; tabbed lower edge.
h: 15¼ in. (38.7 cm.)
Mrs. Alice F. Schott Bequest
M.67.8.99
Exh: U
See plate 6

80
STOMACHER
France, third quarter of 18th century
Red, green, and brown brocaded silk, in stylized
plant motif, on red and brown shot-silk
diapered ground; linen lined; fully boned.
h: 10 in. (25.5 cm.)
Mrs. Alice F. Schott Bequest
M.67.8.100

81
STOMACHER
Italy, early 18th century; altered in 19th century
Venetian linen point lace.
h: 15¾ in. (40 cm.)
Gift of Mrs. Gabriella K. Robertson and
Mrs. Marlene P.L. Toeppen
63.2.3

82
STOMACHER
France, mid-18th century
Mauve and peach ombré ribbon; yellow and
white silk thread flowers; shaded green fly
fringe and blond lace; on pale blue silk damask;
blond lace edging.
h: 15 in. (38.1 cm.)
Gift of Mrs. Gabriella K. Robertson and
Mrs. Marlene P.L. Toeppen
63.2.5
See plate 4

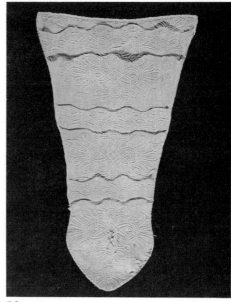

83
STOMACHER
England, early 18th century
White silk thread corded quilting on white linen;
three matching scalloped horizontal bands for
inserting fichu.
h: 13½ in. (34.5 cm.)
Gift of Dr. Alessandro Morandotti
M.59.21.4

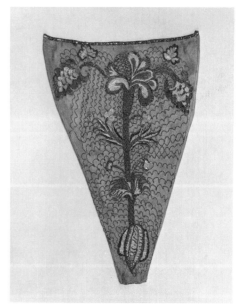

84
STOMACHER
England, first half of 18th century
Shaded silk polychrome and metallic thread
embroidery on yellow silk.
h: 13½ in. (34.5 cm.)
Gift of Arditti & Mayorcas
60.55

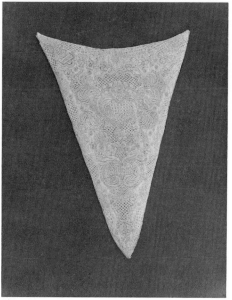

85

STOMACHER
England, c. 1700–1725
Polychrome silk and silver metallic thread floral appliqués on silver net on cream silk taffeta; silver fringe edging; paper backing.
h: 17¼ in. (43.9 cm.)
Gift of Mr. Jack Cole
63.24.4

86

STOMACHER
Italy (?), second quarter of 18th century
Shaded yellow and pink silk and metallic thread embroidery, in stylized floral motifs, on natural linen; metallic thread edging.
h: 12¼ in. (31.2 cm.)
Costume Council Fund
M.64.83.1b

87

STOMACHER
Italy, second quarter of 18th century
Cream silk embroidery in a variety of stitches on cream silk.
h: 12¼ in. (31.2 cm.)
Gift of Mrs. Gabriella K. Robertson and Mrs. Marlene P.L. Toeppen
63.2.4

88

STOMACHER FOR A CHURCH FIGURE
France, mid-18th century
Polychrome silk and gold metallic thread embroidery on cream silk satin; gold metallic lace border.
h: 10½ in. (26.7 cm.)
Gift of Mrs. Gabriella K. Robertson and Mrs. Marlene P.L. Toeppen
63.2.6

89*

ENGAGEANTES (pair)
England, c. 1760
Double sleeve ruffles of white cotton embroidery (chain, darning stitches, and drawnwork) in floral spray motif on white cotton.
a, b: 10 x 20 in. (24.4 x 50.9 cm.)
Gift of Mrs. Henry Salvatori
M.79.19.6a,b
Exh: S
See fig. 41

90

ENGAGEANTES (pair)
England, c. 1760
Single sleeve ruffles of white cotton embroidery (satin and darning stitches) in floral and trellis motif on white cotton ground.
a, b: 13¾ in. (35 cm.)
Costume Council Fund
M.81.143.4a,b

91

ENGAGEANTES (pair)
France, mid-18th century
Single sleeve ruffles of white cotton Dresden work on white linen.
a: 6½ x 34 in. (16.5 x 86.3 cm.)
b: 2 x 28 in. (5 x 71.1 cm.)
Costume Council Fund
M.64.85.10a,b

*Measurements for ungathered engageantes and cuffs are taken height by width. Measurements for gathered engageantes and cuffs consist of the diameter of the object at its greatest width.

92
ENGAGEANTES (pair)
England, c. 1750–60
Single sleeve ruffles of white cotton embroidery (running, darning stitches, and drawnwork) in floral and stem design on white cotton.
a: 15½ in. (39.3 cm.)
b: 16¾ in. (42.5 cm.)
Costume Council Fund
M.81.97.2a,b

93
ENGAGEANTES (pair)
Germany, mid-18th century
Single sleeve ruffles of white cotton Dresden work on white linen.
a: 6½ x 36⅞ in. (16.5 x 93.7 cm.)
b: 6⅜ x 37 in. (16.2 x 94 cm.)
Costume Council Fund
M.81.97.3a,b

94
ENGAGEANTES (pair)
Germany, mid-18th century
Single sleeve ruffles of white cotton Dresden work, in a wide variety of ground stitches, on white linen.
a: 35 x 7⅛ in. (89 x 18.1 cm.)
b: 34¼ x 7¼ in. (86.7 x 18.4 cm.)
Costume Council Fund
M.81.97.1a,b
See fig. 30

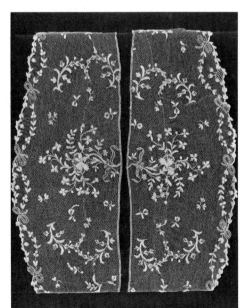

95
ENGAGEANTES (pair)
France, c. 1765–75
Single sleeve ruffles of linen needle lace (*point d'Argentan*).
a: 7 ¾ x 37 in. (19.6 x 93.9 cm.)
b: 7 ¾ x 36 in. (19.6 x 91.4 cm.)
Costume Council Fund
M.66.72a,b

96
ENGAGEANTES (pair)
France, c. 1770
Double sleeve ruffles of linen needle lace (*point d'Alençon*).
a: 39 x 6¾ in. (99.1 x 17.1 cm.)
b: 39 x 3 in. (99.1 x 7.1 cm.)
c: 39 x 6½ in. (99.1 x 16.5 cm.)
d: 38 x 3¼ in. (96.5 x 8.2 cm.)
Costume Council Fund
M.81.143.1a–d

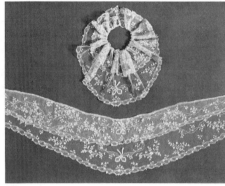

97
ENGAGEANTES (pair)
France, c. 1770
Triple sleeve ruffles of linen needle lace (*point d'Alençon*).
a: 8¾ x 47¼ in. (22.2 x 120 cm.)
b: 8¾ x 47¼ in. (22.2 x 120 cm.)
c: 6⅛ x 38½ in. (15.9 x 97.8 cm.)
d: 6¾ x 42 in. (17.1 x 106.7 cm.)
e: 6¼ x 42¾ in. (15.8 x 108.9 cm.)
f: 5¼ x 38 in. (13.4 x 96.1 cm.)
Costume Council Fund
M.81.143.2a–f
See fig. 40

98
ENGAGEANTES (pair)
France, c. 1750
Single sleeve ruffles of white cotton Dresden work on white linen.
a, b: 8½ x 13½ in. (21.6 x 34.5 cm.)
Purchased with Funds Provided by Mr. and Mrs. John Jewett Garland
M.57.8.19a,b

98a
ENGAGEANTES (pair)
England, c. 1760
Single sleeve ruffles of white cotton embroidery (darning stitch and drawn or pulled fabric work) on white cotton.
a, b: 8½ x 19½ in. (21.6 x 49.5 cm.)
Costume Council Fund
M.82.26.2a,b

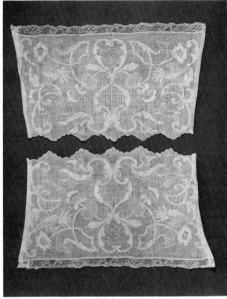

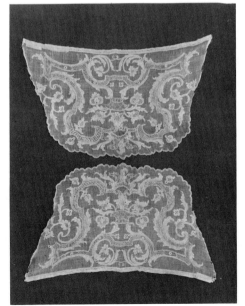

99
ALB CUFFS (pair)
France, c. 1750
White cotton Dresden work on white linen; trimmed with Mechlin bobbin lace.
a, b: 8½ x 14 in. (21.6 x 35.5 cm.)
Purchased with Funds Provided by Mr. and Mrs. John Jewett Garland
M.57.8.17a,b
Exh: U

100
ALB CUFFS (pair)
France, c. 1750
White cotton Dresden work on white linen.
a, b: 7¼ x 13½ in. (17 x 34.5 cm.)
Purchased with Funds Provided by Mr. and Mrs. John Jewett Garland
M.57.8.18a,b

101
BABY'S CUFF (one of pair)
England, first half of 18th century
Linen bobbin lace attached to linen band.
4 x 3½ in. (10.1 x 8.9 cm.)
Gift of Miss Margaret Isabel Fairfax MacKnight
49.45.8

101a
BABY'S MITT (one of pair)
England, first half of 18th century
Linen bobbin lace; open mitt with thumb and
gathered cuff; linen-lined band.
4¼ x 3½ in. (10.8 x 8.9 cm.)
Gift of Miss Margaret Isabel Fairfax MacKnight
49.45.7
Pub: 20, p. 35 (ill.)

102*
FICHU (triangular)
England, c. 1770–80
White cotton darning stitch embroidery on fine
white cotton.
8½ x 52 in. (21.6 x 131.1 cm.)
Costume Council Fund
M.59.25b

103
FICHU (triangular)
England, late 18th century
Fine white linen; bobbin lace on two edges.
28¼ x 59 in. (71.8 x 150 cm.)
Gift of Miss Helen Doud
CR.169.60.1

104
FICHU (triangular)
England, early 19th century
White cotton padded satin and stem stitch
embroidery on white cotton mull; pulled fabric
work edging.
46½ x 92¼ in. (118 x 234 cm.)
Helen Crocker Russell Bequest
M.67.50.33

*Measurements for fichus are taken height by
width.

105
FICHU (triangular)
England, c. 1800
White cotton embroidered scalloped edges
on white cotton mull.
15 x 50 in. (38.1 x 127 cm.)
Gift of Miss Mary E. Nicoll
CR.157.60.6

106
FICHU (triangular)
England, late 18th century (detail)
Heavy white cotton stem, satin, and knotted
stitches on fine white cotton mull.
37 x 83½ in. (94 x 212 cm.)
Costume Council Fund
M.80.190.5

107
FICHU (square)
England, late 18th century
White cotton chain and knotted stitch
embroidery on white cotton mull; reverse-side
placement of embroidery permits correct
positioning of design when fichu is folded
triangularly.
36½ x 37½ in. (92.8 x 95.3 cm.)
Costume Council Fund
M.80.190.6
See fig. 31

108
FICHU (rectangular)
England, c. 1780–85
White cotton padded satin and stem stitch
embroidery on white cotton mull; narrow bobbin
lace edging.
109½ x 19 in. (278 x 48.5 cm.)
Costume Council Fund
M.81.97.14

109
FICHU (shaped)
Holland (?), second half of 18th century
Polychrome shaded silk floral embroidery on
thin white silk.
28¾ x 28¼ in. (72 x 71.5 cm.)
Purchased with Funds Provided by
Mr. and Mrs. Marvin M. Chesebro
M.82.23
See plate 11

110
FICHU (shaped)
Flanders, c. 1780–90
White linen trimmed with Brussels bobbin lace.
58 x 20½ in. (147.3 x 52.1 cm.)
Costume Council Fund
M.64.85.11

110a
FICHU (crossover)
England, c. 1780–90
White cotton with small turned-down collar;
narrow self-ruffle edging; worn crossed over
front of bodice and fastened at center-back
waist.
75 x 10 in. (196 x 25.4 cm.)
Costume Council Fund
M.82.26.1

111
APRON
England, c. 1730–40
Polychrome silk and padded silver gilt thread
embroidery on ivory silk.
18 x 37½ in. (45.7 x 95.3 cm.)
Costume Council Fund
M.80.190.7
Exh: T
See plate 12

112
APRON (broad)
England, mid-18th century
White cotton chain stitch embroidery on white
cotton mull; pulled fabric work corners; bobbin
lace edging.
35 x 52⅜ in. (89 x 133 cm.)
Costume Council Fund
M.81.97.16

113
APRON
England, c. 1760
White cotton chain stitch embroidery on white
cotton mull.
26 x 67 in. (66 x 170 cm.)
Costume Council Fund
M.81.97.17

113a
APRON
England, c. 1725
White cotton stem and satin stitch embroidery
on white cotton mull; central motif of cipher
within heart, surmounted by crown and flanked
by cherubs; needle lace edging.
37 x 28 in. (94 x 71.2 cm.)
Costume Council Fund
M.81.143.3

113b
APRON
England, mid-18th century
White cotton chain and stem stitch embroidery
on white linen.
36 x 41 in. (91.4 x 104.2 cm.)
Gift of Miss Margaret Isabel Fairfax MacKnight
49.45.4

116
POCKETS (pair)
Italy, mid-18th century
Rust-colored silk chain stitch embroidery, of
floral and leaf design, on quilted white silk;
white silk binding; backed with rust linen.
14¾ x 8 in. (37.4 x 20.3 cm.)
Gift of Dr. Alessandro Morandotti
M.59.21.1a,b

118
POCKET (one of pair)
Scotland, 1759
Polychrome silk chain stitch and fishbone stitch,
in floral and bird motif, on natural linen;
embroidered with initials "S.M." and "1759."
14⁵⁄₁₆ x 10½ in. (36.3 x 26.7 cm.)
Anonymous Gift
A.1654.41.20
Pub: 36, pl. 33

114
APRON
England, c. 1730–40
Multicolored silk and metallic thread
embroidery on white silk taffeta.
18 x 38 in. (45.7 x 96.5 cm.)
Costume Council Fund
M.59.24.7; ex-coll. Doris Langley Moore
Exh: R

115
APRON
England, c. 1740
Multicolored shaded silk embroidery on yellow
silk taffeta; pink silk fringe edging.
20½ x 41½ in. (50.1 x 105.4 cm.)
Gift of Mrs. Murray Ward
M.79.96
Exh: S

117
POCKETS (pair)
England, c. 1790–1800
Light olive-colored silk taffeta; block printed to
shape with black Greek key borders; Directoire
style; attached to brass rings; joined by silk
ribbon ties.
10½ x 6 in. (26.7 x 15.2 cm.)
Mrs. Alice F. Schott Bequest
CR.448.67.63a,b

119
POCKETS (pair)
England, mid-18th century
Yellow, red, and green silk embroidery, in floral
and peacock motif, on natural linen; backed
with scraps of blue and white linen.
15½ x 8 in. (39.3 x 20.3 cm.)
Mrs. Alice F. Schott Bequest
M.67.8.89a,b

120

POCKET (one of pair)
Colonial America, 1718
Shades of red, yellow, and brown crewel wool embroidery on homespun linen, primarily in chain stitch; slit bound with a strip pieced of four cotton prints; edge bound with sprigged white linen print.
16¾ x 10¼ in. (42.5 x 26 cm.)
Mrs. Alice F. Schott Bequest
M.67.8.91

121

POCKETS (pair)
England, 1753
Polychrome wool crewel embroidery, primarily in chain stitch, on linen and cotton; gold silk binding; linen and cotton backs.
13¾ x 8¼ in. (34.9 x 21 cm.)
Mrs. Alice F. Schott Bequest
M.67.8.90a,b

122

POCKET (one of pair)
Colonial America, early 18th century
Shaded red, yellow, and tan wool crewel embroidery, of basket of flowers with birds and meandering vine border, in varied stitches on fine cotton; linen back, binding, and ties.
14⅜ x 11½ in. (37.1 x 29.2 cm.)
Mrs. Alice F. Schott Bequest
M.67.8.92

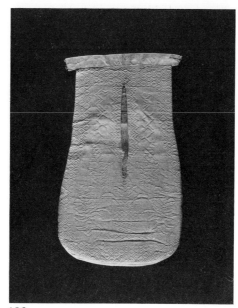

123

POCKET (one of pair)
France, c. 1780–1800
White cotton machine-woven version of Marseilles quilting; plain cotton back.
12¾ x 8 in. (32.4 x 20.3 cm.)
Gift of Mrs. Sara A. Bicknell
A.5123.23

124

POCKET (one of pair)
England, c. 1770–80
White cotton sateen with topstitched edges; opening finished with buttonhole stitch; plain cotton back; linen tape ties.
14 x 11¼ in. (35.6 x 28.6 cm.)
Costume Council Fund
M.59.25d

125

POCKET (one of pair)
Colonial America, mid-18th century
Plain linen front and back; linen binding and ties.
13½ x 10 in. (34.3 x 25.4 cm.)
Gift of Mrs. Sara A. Bicknell
A.5123.24

126

POCKET (one of pair)
United States, late 18th century
White cotton dimity; slit base finished with buttonhole stitch; tan linen twill tape ties; plain cotton back.
16 x 11¼ in. (40.6 x 28.6 cm.)
Gift of Mrs. Henrietta H. Partridge and Miss Lora Partridge Lehman
37.15.4

127

CORSET
England, c. 1730–40
Pastel blue silk moiré; mock lacing in front; fully boned; coarse linen lining.
cb: 15 in. (38 cm.)
Costume Council Fund
M.57.24.1; ex-coll. Doris Langley Moore
Exh: C
Pub: 14, p. 3 (ill.)
See plate 14

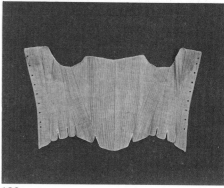

128

CORSET
Colonial America, 1730–40
Tan linen; fully boned; linen lining.
cb: 15½ in. (39.5 cm.)
Gift of Miss Eleanor Bissell
42.16.39

129

CORSET
England (?), late 18th century
Coarse beige linen; fully boned with reed; unfinished; unlined.
cb: 13½ in. (34.3 cm.)
Gift of Miss Madeline Frances Wills
A.2246.30.6

130

CORSET (doll)
England, mid-18th century
Multicolored silk brocade; red silk ribbon edging; fully boned; brown printed cotton lining.
cb: 3⅜ in. (8.5 cm.)
Gift of Mrs. Stanley Bergerman
CR.304.64.1

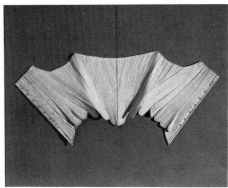

131
CORSET
England, c. 1790
Beige cotton; fully boned; linen lining.
cb: 13 in. (33 cm.)
Mrs. Alice F. Schott Bequest
CR.448.67.134

132
CORSET
France, c. 1750
Multicolored floral silk brocaded on patterned cream silk ground; fully boned; sham lacing in front; hip pads; linen lining.
cb: 16½ in. (42 cm.)
Gift of Mr. Jack Cole
63.24.5
Exh: H

133
CORSET (child)
Spain, c. 1740
Brown patterned silk brocade; partially boned; coarse linen lining.
cb: 7¼ in. (18.5 cm.)
Mrs. Alice F. Schott Bequest
M.67.8.105

134
CORSET (child)
Italy, mid-18th century
Dark blue silk taffeta; yellow silk ribbon edging; fully boned; fine white linen lining.
cb: 8⅝ in. (22 cm.)
Mrs. Alice F. Schott Bequest
M.67.8.106

135
CORSET
Italy, c. 1750
Blue and pink shot-silk; fully boned; yellow silk ribbon trimming; cotton lining.
cb: 16 in. (40 cm.)
Gift of Edward Maeder
M.81.220.1
See plate 15

136
CORSET
Central Europe, c. 1790
Multicolored silk floral motif brocaded on brown silk patterned ground; partially boned; linen lining.
cb: 11⅜ in. (28.9 cm.)
Mrs. Alice F. Schott Bequest
CR.448.67.234

137
CORSET (statue figure)
Italy, c. 1730–40
Multicolored silk and metallic thread floral design embroidered on cream silk satin; fully boned; linen lined.
cb: 9¼ in. (23.5 cm.)
Mrs. Alice F. Schott Bequest
M.67.8.107

138
CORSET
Ireland, mid-18th century
Natural glazed linen; fully boned with whalebone; spot-printed linen lining.
cb: 15½ in. (39.4 cm.)
Gift of Eliza A. Faries
A.1533.26.2

139
STAYS (pair)
Italy, mid-18th century
Multicolored silk brocaded on white silk ground; front lacing; blue and gold striped cotton tie; fully boned; linen lined.
cb: 16¾ in. (42.5 cm.)
Mrs. Alice F. Schott Bequest
M.67.8.104

140
STAYS (pair)
France, mid-18th century
Multicolored floral pattern brocaded on blue silk ground; pink silk lacing; fully boned; linen lined.
cb: 12¼ in. (31 cm.)
Mrs. Alice F. Schott Bequest
M.67.8.102

141
STAYS (pair)
Italy, late 18th century
Multicolored floral pattern brocaded on ivory silk ground; green silk ribbon lacing; fully boned; linen lined.
cb: 7⅝ in. (19.4 cm.)
Mrs. Alice F. Schott Bequest
M.67.8.101

142
STAYS (pair)
Italy, second half of 18th century
Deep red silk velvet; yellow silk ribbon
trimming; fully boned; linen lined.
cb: 14⅝ in. (37.2 cm.)
Mrs. Alice F. Schott Bequest
CR.448.67.232

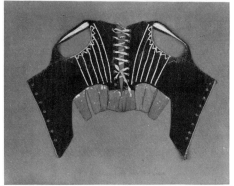

143
STAYS (pair)
Italy, second half of 18th century
Deep red silk velvet; yellow silk ribbon
trimming; fully boned; linen lined.
cb: 14½ in. (37 cm.)
Mrs. Alice F. Schott Bequest
CR.448.67.233

144
STAYS (pair)
France, c. 1760
Multicolored floral silk pattern brocaded on red
silk satin ground; white leather edging; fully
boned; linen lined.
cb: 15 in. (38.5 cm.)
Mrs. Alice F. Schott Bequest
M.67.8.103

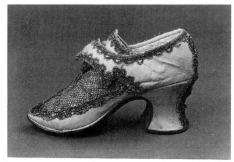

145*
SHOES (pair)
England, c. 1700–1715
Pale green silk satin with silver lace and sequins.
4½ x 8¼ in. (11.5 x 21 cm.)
Costume Council Fund
M.64.85.7a,b

*Height precedes length in all shoe
measurements.

146
CHILDREN'S SHOES (pair)
England, c. 1700–1730
Red thread embroidered in "queen's stitch";
metallic gold braid.
2 x 5 in. (5 x 12.7 cm.)
Mrs. Alice F. Schott Bequest
M.67.8.170a,b
Exh: U

147
SHOE (one of pair)
England, c. 1720
Silver braid in multiple rows on white silk satin.
4½ x 8½ in. (11.5 x 21.6 cm.)
Mrs. Alice F. Schott Bequest
M.67.8.142

148
SHOES (pair)
England, c. 1720–30
Polychrome large floral silk brocade on cream
ground; green silk trim.
4 x 9 in. (10.2 x 22.9 cm.)
Mrs. Alice F. Schott Bequest
M.67.8.133a,b
See plate 18a

149
SHOES (pair)
England, c. 1720–30
Red Moroccan leather; upturned pointed toe.
4¼ x 9 in. (10.8 x 22.9 cm.)
Costume Council Fund
M.82.26.4a,b

150
SHOES (pair)
England, c. 1750–60
Green silk damask; floral pattern; dark green
silk trim.
4½ x 9 in. (11.5 x 22.9 cm.)
Costume Council Fund
M.80.70.2a,b

151
CLOG (one of pair)
England, c. 1750–70
Rose and cream silk brocade in floral pattern.
2½ x 7½ in. (6.4 x 19.1 cm.)
Gift of Miss Nellie Flaskell
A.6289.52.1

152
SHOES (pair)
England, c. 1740–50
Green silk damask (Spitalfields); green silk trim.
4¾ x 9½ in. (12.1 x 24.1 cm.)
Costume Council Fund
M.81.71.1a,b
Exh: T
See plate 18b

153
WEDDING SLIPPERS (pair)
Colonial America, c. 1740
Rose, black, and white silk brocade.
4 x 9 in. (10.2 x 22.9 cm.)
Gift of Miss Eleanor Bissell
42.16.43a,b
Pub: 13, p. 12 (ill.)

154
SHOES (pair)
France, c. 1740–55
Multicolored floral silk brocade on blue green ground; white silk trim; white leather-covered heel.
4½ x 9¼ in. (11.5 x 23.5 cm.)
Gift of Mr. Jack Cole
63.24.7a,b
Exh: R

155
SHOE (one of pair)
Colonial America, mid-18th century
Yellow silk brocade with yellow silk trim; bottom of heel covered with white kid to prevent slipping on wood floors.
5 x 7¾ in. (12.8 x 19.7 cm.)
Gift of Florence Alden Stoddard and Katharine Alden Stewart
M.79.253.1

156
SHOES (pair)
England, c. 1750–65
Yellow silk satin.
4¾ x 8¾ in. (12.1 x 22.3 cm.)
Costume Council Fund
M.81.71.2a,b
Exh: T

157
SHOES (pair)
England, c. 1765–70
Polychrome floral silk brocade on dark green ground; dark green silk trim.
4 x 9 in. (10.2 x 22.9 cm.)
Costume Council Fund
M.59.24.26a,b; ex-coll. Doris Langley Moore
Exh: N, Q

158
SHOES (pair)
France, c. 1765–75
Green and black scattered sprig motif on rose beige cut and uncut diaper-patterned silk velvet; shot with metal thread strips.
4½ x 9½ in. (11.5 x 24.1 cm.)
Mrs. Alice F. Schott Bequest
M.67.8.128a,b

159
SHOES (pair)
Colonial America, c. 1770
Yellow and beige silk damask in floral pattern; white kid-covered heel.
4¾ x 6¼ in. (12.1 x 16 cm.)
Gift of Mrs. Marie Tuttle
61.27.1a,b

160
SHOES (pair)
Colonial America, c. 1772
White and green striped floral brocade on white silk ground; pink silk trim.
5½ x 8¼ in. (14 x 21 cm.)
Gift of Mrs. Frank H. White
A.5548.46.7a,b

161
SHOES (pair)
Colonial America, c. 1770–80
Polychrome floral silk brocade on dark green ground; white silk trim.
4¼ x 9 in. (10.8 x 22.9 cm.)
Costume Council Fund
M.81.71.4a,b
See plate 17

162
SHOES (pair)
Holland, c. 1770–80
Polychrome and gold brocade on pale blue silk ground; white silk trim; white kid-covered heel.
4½ x 8½ in. (11.5 x 21.5 cm.)
Mrs. Alice F. Schott Bequest
M.67.8.126a,b

163
MULES (pair)
Germany or Italy, c. 1770–80
White floral silk brocade on blue ground; pink ribbon ruching.
2¾ x 8¼ in. (7 x 21 cm.)
Mrs. Alice F. Schott Bequest
M.67.8.125a,b

164
SHOES (pair)
England, c. 1770–80
Yellow floral embroidery on black silk satin; yellow silk trim.
4½ x 8½ in. (11.5 x 21.5 cm.)
Gift of Mr. Jack Cole
CR.268.63.6a,b
See plate 18c, fig. 72

165
SHOES (pair)
England, c. 1775–85
Sky blue spotted silk upper; white spotted silk-covered heel; white silk trim; label: "G. Tarington, [shoe] Maker No. 39 in the Poultry."
4 x 9½ in. (10.2 x 24.1 cm.)
Mrs. Alice F. Schott Bequest
M.67.8.129a,b

166
SHOES (pair)
United States, c. 1785–90
Drab brown spotted silk upper with green silk trim; padded bow with copper and silver gilt passementerie; white kid-covered heel.
4½ x 8 in. (11.5 x 20.3 cm.)
Gift of Mrs. J.F. Donald
M.82.57a,b

167
SHOES (pair)
England, c. 1780–85
White and beige striped and polychrome floral silk brocade on sky blue ground; white silk satin latchets and covered heel.
4½ x 9 in. (11.5 x 22.9 cm.)
Costume Council Fund
M.81.71.3a,b
Exh: T

168
SHOES (pair)
England, c. 1785–90
Cream silk twill with silver metallic stripes; self-covered heel; white silk trim.
3¾ x 9½ in. (9.5 x 24.1 cm.)
Mrs. Alice F. Schott Bequest
M.67.8.130a,b

169
SHOES (pair)
England, c. 1785–90
White silk satin; narrow self-covered heel.
4¼ x 9½ in. (10.8 x 24.1 cm.)
Costume Council Fund
M.81.71.7a,b

170
SHOES (pair)
England, c. 1785–95
Beige and white embroidery on olive striped white cotton; olive silk trim and bow; low leather-covered heel; known as "ticking shoe."
2½ x 10¼ in. (6.4 x 26 cm.)
Costume Council Fund
M.59.24.30a,b; ex-coll. Doris Langley Moore
Exh: U

171
SHOES (pair)
England, c. 1785–95
Black silk satin; pointed toe; drawstring at upper edge.
3½ x 10 in. (8.9 x 25.4 cm.)
Gift of Colonel and Mrs. George J. Denis
26.1.18a,b

172
SHOES (pair)
France, c. 1780
Multicolored floral brocade on yellow green silk satin ground; self-covered heel; white silk trim; tongue edge decorated with white silk ruching.
5¼ x 9½ in. (13.3 x 24.1 cm.)
Mrs. Alice F. Schott Bequest
M.67.8.127a,b

173

SHOES (pair)
England (London), c. 1795
Olive green kid sandal shoe; yellow cutout and embroidered design on vamp; yellow silk ruching; label: "Ledger, Boot & Shoe Maker No. 41 Theobald's Road, New Bedford Row, London."
2½ x 10½ in. (6.4 x 26.7 cm.)
Costume Council Fund
M.59.24.28a,b; ex-coll. Doris Langley Moore

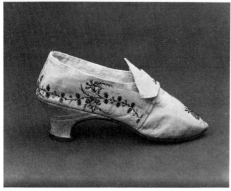

174

SHOES (pair)
France, c. 1780–85
Polychrome floral brocade with white stripes on white silk ground; white silk trim.
4¼ x 9½ in. (10.8 x 24.1 cm.)
Costume Council Fund
M.59.24.27a,b; ex-coll. Doris Langley Moore
Exh: R

175

SHOES (pair)
France, c. 1785–95
Black silk satin with pointed toe; drawstring at upper edge.
3¾ x 9¼ in. (9.5 x 23.5 cm.)
Gift of Hazel Steadman Burkhardt
A.507.3a,b

176

OVERSHOES (pair)
France, c. 1785–95
Black leather with leather-covered spring attachment for heel.
1 x 9 in. (2.5 x 22.9 cm.)
Costume Council Fund
M.82.8.7a,b

177

SHOES (pair)
France, c. 1788–92
Moroccan black leather; sharply pointed toe; ¼-inch wedge heel.
2 x 9½ in. (5 x 24.1 cm.)
Gift of Hazel Steadman Burkhardt
A.507.2a,b

178

SHOES (pair)
England, c. 1796–97
Olive green, rose, and brown striped leather; black leather-covered heel; black silk trim.
2½ x 11 in. (6.4 x 28 cm.)
Mrs. Alice F. Schott Bequest
M.67.8.132a,b

179

SHOES (pair)
France, c. 1799–1805
Green leather slippers; no heel; blue green silk ribbon ruching and ties.
2½ x 9 in. (6.4 x 22.9 cm.)
Mrs. Alice F. Schott Bequest
M.67.8.145a,b

180

SHOES (pair)
England, c. 1793–98
White silk with gold sequins and gold braid; self-fabric bow; low, white silk satin-covered heel.
2½ x 10 in. (6.4 x 22.9 cm.)
Costume Council Fund
M.59.24.29a,b; ex-coll. Doris Langley Moore
Exh: U
See plate 52

181

SHOE BUCKLES (pair)
England, c. 1780–85
Transparent faceted paste stones set in silver; steel chape.
1⅞ x 3¼ in. (4.7 x 8.2 cm.)
Costume Council Fund
M.59.24.27c,d; ex-coll. Doris Langley Moore

182

SHOE BUCKLES (pair)
England, c. 1780–90
Transparent faceted paste stones set in silver; steel chape.
1¾ x 3¼ in. (4.5 x 8.2 cm.)
Costume Council Fund
M.80.70.3a,b

183

HAT (*bergère*)
England, mid-18th century
Flat straw with wide, round brim; underside lined with floral brocade on brown silk ground; red silk satin ribbon and bow.
diam: 16 in. (40.7 cm.)
diam. of tip: 4⅜ in. (11.8 cm.)
d. of crown: ¼ in. (.8 cm.)
Costume Council Fund
M.64.85.3

184

HAT (*bergère*)
England, mid-18th century
Natural straw with wide, round brim.
diam: 18½ in. (47 cm.)
diam. of tip: 5¼ in. (13.4 cm.)
d. of crown: ⅞ in. (2.2 cm.)
Costume Council Fund
M.57.24.3; ex-coll. Doris Langley Moore
Exh: D
Pub: 26, p. 9 (ill.)

185*

CALASH
United States, c. 1790
Brown silk and wool challis; light green and blue
silk ribbon ties.
16½ x 13 in. (42 x 33 cm.)
Gift of Mrs. Frank H. White
A.5548.4

186

HOOD
United States, c. 1775
Padded and quilted dark green silk sarcenet.
23 x 16 in. (58.4 x 40.6 cm.)
Gift of Mrs. Willard Larson
59.20.3

187

CALASH
England, c. 1770
Brown silk taffeta; lined with rose shot-silk.
21½ x 17 in. (54.6 x 43.2 cm.)
Costume Council Fund
M.59.24.4; ex-coll. Doris Langley Moore

*Calash, hood, and other flexible hat
measurements are taken when the hat is in a
collapsed state; height precedes width.

188

BONNET
United States, c. 1795
Woven straw with wide brim; red silk satin
ribbon tie; style known in the 19th century as
"shovel bonnet."
11½ x 13 in. (29.2 x 33 cm.)
Gift of Mrs. Elizabeth Buck
M.82.66

189

HAT (cartwheel)
Colonial America, c. 1730–50
Gray wool felt with flat, round brim;
Quaker style.
diam: 17⅞ in. (45.5 cm.)
diam. of tip: 5⅞ in. (15 cm.)
d. of crown: ⅜ in. (1.6 cm.)
Gift of Mr. and Mrs. R. L. Dixon
A.4165.1

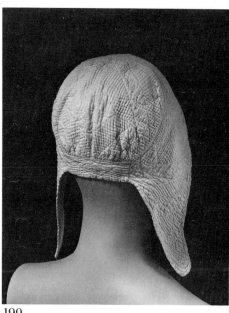

190

NIGHTCAP
England, early 18th century
Quilted white linen; lappets to shoulder.
12½ x 8¼ in. (31.7 x 21 cm.)
Costume Council Fund
M.80.190.4

191

HAT (wood chip)
England, c. 1750
Pink silk over woven split wood strips; flat,
round brim; white cut paper flowers on pink silk
under white silk tulle covering.
diam: 16⅞ in. (43 cm.)
d. of crown: ¼ in. (.8 cm.)
Costume Council Fund
M.82.8.8
See figs. 70, 71

192

LETTER CASE
United States, c. 1800
Multicolored design of flowers, grapes, and
berries in petit point embroidery on white silk.
4½ x 6¼ in. (11.4 x 15.8 cm.)
Gift of Mrs. Thomas H. Truslow
62.13.2

193

POCKETBOOK
United States, 1799
Polychrome silk landscape embroidered on white
silk satin; stamped gold leaf initials "J.G.L." and
year "1799."
6 x 4⅞ in. (15 x 12.3 cm.)
Gift of Mrs. Irene Salinger in Memory of
Her Father, Adolph Stern
54.104.134

194
POCKETBOOK
Germany, c. 1780–1800
Polychrome silk ribbon embroidery in floral motif on white silk; centered medallion silhouette of woman's head; initials T and E embroidered on back.
6½ x 4¾ in. (16.5 x 12 cm.)
Gift of Mrs. Stanley Bergerman
M.64.75.2

195
INDISPENSABLE
England, c. 1799
Polychrome silk ribbon and floss, colored foil bullion, and sequin floral embroidery on white silk; white silk and silver metallic lace edging.
10 x 12½ in. (25.4 x 31.8 cm.)
Costume Council Fund
M.80.70.5
See plate 46

195a
INDISPENSABLE
France, c. 1799
Polychrome floral silk embroidery on cream silk satin brocade; silk fly fringe braid; drawstring closure.
9 x 9 in. (22.9 x 22.9 cm.)
Promised Gift of
Mr. and Mrs. Robert D. Mathey
TR.5824.2

196
DISPATCH CASE
France, c. 1780–90
Gold-stamped Directoire motif on red leather with inlaid tortoise shell; silver clasps.
5¼ x 7 in. (13.3 x 17.8 cm.)
Costume Council Fund
M.80.186
Exh: T
See plate 8

196a
PURSE
France, c. 1780
Polychrome *sablé* beaded floral and meandering vine motif; white silk lining.
9 x 8½ in. (22.8 x 21.6 cm.)
Promised Gift of the Costume Council
TR.5947

196b
LETTER CASE
England, c. 1790
Cream, green, yellow, and peach silk brocaded on cream and brown silk satin striped ground; cream silk and gilt metal threadribbon binding and strap.
4⅜ x 7½ in. (11.1 x 19 cm.)
Costume Council Fund
M.81.97.4

196c
DISPATCH CASE
France, c. 1800
Gold-stamped Directoire motif on black textured leather; brass and tortoise shell inlay; silver clasps.
5½ x 6⅝ in. (14 x 16.8 cm.)
Gift of Mr. Michael Hall
M.82.50

197*
FAN
France, mid-18th century
Painted garden scene on vellum mount backed with painted silk; carved and stained ivory sticks and guards.
9⅜ in. (24.3 cm.)
Gift of Mr. and Mrs. John Jewett Garland
M.59.9.3

198
FAN
France, c. 1770
Painted landscape with seated lovers on pressed, perforated paper mount with gold foil and silver sequins.
10¼ in. (26 cm.)
Gift of Mrs. John S. Griffith
CR.36.59.15

199
FAN
France, c. 1770–80
Silver sequin floral embroidery and painting on paper mount; pierced amber sticks and guards; glass magnifier in guard.
10½ in. (26.6 cm.)
Eva B. Zobelein Bequest
CR.70.40

200
FAN
France, second half of 18th century
Painting of "Zeus and the Heavenly Host" on paper mount; carved and painted ivory sticks and guards.
11¼ in. (28.5 cm.)
Gift of Mrs. Meyer Rosenfield
CR.62.56.3

201
FAN
France, c. 1780
Painted oriental scenes in grisaille on paper mount; ivory sticks and guards.
10½ in. (26.6 cm.)
Gift of Mrs. Meyer Rosenfield
CR.62.56.1

202
FAN
Italy, 1779
Painted scene of Mt. Vesuvius with tombs of "Virgilia" and "Cicerone" on reverse on vellum; dated "Aug. 8, 1779"; ivory sticks and guards.
10⅛ in. (25.7 cm.)
Gift of Mrs. Lillian Burkhart Goldsmith
A.2071.29.5

203
FAN
France, late 18th century
Painted and gilt mythological scene on beige vellum; polychrome-painted, carved, and pierced ivory sticks with vignettes of birds, floral designs, and figures.
10½ in. (26.6 cm.)
Gift of Mrs. Harry D'Arrast
M.76.8.2

*For fans, the measurement cited is the radius.

204

FAN

France, first quarter of 18th century
Black, white, pink, and gilt gouache drawing
(grisaille) and cut paper chinoiserie scenes on
silk; grisaille chinoiserie scenes also on ivory
sticks; mother-of-pearl inlay on ivory guards.
10½ in. (26.6 cm.)
Costume Council Fund
M.81.245.1

205

FAN

France, c. 1720
Polychrome-painted and lacquered scenes of a
battle and mounted riders on ivory sticks; *brisé*
paste rivet.
6½ in. (16.5 cm.)
Gift of Mrs. Walter Jarvis Barlow
40.14.17

206

FAN

France, c. 1780
Painted central medallion of romantic scene,
flanked by rondels of cherubs, embroidered with
gold metallic thread, ombré silk ribbon, and
sequins on cream silk; pierced and gilded bone
sticks and guards; paste rivet.
9¾ in. (24.7 cm.)
Purchased with Funds Provided by
Dr. and Mrs. Miguel A. Llanos
M.81.245.4

206a

FAN

France, c. 1800
Cream silk, silver and gilt sequins, spangles, and
paillettes in festoons on gilt metallic mesh
mount; gilt mother-of-pearl sticks and guards.
8½ in. (21.5 cm.)
Costume Council Fund
M.81.245.6

206b

FAN

France (?), mid-18th century
Printed 17th-century scenes on parchment
mount; pierced and painted floral and bird
designs on bone sticks and guards.
11¾ in. (30 cm.)
Costume Council Fund
M.81.245.2

206c

FAN

France, c. 1750
Painted group of children wearing Turkish and
antique Roman costumes on paper mount;
carved and pierced animals and birds on bone
sticks and guards.
11¼ in. (28.5 cm.)
Costume Council Fund
M.81.245.3

207

MUFF COVER

England, c. 1780
Handpainted sepia landscape, with multicolored
roses, pansies, forget-me-nots, leaves, and bows,
on white silk satin; trimmed with silver gilt
threads and silver sequins.
23 x 18¼ in. (58.4 x 45.4 cm.)
Gift of Mrs. Henry Salvatori
M.79.17.7
Exh: S

208

MUFF COVER

France, mid-18th century
Polychrome silk and silver couched and satin
stitch embroidery, with silver gilt sequins, on
white silk satin; edged with silver lace; white
ribbon drawstrings.
12 x 10¼ in. (30.5 x 26 cm.)
Mrs. Alice F. Schott Bequest
CR.448.67.62

209

MITTENS (pair)

England, c. 1700–1724
Yellow silk backstitch embroidery, in all-over
floral and scroll tracery pattern, on white linen;
edges bound with green silk ribbon.
13½ x 5½ in. (34.3 x 14 cm.)
Costume Council Fund
M.80.43.4a,b
Exh: T

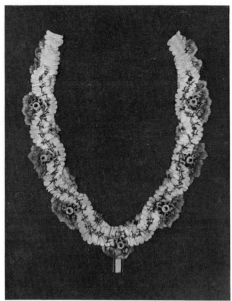

210
DRESS ROBING
England, c. 1740–50
Polychrome silk floss flowers and fly fringe on pinked ruched yellow silk, in alternate meanders with white silk gauze lace.
42¾ x 3⅜ in. (108.5 x 9 cm.)
Costume Council Fund
M.81.97.6
Exh: T

210a
DRESS ROBING
Italy, mid-18th century
Polychrome silk shaded satin stitch embroidery in branch floral pattern on yellow silk satin; rose and white silk bobbin lace edging; lined with pink patterned silk.
25½ x 10¾ in. (64.8 x 27.3 cm.)
Gift of Mrs. Gabriella K. Robertson and Mrs. Marlene P.L. Toeppen
63.2.13

211
FICHU BUCKLE
England, c. 1780–90
Transparent faceted paste stones set in silver; silver and gilt chased design; steel fitting and chape.
2 x 2 in. (5 x 5 cm.)
Costume Council Fund
M.80.92.5

211a
FICHU BUCKLE
England, c. 1770–90
Transparent faceted paste stones set in silver-plated copper base; anchor chape.
3⅜ x 2½ in. (8.1 x 6.3 cm.)
Gift of Mexicer Brown IV
M.81.109.8

211b
FICHU BUCKLE
England (?), c. 1785–90
Orange, blue, and black horizontal striped glass, possibly Vauxhall; surrounded by a double row of faceted paste stones; set in oval silver frame.
3⅜ x 2⅝ in. (9.2 x 6.7 cm.)
Costume Council Fund
M.80.92.4

212
SEWING BASKET
Portugal (Lisbon), c. 1787
Pale blue silk pouch, with drawstring top, attached to white silk satin two-sided base with multicolored silk, gold, metallic, and sequin embroidery and red paste stones; each side of base has a red wax seal. This basket is believed to have been commissioned by Admiral Sir Charles Cotton Baronet (1753–1811) for his wife, Philadelphia, whom he married in 1788. One seal is that of the Cotton family. The other is the seal of the Order of Bridgettine nuns (Syon House, England, and Lisbon, Portugal), who probably executed the work. Basket is in original bentwood box painted with landscape scenes.
basket: 15½ x 15 in. (39.3 x 38.1 cm.)
box: h: 5 in. (12.7 cm.); w: 15½ in. (39.3 cm.); d: 8¾ in. (22.2 cm.)
lid: 8¼ x 15 in. (21 x 38.1 cm.)
Gift of Mr. and Mrs. Michael Laykin
M.81.94a–c
Exh: T
See plate 3

212a
SEWING BASKET
England, late 18th century
Natural, blue, and gold joined strips of raffia bobbin lace attached to openwork basket of raffia-covered reeds; blue, red, and gold raffia flowers on basket and tassels; drawstring closure.
16½ x 10 in. (41.9 x 25.4 cm.)
Promised Gift of the Costume Council
TR.3630.2

212b
NEEDLE HOLDER AND PINCUSHION
United States (Pennsylvania), 1796
Red, pink, and green silk floral and strawberry motif embroidered on white silk satin; silver gimp; white silk tassels; documented purchase in Bethlehem, Pennsylvania (1796), at a Moravian school.
4½ x 2½ in. (11.4 x 6.4 cm.)
Gift of Mrs. Frank H. White
A.5548.46.15

213*
SUIT (coat, waistcoat, and breeches)
England, c. 1760
Ivory cut *chiné* silk velvet with small floral diaper pattern in pink, orange, green, and black on pink silk ground; self-covered buttons; suit of ditto.
cb: 41½ in. (105.4 cm.)
Costume Council Fund
M.80.117a–c

214
SUIT (coat, waistcoat, and breeches)
England, c. 1760–70
Multicolor silk, satin stitch floral embroidery in border pattern on yellow green ribbed silk; self-covered embroidered buttons; standing collar.
cb: 41¾ in. (106 cm.)
Costume Council Fund
M.61.5a–c
Exh: L

215
SUIT (coat and breeches)
England, c. 1780–90
Beige diaper-patterned *ciselé* silk velvet; self-covered buttons; high standing collar; suit of ditto.
cb: 40 in. (105 cm.)
Costume Council Fund
M.59.24.20a,b; ex-coll. Doris Langley Moore
Exh: D, L
Pub: 26, p. 9 (ill.)

216
LIVERY SUIT (coat, waistcoat, and breeches)
Ireland, c. 1790–1800
Forest green wool broadcloth coat; silver gilt galloon trim and gilt brass buttons with family crest on coat and waistcoat; high standing collar; bright yellow wool broadcloth waistcoat; bright yellow wool plush breeches; belonged to the Earl of Charleville, Belvedere, Mullingar, County Westmeath, Republic of Ireland.
cb: 41½ in. (105.5 cm.)
Costume Council Fund
M.81.5a–c
See plate 7

217
COAT
England, c. 1750–60
Olive drab wool broadcloth with silver satin stitch and sequin embroidery; silk-covered silver thread and sequin embroidered buttons; turned-down collar.
cb: 40½ in. (103 cm.)
Costume Council Fund
M.79.245.3

218
BANYAN
England, c. 1740
Sky blue floral and lace patterned silk damask; Spitalfields; double row of self-covered buttons; double-breasted.
cb: 39½ in. (100 cm.)
Gift of Mrs. Henry Salvatori
M.79.140

219
BANYAN
England, second quarter of 18th century
Deep green large floral-and-leaf patterned silk damask; Spitalfields; green silk passementerie frogs.
cb: 44½ in. (113 cm.)
Costume Council Fund
M.79.245.1

220
SUIT (coat, waistcoat, and breeches)
England, c. 1780–85
Gray beige wool broadcloth coat; broad turned-down collar; cream silk satin waistcoat and breeches; cloth-of-silver covered buttons and silver braid on all three pieces.
cb: 46 in. (117 cm.)
Costume Council Fund
M.63.54.13a–c; ex-coll. Doris Langley Moore
Pub: 3, p. 314, pl. 781

221
BANYAN AND WAISTCOAT (sleeved)
England, c. 1760–80
Pink, green, pale yellow, and cream meandering realistic floral pattern on pale green diapered silk ground; self-covered buttons; double-breasted; standing collar; matching sleeved waistcoat with short standing collar, fully lined with heavy wool flannel.
cb: 53 in. (134.8 cm.)
Costume Council Fund
M.63.53a,b
Exh: H, J, N
Pub: 30, pl. 24
See plate 35

222
SUIT (coat, waistcoat, and breeches)
England, c. 1785
Silver braid, sequins, and colored foil trim on salmon pink ribbed silk; braid, sequin, and foil embroidered buttons; standing collar on coat and waistcoat.
cb: 41 in. (104 cm.)
Mrs. Alice F. Schott Bequest
CR.448.67.8a–c

223
COAT
England, c. 1785–95
Dusty rose wool and silk bombazine; cloth-of-gold covered buttons; turned-down collar.
cb: 41 in. (104 cm.)
Costume Council Fund
M.61.9.5; ex-coll. Doris Langley Moore

*Unless otherwise indicated, all measurements are for the coat only.

224

COAT

England, c. 1785–95

Deep red wool broadcloth; gold metallic braid trim on coat and covered buttons; turned-down collar.

cb: 41 in. (104 cm.)

Costume Council Fund

M.61.9.4; ex-coll. Doris Langley Moore

225

COAT (Macaroni)

England, c. 1790–1800

Lavender, pink, green, and yellow rose floral brocade on cream silk patterned damask ground; original mother-of-pearl, silver crescents, and paste buttons removed; high standing collar.

cb: 42½ in. (108 cm.)

Gift of Dorothy Dixon

M.82.80.3

226

COAT (musician's?)

England, c. 1750

Red corded silk with elaborate red silk frogs and tassels; narrow standing collar.

cb: 40½ in. (103.8 cm.)

Max Berman and Sons, Inc., London

M.82.13.1

227

COAT

England, c. 1785

Cream, pink, and green miniature leaf and bud silk embroidery on sapphire blue silk satin; matching self-covered embroidered buttons; narrow standing collar.

cb: 40½ in. (102.9 cm.)

Mrs. Alice F. Schott Bequest

CR.448.67.2

228

COAT

Italy, c. 1785–95

Yellow, cream, and pink floral satin stitch, silk embroidery on moss green silk velvet; matching self-covered embroidered buttons; high standing collar.

cb: 44¾ in. (113.8 cm.)

Mrs. Alice F. Schott Bequest

CR.448.67.239

229

COAT

England, c. 1790–1800

Pastel leaf and blossom design in silk satin stitch embroidery over silk tulle on brown drab wool broadcloth; matching self-covered embroidered buttons; high standing collar.

cb: 43¼ in. (109.9 cm.)

Costume Council Fund

M.71.47.1

Pub: 27, p. 56, pl. 66

230

COAT AND WAISTCOAT (sleeved)

France, c. 1740–50

Gold metallic, blue, green, and black elaborate border design, of flowers and simulated gold lace woven to shape in *ciselé* silk and velvet, on pale lavender ground; fabric woven in Lyon; matching sleeved waistcoat; brass buttons.

cb: 41 in. (104 cm.)

Costume Council Fund

M.57.35a,b

Exh: C, G, J

Pub: 14, p. 7 (ill.); 26, p. 8 (ill.); 32, p. 40, pl. 24

231

COAT AND WAISTCOAT

France, c. 1760

Silver and gold metallic floral and fur motif, woven to shape on crimson silk satin ground; all-over pattern of red silk chenille flowers and red silk-wrapped metal thread brocaded leaves; fabric woven in Lyon; metallic cloth-covered buttons; narrow standing collar; matching waistcoat.

cb: 42 in. (106.6 cm.)

Costume Council Fund

M.59.29.1a,b

Exh: D

Pub: 16, p. 358, pl. 12 (ill.); 12, p. 12 (ill.)

232

SUIT (coat, waistcoat, and breeches)

France or Germany, c. 1730–50

Blue silk chenille, cream pale and dark blue floral, and lace motif woven to shape on pink and cream basket-patterned silk ground; fabric woven in Lyon; large steel gilt and paste buttons.

cb: 40¼ in. (102.2 cm.)

Costume Council Fund

M.59.29.2a–c

Exh: D, J

233

SUIT (coat, waistcoat, and breeches)

France, c. 1765–69

Cream cut-silk velvet with green and brown border pattern of leaves, woven to shape, and embroidered with silver sequins and bullion; self-covered, woven-to-shape, embroidered buttons; narrow standing collar; matching waistcoat and breeches.

cb: 45½ in. (115.5 cm.)

Costume Council Fund

M.59.24.23a–c; ex-coll. Doris Langley Moore

Exh: D, K

Pub: 12, p. 14 (ill.); 26, p. 9 (ill.)

234

COURT SUIT (coat, waistcoat, and breeches)

France, c. 1780–90

Pale blue and black vertical stripe-patterned silk with cream silk, silver metallic thread, sequin, and paste embroidery; large, cream silk satin elaborately embroidered buttons; high standing collar; cream silk faille waistcoat with matching embroidery.

cb: 44¼ in. (112.5 cm.)

Gift of Mrs. Murray Ward

M.73.33.1a–c

Exh: N

Pub: 30, pl. 27

235

SUIT (coat and breeches)

France, c. 1785–89

Moss green vertically striped cut silk velvet on pink silk ground; high standing collar.

cb: 43½ in. (110.5 cm.)

Gift of Mrs. Dorothy Jeakins

M.67.56.3a,b

236

SUIT (coat and breeches)

France, last quarter of 18th century

Silver thread, sequins, and paste embroidery of wheat and flower motif on green and brown corded silk; large foil-covered and embroidered buttons; high standing collar.

cb: 43¾ in. (111 cm.)

Gift of Mrs. Aldrich Peck

M.56.7a,b

Exh: B, D

Pub: 12, p. 12 (ill.)

237
SUIT (coat, waistcoat, and breeches)
France, 1780–90
Rich and colorful shaded silk embroidery with forget-me-nots, Queen Anne's lace, and fern fronds on deep brown, cut silk velvet with all-over trefoil brown satin ground; self-covered embroidered buttons; high standing collar; matching embroidered waistcoat and breeches.
cb: 42 in. (106.6 cm.)
Purchased with Funds Provided by
Mr. and Mrs. John Jewett Garland
M.63.51a–c
Exh: G, Q
Pub: 32, pl. 36
See plates 37, 38

238
COAT
Italy, c. 1790–95
Blue, pink, yellow, and black vertical ombré satin stripe on brown silk ground; self-covered buttons; high standing, turned-down collar.
cb: 43¼ in. (110 cm.)
Gift of Mrs. Willard Larson
M.75.83

239
COAT
France, third quarter of 18th century
Uncut red silk velvet with border and pockets in stylized floral cut-pattern motif; woven to shape; standing collar.
cb: 41 in. (104.2 cm.)
Mrs. Alice F. Schott Bequest
CR.448.67.4

240
COAT
France, c. 1770–85
Blue gray cut silk velvet on leaf-patterned cloth-of-silver *droguet* ground; self-covered buttons; cream silk piping; high standing collar.
cb: 46 in. (116.9 cm.)
Costume Council Fund
M.59.23.1
Exh: G
Pub: 32, p. 40, pl. 25

241
COURT COAT
France, c. 1790–1800
Multicolored silk knotted and satin stitch embroidery, in exotic plant and leaf pattern, on olive green and deep brown spot-patterned silk; self-covered embroidered buttons; high standing collar.
cb: 41½ in. (105.4 cm.)
Costume Council Fund
M.59.24.24; ex-coll. Doris Langley Moore

242
COURT COAT
France, c. 1790–1800
Multicolored silk and silver thread embroidery, with colored sequins, glass paillettes, and faceted glass stones, on greenish brown uncut vertical-patterned silk velvet on brown silk satin ground; self-covered embroidered buttons; high standing collar.
cb: 41½ in. (105.4 cm.)
Costume Council Fund
54.93; ex-coll. Rodman Wanamaker
Exh: D, G
Pub: 19, p. 42 (ill.); 12, p. 14 (ill.); 32, p. 42, no. 27 (ill.)

243
COURT COAT
France, c. 1790–1800
Multicolored silk embroidery with sequins, faceted stones, and applied lace on purple, blue, and black patterned silk velvet.
cb: 43¼ in. (109.9 cm.)
Gift of Mrs. Murray Ward
M.73.33.2

244
COAT
France, c. 1785–1800
Yellow heavily padded silk satin stitch, silver gilt sequins, and metallic bullion embroidery in stylized leaf pattern on brown wool broadcloth; self-covered embroidered buttons; high standing collar.
cb: 43½ in. (110.5 cm.)
Gift of Max Berman and Sons, Inc., London
M.82.13.2

245
COAT
France, c. 1790–1800
Black diaper-patterned silk velvet on wine and emerald green silk satin ground; self-covered buttons; high standing collar.
cb: 43½ in. (110.5 cm.)
Gift of Mrs. Grace A. Moody
52.43.1

246
LIVERY COAT (?)
France, late 18th century
Green silk satin stripes on gold brown silk taffeta ground; deep green scallop-edged velvet and silk satin ribbon galloon trim; narrow standing collar.
cb: 38¾ in. (98.4 cm.)
Promised Gift of Dr. and Mrs. Pratapaditya Pal
L.79.34.5

247
COAT
France, c. 1795
Purple silk satin vertical stripes on black wool ground; purple silk piping; high standing collar; Directoire style.
cb: 44½ in. (113 cm.)
Promised Gift of Dr. and Mrs. Pratapaditya Pal
L.79.34.7

248
COURT COAT AND WAISTCOAT
Italy, c. 1800
Silver heavily padded embroidery in acorn, oak leaf, and varying leaf motifs on cerise wool broadcloth; self-covered buttons heavily embroidered with silver thread and bullion; high standing collar; cloth-of-silver waistcoat with matching silver embroidery and self-covered embroidered buttons; high standing collar.
cb: 43¼ in. (109.9 cm.)
Costume Council Fund
M.80.60a,b

249
BANYAN
Italy, late 18th century
Silver metallic and coral silk meandering brocaded stripes on patterned purple silk *gros de Tours* ground; diaper-patterned brown cotton lining; elaborate green silk and silver frogs, for turn-back front, which attach to self-covered buttons.
cb: 46 in. (116.8 cm.)
Mrs. Alice F. Schott Bequest
M.67.8.1

250
BANYAN
Italy, c. 1760–80
Green and pink shot-silk taffeta; double-breasted with attached single-breasted waistcoat; self-covered buttons.
cb: 46½ in. (118.1 cm.)
Costume Council Fund
M.82.19

251
LIVERY COAT
Italy, c. 1800
Red and black lions and cardinal insignia woven into heavy cream silk galloon on cerise wool broadcloth; copper gilt buttons; high standing collar; lined with cream twill glazed wool.
cb: 46 in. (116.9 cm.)
Gift of Mr. and Mrs. William J. Robertson
M.74.116

252
SUIT (coat and waistcoat)
Italy, c. 1770–80
Green, rose, and black shot-silk with minute diaper pattern; self-covered buttons; standing collar; matching waistcoat.
cb: 44½ in. (113.1 cm.)
Purchased with Funds Provided by
Mrs. Nancy Yewell
M.82.43a,b
Exh: Genoa, Italy, 1892

252a
COAT
Italy (Venice), c. 1795
Heavy claret red silk with pale yellow graduated vertical pinstripes; large self-covered buttons; turned-down collar; Directoire style.
cb: 40 in. (101.6 cm.)
Gift of Edward Maeder
M.81.220.2

253
COAT
United States (Boston), c. 1795–1800
Pale blue and dark green vertical stripes on moss green silk taffeta ground; self-covered buttons; high turned-down collar; Directoire style.
cb: 44 in. (112 cm.)
Gift of Mrs. Willard Larson
M.61.13

254
COAT
German (?), c. 1720–30
Purple cut silk velvet; very wide boot cuffs; self-covered buttons.
cb: 43½ in. (110.5 cm.)
Purchased with Los Angeles County Funds
62.6.2
Exh: G
Pub: 32

255
MILITARY UNIFORM (tailcoat, trousers, and knee breeches)
United States, c. 1830
Deep blue wool broadcloth tailcoat; pocket flaps and high standing collar heavily embroidered with silver bullion and sequins; cast brass buttons with military insignia; cream wool broadcloth trousers and knee breeches.
cb: 40 in. (101.7 cm.)
Gift of Mr. and Mrs. Cornelius Willis
M.65.8a–c

256
COURT SUIT (coat, waistcoat, knee breeches, and hat)
England, 1858
Deep blue wool broadcloth coat; cut steel buttons and corded false buttonholes; high standing collar; polychrome silk floral embroidery on cream silk faille waistcoat with self-covered embroidered buttons; matching deep blue wool knee breeches; black silk faille hat; entire suit cut and decorated in 18th-century style.
cb: 36⅝ in. (93 cm.)
Gift of Mrs. James P. Rock
M.72.72a–d

257
LIVERY COAT (cutaway)
England, late 18th century
Fine aubergine wool broadcloth; cut steel buttons; corded false buttonholes; high standing collar.
cb: 39¾ in. (101 cm.)
Gift of the Los Angeles Fashion Group, Inc.
M.49.1.1

258
WAISTCOAT
England, c. 1720–35
Shaded polychrome silk floral embroidery on linen; large corded buttonholes and metallic thread-covered buttons; twill silk lining; home manufacture.
cb: 36 in. (91.1 cm.)
Costume Council Fund
M.63.54.11

259
WAISTCOAT
England, c. 1725–50
Quilting (cording and stuffed work), embroidery, and drawn fabric work on linen; Dorset thread buttons; linen lining.
cb: 28 in. (71.2 cm.)
Costume Council Fund
M.66.8

260
WAISTCOAT (sleeved)
Central Europe, c. 1730
Metallic gold embroidery (satin stitch and other forms) on deep red silk velvet; sleeves and back replaced; silk taffeta lining.
cf: 34 in. (86.4 cm.)
cb: 22¼ in. (56.5 cm.)
Costume Council Fund
M.79.245.2
See plates 41, 42

261
WAISTCOAT (sleeved)
England, c. 1730
Buff wool with gold galloon braid trim; gold metallic embroidery buttons; bombazine, cotton, and linen linings.
cb: 35½ in. (90.2 cm.)
Costume Council Fund
M.81.135.1

262

WAISTCOAT

France or Italy, c. 1730–40

Terracotta and cream silk meandering floral-diaper pattern and silver threads brocaded on patterned beige silk ground; silver metallic embroidered buttons and silver corded buttonholes; five stitched eyelet holes on front of sleeve opening.

cb: 35 in. (88.9 cm.)

Gift of The Fashion Group, Inc., Los Angeles

52.44

263

WAISTCOAT

England, c. 1750–70

Black outlined floral and geometric pattern, warp-dyed, on cream and coral cut silk velvet ground; self-covered buttons; linen and cotton mixture lining.

cb: 30 in. (76.2 cm.)

Costume Council Fund

M.59.24.21; ex-coll. Doris Langley Moore

Exh: G

Pub: 32, p. 45, pl. 31

264

WAISTCOAT

England, c. 1745–50

"Gentleman's pink" elaborate stylized floral pattern in corded and stuffed quilted silk taffeta; self-covered buttons; relined in 19th century.

cb: 33¼ in. (84.5 cm.)

Gift of Mrs. Henry Salvatori

M.79.85

Exh: T

265

WAISTCOAT

Colonial America, c. 1750–60

Beige diaper pattern of stylized blooms and flowers in silk *gros de Tours*; self-covered buttons; bombazine and linen lining.

cb: 28¼ in. (71.8 cm.)

Gift of The Fashion Group, Inc., Los Angeles

52.45

266

WAISTCOAT

France, c. 1750–70

Dark red silk satin; woven to shape; pocket and front edge ornamentation of twisted floral design in silver metallic and cream silk with false watered pattern woven in ground; basket buttons; glazed wool twill and cotton linen lining.

cf: 31 in. (78.8 cm.)

Gift of Pacific Palisades Girl Scouts #35

66.2

267

WAISTCOAT (sleeved)

France, c. 1760–70

Polychrome floral sprigs and designs of ribbons, swags, and tassels in silk chain stitch on red and cream shot-silk taffeta; self-covered embroidered buttons; linen sleeves and lining.

cf: 31¼ in. (79.4 cm.)

Mrs. Alice F. Schott Bequest

M.67.8.6

268

WAISTCOAT

France, c. 1770–80

Polychrome silk embroidery, with metal thread sequins and blue and black velvet ribbon, on cream silk satin ground; self-covered embroidered buttons; silk taffeta and linen lining.

cb: 23½ in. (59.7 cm.)

Gift of Major General and Mrs. R.G. Fergusson

CR.72.20.1

269

WAISTCOAT

France, c. 1770–1800

Polychrome silk, satin stitch floral embroidery, in border design and all-over pattern, on ivory silk faille ground; self-covered embroidered buttons; twill silk, cotton, and linen lining.

cf: 27½ in. (69.9 cm.)

Costume Council Fund

M.55.23.1

270

WAISTCOAT

France, c. 1775–85

Cloth of silver with sequins, bullion, and paste embroidery; self-covered embroidered buttons; silk and linen lining.

cf: 27½ in. (69.9 cm.)

Gift of Mr. G.S. Stuart

62.28

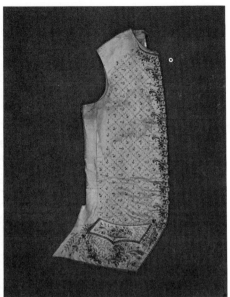

271

WAISTCOAT

England, c. 1775–85

Polychrome silk embroidery of floral and feather all-over pattern, and trellis motif with small silk flowers, on cream silk satin ground; twill silk and lamb's wool padded linen lining.

cf: 29½ in. (75 cm.)

Costume Council Fund

M.64.78

272

WAISTCOAT

Italy, c. 1780

Polychrome silk floral and couched silk trellis border with sequins and black silk chenille; spot embroidery, sequin, and feather all-over pattern on cream silk satin; brushed cotton lining.

cf: 25¾ in. (65.5 cm.)

Mrs. Alice F. Schott Bequest

CR.448.67.6

273

WAISTCOAT

England, c. 1780

Gray and cream silk ribbon pattern, woven to shape, on vertical striped cream silk ground; reembroidered with silver sequins; silver and silk metallic embroidered buttons; linen lining.

cf: 27 in. (68.6 cm.)

Gift of Dorothy Jeakins

M.67.56.3c; ex-coll. Lord Hugo Rumbold

274

WAISTCOAT

England, c. 1780

Multicolored floral silk embroidery on cream silk satin; self-covered embroidered buttons; linen lining.

cf: 23 in. (58.5 cm.)

Mrs. Alice F. Schott Bequest

CR.448.67.3

275

WAISTCOAT

France, c. 1780–90

Green, brown, and rust silk satin stitch, in heavily embroidered floral pattern, on cream silk satin; self-covered embroidered buttons; high standing collar; linen lining.

cf: 21 in. (53.4 cm.)

Gift of Mrs. Murray Ward

M.73.33.3

276

WAISTCOAT

France, c. 1790–1800

Pink and green silk thread and ribbons, silver thread, and silver sequin embroidery, in floral and meandering pattern, on cream silk taffeta; self-covered embroidered buttons; high standing collar; linen lining.

cf: 19¾ in. (52 cm.)

Gift of Doris Langley Moore

M.59.20

277

WAISTCOAT

England, c. 1780–90

Polychrome floral and figure-eight knot pattern of silk and metallic thread and sequin embroidery on cream silk repp; cloth-of-silver buttons embroidered with sequins.

cb: 28½ in. (72.4 cm.)

Costume Council Fund

M.59.23.3

278

WAISTCOAT

England, c. 1785–95

Polychrome silk floral satin stitch embroidery on white silk faille; self-covered embroidered buttons; high standing collar; cotton lining.

cf: 22½ in. (57.2 cm.)

Mrs. Alice F. Schott Bequest

M.67.8.4

279
WAISTCOAT
France, c. 1790
Multicolored striped, warp-patterned cut silk velvet, with miniature floral design, on cream silk satin ground; double row of self-covered buttons; standing collar; brushed cotton and linen lining. (*See also* cat. no. 54.)
cf: 25 in. (63.5 cm.)
Promised Gift of Dr. and Mrs. Pratapaditya Pal
L.80.37.1

280
WAISTCOAT
Spain (?), c. 1790
Polychrome silk, satin stitch, bold floral embroidery on pale green silk satin; self-covered buttons; high standing collar; silk and linen lining.
cf: 22¼ in. (56.6 cm.)
Gift of Mrs. Norman Topping
M.65.55

281
WAISTCOAT
England, c. 1790–1800
Red and green printed cotton floral ribbon border; bow and tassel motif embroidered, in silver and gold chain stitch and silk, on vertical striped cream cotton dimity; double row of self-covered embroidered buttons; standing collar; cotton lining.
cf: 20½ in. (52.1 cm.)
Costume Council Fund
M.63.54.12

282
WAISTCOAT
France, c. 1790–1800
Pale blue, green, gold, and cream embroidery with ribbon appliqué and tulle in stylized pattern on cream silk faille; silk thread buttons; high standing collar; cotton and linen lining.
cf: 23 in. (58.5 cm.)
Gift of Mrs. Murray Ward
M.73.33.4

283
WAISTCOAT
England, c. 1790–1800
Brown printed-to-shape border, with bow and tassel design, on horizontal striped cream cotton; double row of self-covered printed buttons and buttonholes; standing collar; linen lined.
cf: 24½ in. (62.3 cm.)
Gift of Mr. Jack Cole
M.63.24.6

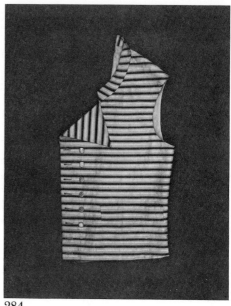

284
WAISTCOAT
England, c. 1790–1810
Red, blue, and green ombré horizontal striped wool with narrow cream silk figured ribbon; double row of silver metallic buttons; cotton lining.
cf: 20¼ in. (51.5 cm.)
Costume Council Fund
M.59.23.4

285
WAISTCOAT
Germany, c. 1797–1804
Deep red silk velvet; double-breasted; self-covered buttons; standing collar; linen lining.
cf: 20½ in. (52.1 cm.)
Gift of Anna Bing Arnold
60.46.13

286

WAISTCOAT

France, c. 1795–1800

Elaborate polychrome floral silk embroidery, ribbon appliqué, and silk chenille threads on diaper-patterned cream silk; self-covered embroidered buttons; high standing collar (removed); brushed linen and cotton lining.

cf: 21 in. (53.4 cm.)

Costume Council Fund

M.55.23.2

Exh: D, N

Pub: 12, p. 9 (ill.); 27, p. 56, pl. 66

287

WAISTCOAT AND SASH

France, c. 1800–1805

Polychrome silk embroidery and silk appliqué of printed hand-colored engravings on cream silk faille; plum-colored ribbon sash with embroidered appliqué of printed engraving of fairy scenes, outlined with pressed paper paillettes; self-covered embroidered buttons; high standing collar; linen lining.

cf: 22¼ in. (56.5 cm.)

l. of sash: 120 x 4½ in. (317.5 x 11.5 cm.)

Costume Council Fund

M.59.28.6a,b

Exh: E, M

Pub: 23, p. 28, pl. 38 (ill.); 31, p. 103 (ill.)

288

CHILD'S WAISTCOAT

England, late 18th century

Polychrome chain stitch silk embroidery on cream silk satin; recut from an adult waistcoat; self-covered buttons; standing collar; glazed cotton lining.

cf: 14½ in. (36.9 cm.)

Mrs. Alice F. Schott Bequest

M.67.8.12

289

WAISTCOAT

United States, c. 1800

Silver thread grape design, with green and white silk embroidered leaves, on white vertically striped cotton dimity; self-covered embroidered buttons; standing collar; linen lining.

cf: 25 in. (63.5 cm.)

Gift of Mrs. Emma Hardy Hill

57.39

290

WAISTCOAT

France, c. 1800

Slate blue woven design of mounted and foot soldiers in curved rows, marching left on one side and right on the other, on cream silk moiré ground; self-covered buttons; high standing collar; cotton lining.

cf: 19¼ in. (49 cm.)

Gift of Mrs. Harry Lenart

65.4

291

WAISTCOAT

England, c. 1780

Multicolored silk floral embroidery on cream silk faille; self-covered buttons; linen lining.

cf: 25 in. (63.5 cm.)

Costume Council Fund

M.59.23.2

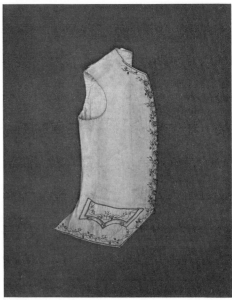

292

WAISTCOAT

England, c. 1780–90

Pink, green, and brown floral chain stitch silk embroidery on beige ribbed silk; self-covered embroidered buttons; linen and cotton linings.

cf: 24 in. (61 cm.)

Gift of Mrs. Patricia E. Bye

61.14

293

WAISTCOAT

Holland (?), c. 1730

Blue, pink, and yellow floral design brocaded on cream silk damask ground; metallic and embroidered buttons; corded metallic buttonholes; lining replaced in 19th century.

cf: 29 in. (73.7 cm.)

Costume Council Fund

M.81.97.10

294
WAISTCOAT (sleeved)
Spanish Colonial (Bolivia), c. 1720–30
Brown *ciselé*, cut and uncut, floral patterned silk velvet; sleeves and back of patterned twill silk c. 1700–1715; cloth-of-silver covered wood buttons; red wool twill and striped native Bolivian wool twill lining.
cf: 32 in. (81.3 cm.)
Promised Gift of Cathy Glynn Benkaim
TR.5335

295
WAISTCOAT
United States, c. 1800
Multicolored floral design in silk, satin stitch on cream silk satin; embroidered self-covered buttons; high standing collar; brushed cotton lining.
cf: 22 in. (57.2 cm.)
Gift of The Fashion Group, Inc., Los Angeles
52.46

296
WAISTCOAT
England, c. 1775–85
Pink, blue, brown, and green floral chain stitch embroidery on pale yellow silk shagreen; self-covered embroidered buttons; high standing collar; heavy cotton lining.
cf: 28 in. (72.1 cm.)
Promised Gift of Dr. and Mrs. Pratapaditya Pal
L.79.34.4

297
WAISTCOAT
England, c. 1775–85
Pink and mauve chain stitch border, with silver gilt sequins, on silver metallic vertical stripes on tan silk satin ground; self-covered embroidered buttons; silk plush and cotton-linen flannel lining.
cf: 26 in. (67.3 cm.)
Promised Gift of Dr. and Mrs. Pratapaditya Pal
L.79.34.2

298
WAISTCOAT
France, c. 1760–70
Pink, silver, and green floral brocade pattern woven to shape on cream silk faille ground; self-covered and embroidered buttons; linen lining.
cf: 25 in. (64.2 cm.)
Promised Gift of the Costume Council
TR.5827

299
WAISTCOAT
France, c. 1780–90
Multicolored feather and floral border pattern of satin stitch silk embroidery on cream silk satin ground; self-covered embroidered buttons; cotton-linen lining.
cf: 19 in. (48.3 cm.)
Gift of Mrs. Hildegarde Lindsay
M.80.282.2

300
WAISTCOAT
England, c. 1795
Lavender, pink, and yellow silk embroidery on vertically striped white cotton dimity; self-covered embroidered buttons; standing collar; linen lining.
cf: 20 in. (49.9 cm.)
Gift of Stephanie Kline Morehouse
M.82.12.1

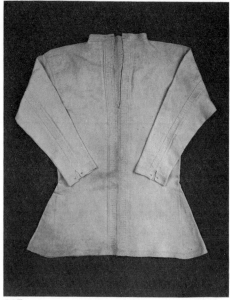

301
WAISTCOAT
England, c. 1795
Green, lavender, and yellow feather motif silk
embroidery on white vertical and horizontal
striped cotton dimity; self-covered embroidered
buttons; standing collar; linen lining.
cf: 21 in. (53.4 cm.)
Gift of Stephanie Kline Morehouse
M.82.12.2

302
WAISTCOAT
England, c. 1740–50
Oyster linen, quilted (cording and stuffed work),
with embroidery and drawn fabric work in
elaborate design of floral and stylized leaves;
buttons removed; linen lining.
cf: 29 in. (73.7 cm.)
Costume Council Fund
M.71.47.2

303
WAISTCOAT (sleeved)
France, c. 1740–50
Blue, cream, and metallic floral-and-feather
patterned brocade on pale blue silk faille
ground; silver and silk embroidered corded
buttons; linen and silk lining.
cf: 27 in. (68.6 cm.)
Mrs. Alice F. Schott Bequest
M.67.8.11

304
WAISTCOAT (sleeved)
France (?), c. 1750
Polychrome brocaded silk in floral design on
cream silk diapered and ribbed ground; silver
paillette and corded buttons; silk and linen
lining.
cf: 27 in. (68.6 cm.)
Gift of Mrs. Aldrich Peck
M.54.18.4
Pub: 19, p. 41 (ill.); 25, p. 9 (ill.)

305
WAISTCOAT
Italy, c. 1750
Bronze figured silk with meandering pattern on
gros de Tours ground; self-covered buttons; linen
lining.
cf: 28¾ in. (73.1 cm.)
Gift of Edward Maeder
M.81.220.3

306
WAISTCOAT
England, c. 1780
Silk velvet and embroidered appliqué, with
painted metal bullion embroidery, on cream silk
satin; self-covered buttons; silk and cotton
lining.
cf: 28 in. (71.1 cm.)
Gift of Mrs. Harry Robinson
CR.116.62.3; ex-coll. Lord Hugo Rumbold

307
MAN'S SHIRT
England, c. 1650–80
White knitted cotton with geometric pattern on
center front, center back, collar, cuffs, and lower
edge; long sleeves.
cf: 29¾ in. (75.6 cm.)
Costume Council Fund
M.81.135.3

308
POCKETBOOK
Colonial America (Pennsylvania), 1763
Multicolored counted-thread wool embroidery
on linen canvas (known as Irish embroidery in
the 18th century); made by Elizabeth Parker, a
Quaker, of Kennett Square, Westchester County,
Pennsylvania; her initials and "1763" are worked
into the design.
4 x 6 in. (10.1 x 15.2 cm.)
Gift of Mrs. Romona de Jongh
M.79.29

308a
PURSE
Italy, late 18th century
Red silk sprang in tube shape; slit opening;
tasseled ends; worn over belt or sash; known as
"miser's purse."
22½ x 3 in. (57.1 x 7.6 cm.)
Gift of Edward Maeder
M.82.64

309
SHOE BUCKLES (pair)
Colonial America, c. 1770–90
Linear pattern on plated square steel frame;
high arch; blued-steel double chape.
2⅞ x 3¾ in. (7.3 x 9.5 cm.)
Gift of Miss Eleanor Bissell
42.16.17a,b

310
SHOE BUCKLES (pair)
England, c. 1777–85
Double row of faceted cut-steel beads on
rectangular steel frame; accented with three
rows of twisted gilt wire; high arch; probably
from Wolverhampton area.
2⅛ x 5¼ in. (5.4 x 13.3 cm.)
Costume Council Fund
M.80.92.6a,b
Exh: T

310a
SHOE BUCKLES (pair)
England, c. 1780–85
Transparent and blue faceted paste stones set in
silver rectangular frame; steel chape.
2 x 3 in. (5.1 x 7.6 cm.)
Costume Council Fund
M.80.92.3a,b
Exh: T

310b
SHOE BUCKLE (one of pair)
England, c. 1770–85
Square steel frame with rounded corners;
double chape.
2¼ x 2¾ in. (5.7 x 7 cm.)
Gift of Mexicer Brown IV
M.81.109.6

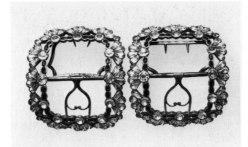

311
SHOE BUCKLES (pair)
England, c. 1780–85
Transparent and blue faceted paste stones set in
silver and gilt; steel fittings; blued-steel chape.
2½ x 2½ in. (6.3 x 6.3 cm.)
Costume Council Fund
M.80.92.1a,b
Exh: T

312
SHOE BUCKLES (pair)
England, c. 1780–1800
Blue faceted paste stones set in brass painted
black; steel spring chape.
2½ x 2⅜ in. (6.3 x 6 cm.)
Costume Council Fund
M.80.92.7a,b

313
KNEE BUCKLE (one of pair)
France, c. 1780–85
Transparent and blue faceted paste stones set in
silver and gilt; chape missing.
1½ x 1½ in. (3.8 x 3.8 cm.)
Costume Council Fund
M.80.92.2

313a
KNEE BUCKLES (pair)
France, c. 1770–80
Transparent faceted paste stones set in silver;
chape missing.
1½ x 1¾ in. (3.8 x 4.5 cm.)
Mrs. Alice F. Schott Bequest
CR.448.67.238a,b

313b
KNEE BUCKLES (pair)
England, c. 1780–90
Transparent faceted paste stones set in silver;
copper back; anchor chape.
1¼ x 1⅜ in. (3.2 x 4.2 cm.)
Mrs. Alice F. Schott Bequest
CR.448.67.237a,b

313c
KNEE BUCKLES (pair)
Colonial America, c. 1770–80
Conch shell discs fastened to brass back with
faceted silver studs; anchor chape.
1½ x 1½ in. (3.8 x 3.8 cm.)
Gift of Miss Eleanor Bissell
42.16.43c,d

313d
STOCK BUCKLE
Colonial America, c. 1755–70
Patterned silver-plated oval frame; chape has
four studs which attach to one end of stock.
2 x 1¼ in. (5.1 x 3.2 cm.)
Gift of Miss Eleanor Bissell
42.16.24

314
BOOTS (pair)
French, late 18th century
Black leather with 6-inch turned-down brown
cuff; heel and sole elaborately patterned with
silver nails in Directoire style; with original box,
made to form.
18 x 10½ in. (45.8 x 26.7 cm.)
Mrs. Alice F. Schott Bequest
M.67.8.187a,b

314a
ECCLESIASTICAL SLIPPERS (pair)
Italy, early 18th century
Red silk velvet with metallic gold galloon.
4½ x 10¾ in. (11.4 x 27.3 cm.)
Costume Council Fund
M.81.195.4a,b

314b
SHOES (pair)
Morocco, late 18th century
Red orange leather with metallic embroidery.
4½ x 10½ in. (11.4 x 26.7 cm.)
Costume Council Fund
M.81.195.1a,b

315
AT-HOME CAP (undress)
Italy, c. 1710–30
Metallic silver brocade on blue and silver lace
patterned silk ground; stiffened and lined with
silk.
d: 8 in. (20.3 cm.)
Mrs. Alice F. Schott Bequest
M.67.8.83

316
AT-HOME CAP (undress)
England, first quarter of 18th century
Multicolored silk and gold metallic embroidery
on white patterned silk.
d: 8 in. (20.3 cm.)
Gift of Mrs. Frederick Kingston
M.61.6
Exh: N
Pub: 30, no. 16 (ill.)
See plate 36

317
NIGHTCAP
Spain, c. 1700
White linen and silver metallic embroidery with
drawnwork on white linen; inscription reads:
"Soy De Don Guyllermo Bumpsted" (I am [the
property] of Don Guyllermo Bumpsted).
d: 18¼ in. (46.3 cm.)
Costume Council Fund
M.59.23.5

318
AT-HOME CAP (undress)
Switzerland, first half of 18th century
Silver metallic and multicolored silk satin
stitch embroidery on green silk satin;
metallic lace trim.
d: 9⅜ in. (23.8 cm.)
Costume Council Fund
M.81.97.12
Exh: T

318a
AT-HOME CAP (undress)
England, c. 1720
Corded quilting in floral and feather motifs on
white linen; gathered brim, high in front;
linen lined.
d: 5¾ in. (14.5 cm.)
Costume Council Fund
M.82.8.5

319
BICORNE
France (Paris), 1790
Black fur felt; black ostrich feather and metallic
galloon trim; leather brow band; silk and leather
lining; made by Dassier by appointment to the
Duc d'Orleans.
d: 15½ in. (39.4 cm.)
circum. of crown: 22 in. (56 cm.)
Mrs. Alice F. Schott Bequest
M.67.8.203

320
TRICORNE
United States, c. 1780
Black beaver felt; black silk ribbon edging;
sheared natural beaver pompons on front cocks;
unlined.
d: 5¾ in. (14.5 cm.)
circum. of crown: 21 in. (53.4 cm.)
Mrs. Alice F. Schott Bequest
M.67.8.204

321
STOCKINGS (pair)
Italy, c. 1800
Pale blue knitted silk with raised silver gilt
embroidery; believed by family tradition to have
been worn by Pope Pius VII (1742–1823); of the
style popular c. 1720–30.
l: 26¼ in. (66.6 cm.)
Purchased with Funds Provided by
Mr. and Mrs. John Jewett Garland
M.57.8.2a,b; ex-coll. Adolfo A. de Segni
See plate 43

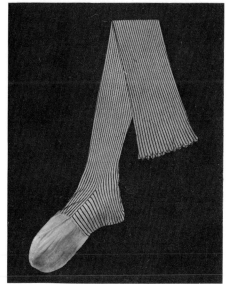

321a
STOCKINGS (pair)
England, c. 1800
Blue and white knitted silk in striped
herringbone pattern; Directoire style.
l: 30¼ in. (77 cm.)
Costume Council Fund
M.81.97.11a,b

321b
STOCKINGS (pair)
England, c. 1750
Blue knitted silk; floral-edged white silk clocks
with crown.
l: 24½ in. (62.2 cm.)
Costume Council Fund
M.82.8.2a,b

321c
STOCKINGS (pair)
England, c. 1760
Blue gray knitted silk with snowflake and crown
design in purl stitch.
l: 23¼ in. (59 cm.)
Costume Council Fund
M.82.8.1a,b

321d
STOCKING
England, c. 1750
Green knitted silk; floral-edged white silk clock
with crown.
l: 24 in. (61 cm.)
Costume Council Fund
M.82.8.3

CHILDREN'S COSTUMES

322
CHILD'S PUDDING CAP
French, c. 1760
Pale gray green silk satin, quilted; metallic silver
bobbin lace trim and ribbon bow.
d: 3 in. (7.6 cm.)
Mrs. Alice F. Schott Bequest
CR.448.67.235

Daniel Chodowieki (German, 1726–1801)
Child Wearing Pudding Cap, 1770 (detail)
Engraving on paper

323
CHILD'S LONG DRESS
England, c. 1760
Cream half-silk satin (linen weft); open front;
half-sleeves.
cb: 31½ in. (80 cm.)
Costume Council Fund
M.80.190.2

324
INFANT'S CHRISTENING GOWN AND
BEARING CLOTH
England, early 18th century
Cream silk satin; cream silk quilting.
cb of a: 33 in. (83.9 cm.)
b: 43½ x 33 in. (110.4 x 83.9 cm.)
Costume Council Fund
M.80.190.3a,b

325
INFANT'S BONNET
France, late 18th century
Multicolored silk and metallic threads brocaded
on light green patterned silk ground; silver
metallic braid trim.
h: 4¼ in. (10.8 cm.)
d: 2 in. (5 cm.)
w: 3½ in. (8.9 cm.)
Costume Council Fund
M.81.71.8

325a
INFANT'S BONNET
England, early 18th century
Light blue silk embroidered with gold metallic
threads in a variety of stitches; gold galloon and
bobbin lace trim.
h: 4 in. (10.2 cm.)
d: 2⅜ in. (6 cm.)
w: 4½ in. (11.5 cm.)
Donated by Adrienne and Elliott Horwitch in
Memory of Estel Schott
M.82.69

325b
INFANT'S BONNET
England, first half of 18th century
White linen hollypoint filling and hemstitching
on white linen.
6 x 5¼ in. (15.2 x 13.3 cm.)
Costume Council Fund
M.81.143.6

325c
INFANT'S BONNET
England, first half of 18th century
White linen; bobbin lace edging.
6½ x 6¼ in. (16.5 x 16 cm.)
Costume Council Fund
M.81.143.7

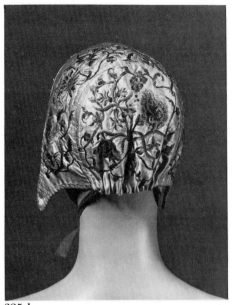

325d
CHILD'S BONNET
England, c. 1750
Multicolored floral silk and metal thread
embroidery on white silk satin ground.
h: 6¼ in. (16 cm.)
d: 4 in. (10.2 cm.)
w: 5 in. (12.2 cm.)
Costume Council Fund
M.81.242.1

326
BOY'S COAT
England, 1788
Pink, black, and green on tan figured cut and
uncut silk velvet; standing collar; self-covered
buttons.
cb: 20¼ in. (51.5 cm.)
Gift of Mrs. Murray Ward
M.70.49

327
BOY'S COAT
England, c. 1780–90
Brown silk corduroy; turned-down collar; self-
covered buttons.
cb: 21⅝ in. (55 cm.)
Costume Council Fund
M.71.47.3

328
BOY'S COAT
France, c. 1795–1805
Black, yellow, white, and red ribbon striped silk
chiné on shaded lavender silk ground; self-
covered buttons; Directoire style.
cb: 30 in. (76.2 cm.)
Mrs. Alice F. Schott Bequest
M.67.8.14

329
BOY'S COAT
Italy, c. 1720–40
Rust wool and cream silk; boot cuffs; self-
covered buttons.
cb: 25 in. (63.5 cm.)
Gift of Sandford and Mary Jane Bloom
M.82.16.3

330
BOY'S COAT
England, c. 1740
Brown silk patterned weave; boot cuffs; turned-
down collar; pewter buttons.
cb: 21 in. (53.3 cm.)
Costume Council Fund
M.82.8.4

331

LAY FIGURE
England, 1769
Wardrobe designer: Ann Whytell (English,
active third quarter of 18th century)
Figure designer: Simon Hennekin (English,
active third quarter of 18th century)
Wooden human figure, jointed with metal
screws at buttocks and back of shoulders;
movement of torso, head, and body extremities
allows the artist to pose the model in its
diminutive clothing—either male or female—in
whatever position and costume required for a
particular portrait; body parts held together
with cotton cord tied at top of head; painted
hair, eyes, and lips; traces of flesh-colored paint
on body; two holes on each side of upper and
lower back torso, one in each breast; hole in back
between buttocks; signed on back of torso: "A.
Whytell's Layman, August 2, 1769."
h: 11½ in. (29.2 cm.)
w: 3¾ in. (9.6 cm.)
d: 2¼ in. (5.7 cm.)
Elsie de Wolfe Foundation
M.79.249.1
See fig. 66a

WARDROBE FOR LAY FIGURE:

WOMEN'S COSTUMES AND ACCESSORIES
Hussar hat and jacket: yellow silk satin, fur trim.
Two dresses: green silk and wool; white
embroidered cotton muslin. Stomacher and
sleeves (pair): yellow silk satin. Engageantes
(pair): white silk and linen lace. Corset: white
linen. Petticoat: white cotton. Two camisoles:
green silk; pink silk satin. Chemise: white linen.
Muff cover: pink silk satin. Shoe: white silk satin
with pink silk rosette. Two hats: brown silk
taffeta with pink satin trim; black wool, also
used for men. Wig: light brown human hair.

MEN'S COSTUMES AND ACCESSORIES
Hussar hat and sleeves: yellow silk satin.
Vandyke waistcoat, sleeves, and knee breeches:
cream silk with pink silk lining. Three waistcoats
and knee breeches: fulled red wool; brown silk
velvet; brown silk. Waistcoat and sleeves: blue
silk satin. Long coat, sleeves, and vest: purple
fulled wool. Long robe: black silk. Two shirts:
white linen. Shoe: black leather. Three wigs:
light brown; dark blond; and dark brown;
human hair.
M.79.249.2–63

332

MADONNA ROBE
Italy (Venice), c. 1700–1725
Polychrome silk in lace-pattern brocade on cloth-
of-gold ground; sleeves and undersleeves
detachable; boned bodice; gold metallic lace and
galloon trim.
a (bodice): 17½ in. (44.4 cm.)
b–c (sleeves): 16 in. (40.7 cm.)
d–e (cuffs): 8⅜ x 9¾ in. (21.2 x 24.8 cm.)
f (skirt): 45⅛ in. (114.35 cm.)
Purchased with Los Angeles County Funds
65.1.1.a–f
Exh: P
Pub: 29, pp. 80, 188–89, pl. 73

333

CHRIST CHILD'S STATUE ROBE
Italy (Venice), c. 1700–1725
Companion piece to cat. no. 332; identical fabric
and trimming.
cb: 17 in. (43 cm.)
Purchased with Los Angeles County Funds
65.1.2

334

INFANT'S STATUE ROBE (?)
France, mid-18th century
Polychrome silk floral brocade on patterned
cloth-of-silver ground; single sleeve ruffles of
self-fabric; gold metallic lace.
cb: 23 in. (58.5 cm.)
Mr. and Mrs. Allan C. Balch Collection
M.45.3.189
Exh: D
Pub: 12, p. 10 (ill.); 26, p. 8 (ill.)

335

STATUE ROBE

England, c. 1701–1725

Elaborate multicolored realistic floral silk embroidery on patterned cloth-of-silver ground; constructed from front of secular dress.

cb: 42¼ in. (107 cm.)

Costume Council Fund

M.56.4

336

STATUE ROBE

Spain, c. 1700

Raised silver gilt embroidered symmetrical design on bodice and skirt front of deep red silk; holes on bodice front where jewelry was sewn when robe was used in processionals.

cf of bodice: 17¾ in. (45.1 cm.)

cb of bodice: 16¾ in. (42.5 cm.)

cb of skirt: 45½ in. (115.6 cm.)

Mrs. Alice F. Schott Bequest

CR.448.67.228a,b

Exh: R

337

CHASUBLE

France, first quarter of 18th century

Polychrome chenille silk floral brocade appliqué, reembroidered with silver gilt threads; raised and padded embroidery of metal scroll shapes and architectural design; linen base and lining.

l: 46 in. (117 cm.)

w: 29 in. (73.6 cm.)

Gift of Mrs. Shannon Crandall, Jr.

M.58.24.1

Exh: U

338

CHASUBLE

France (Lyon), c. 1735–40

Multicolored silk, oversized floral and fruit design with silver metallic ruins, brocaded on yellow silk satin ground; silver galloon; linen lined.

back: 40¼ x 26 in. (102.2 x 66 cm.)

front: 30½ x 22¾ in. (77.5 x 57.8 cm.)

stole: 89 x 8½ in. (260 x 21.4 cm.)

maniple: 34½ x 9 in. (87.6 x 22.9 cm.)

Costume Council Fund

M.81.193.1a–c

339

CHASUBLE

Italy (Bologna), c. 1735–40

Polychrome stylized flowers and apple trees, and Northern Italian architecture with Lombardy poplars, brocaded on olive green silk satin ground; silver orris lace; linen lined.

back: 39½ x 28 in. (100.4 x 71.1 cm.)

front: 30 x 26½ in. (76.2 x 67.3 cm.)

stole: 86½ x 10½ in. (219.8 x 26.6 cm.)

Costume Council Fund

M.81.193.2a,b

See plate 45

340

ALTAR FRONTAL

Italy (Bologna?), c. 1700–1725

Polychrome shaded silk chenille, padded thread, and silver bullion embroidery, in fanciful floral and leaf design on pink silk taffeta shot with silver thread.

44½ x 119¼ in. (113 x 302.9 cm.)

Costume Council Needlework Project Funds

M.80.139, central panel

Costume Council Fund

M.82.25.3a–i, surrounding fragments

See plates 39, 40

341

CHASUBLE

France (?), mid-18th century

Pastel-colored floral satin stitch embroidery on cream silk satin.

cb: 40 in. (101.5 cm.)

Gift of Order of the Holy Cross Mount Calvary, Santa Barbara

61.30

342

ALB (long)

Italy, late 18th century

White pleated linen with darned net flounce and cuffs backed with crimson silk; linen bobbin lace at shoulder and center-front opening; two crimson silk ribbon bows on either side of center-front opening.

58 x 127 in. (147.3 x 322.6 cm.)

Purchased with Funds Provided by Mrs. Helen Fowler

M.82.17

343

ALB (short)

Italy, late 18th century

White pleated linen; linen bobbin lace cuffs, shoulder ruffles, and flounce; chevron-pleated sleeves; red silk ribbon trim.

25 x 114 in. (63.5 x 286.6 cm.)

Purchased with Funds Provided by Nancy Yewell

M.82.20

344
CHASUBLE
France (?), c. 1700–1720
Polychrome silk and metallic threads, in
asymmetrical floral pattern, brocaded on dark
orange silk satin ground.
cb: 40¼ in. (102.2 cm.)
Gift of David L. Woodruff
M.78.102

345
MADONNA CAPE
Spain or France, mid-18th century
Polychrome silk thread, knotted and couched,
and silk chenille floral embroidery on cream silk
satin; yellow silk and gold metallic thread lace
edging.
8¾ x 18½ in. (22.2 x 47 cm.)
Gift of Mrs. Gabriella K. Robertson and
Mrs. Marlene P. L. Toeppen
63.2.9

346
CHASUBLE
Spain, mid-18th century
Shaded peach with blue, yellow, cream, and
green silk floral and fruit bouquet with sprig
motif, on gold and silver metallic thread leaf
pattern, brocaded on peach silk ground; woven
metallic ribbon trim.
cb: 45 in. (114.3 cm.)
Gift of Mrs. Shannon Crandall, Jr.
M.58.24.2

LACE

347
LACE (flounce)
Italy, c. 1700
Linen needle lace, *point de Venise.*
11 x 121 in. (28 x 305.3 cm.)
Gift of Mrs. Helen Crocker Russell
M.67.50.1a

348
LACE (flounce)
Italy, c. 1700
Linen needle lace, *point de Venise.*
8 x 149 in. (20.3 x 378.4 cm.)
Gift of Mrs. Helen Crocker Russell
M.67.50.1b
See fig. 34

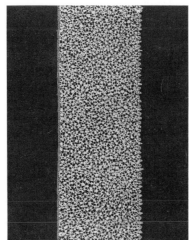

349
LACE (flounce)
Italy, c. 1700 (detail)
Linen needle lace, *point de Venise.*
10 x 59⅝ in. (25.4 x 169.8 cm.)
Gift of Anna Bing Arnold
M.60.46.19

350
LACE (panel)
France, first half of 18th century
Linen needle lace, *point de France;* made into
bonnet back.
6½ x 24 in. (15.9 x 60.9 cm.)
Gift of Mrs. Helen Crocker Russell
M.67.50.21

351
LACE (border)
Italy, late 17th or early 18th century
Linen needle lace.
5 x 126 in. (12.7 x 319.6 cm.)
Gift of Park View Antique Shop (Mrs. J. Lofsky)
M.65.61.11

352
LACE (pair of lappets)
France, c. 1738
Linen needle lace, *point d'Argentan.*
3 x 44 in. (7.6 x 118 cm.)
Gift of Miss Cora E. Sanders
60.39
See fig. 38

353
LACE (panel)
Italy (Venice), c. 1690–1710
Linen needle lace.
23 x 9½ in. (58.4 x 24.1 cm.)
Gift of Anna Bing Arnold
60.46.19

354
LACE (flounce)
Flanders (Brussels), c. 1800
Linen bobbin lace, Valenciennes.
6 x 92 in. (15.3 x 234 cm.)
Gift of Mrs. Helen Crocker Russell
M.67.50.2

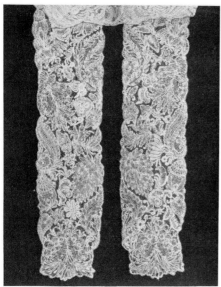

355
LACE (pair of lappets)
Flanders (Brussels),
first quarter of 18th century (detail)
Linen bobbin lace, *point d'Angleterre*.
4½ x 48 in. (11.4 x 122 cm.)
Gift of Mrs. Helen Crocker Russell
M.67.50.22

356
LACE (borders)
Flanders (Brussels), 18th century
Linen bobbin lace, Valenciennes.
4¾ x 25 in. (12.1 x 63.5 cm.)
Gift of Mrs. Helen Crocker Russell
M.67.50.31a,b

357
LACE (lappet fragment)
Flanders, early 18th century
Linen bobbin lace, Binche.
3½ x 21¼ in. (8.9 x 54 cm.)
Gift of Park View Antique Shop (Mrs. J. Lofsky)
M.65.61.1

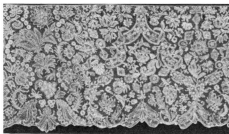

358
LACE (flounce)
Flanders (Bruges?), 18th century (detail)
Linen bobbin lace; picot edge new.
22 x 124 in. (55.8 x 315 cm.)
Gift of Park View Antique Shop (Mrs. J. Lofsky)
M.65.61.4

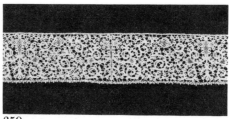

359
LACE (flounce)
Italy (Milan), late 17th–early 18th century (detail)
Linen bobbin lace for church vestment or altar.
4½ x 180 in. (11.4 x 457.2 cm.)
Gift of Park View Antique Shop (Mrs. J. Lofsky)
M.65.61.13

360
LACE (pair of lappets)
Flanders (Mechlin), c. 1738
Linen bobbin lace; joined in middle.
3¾ x 42½ in. (8.2 x 108 cm.)
Gift of Park View Antique Shop (Mrs. J. Lofsky)
M.65.61.6
See fig. 39

361
LACE (pair of lappets)
Flanders (Brussels), first quarter of 18th century
Linen bobbin lace, *point d'Angleterre*.
4½ x 23 in. (11.4 x 58.4 cm.)
Gift of Mrs. Vera W. Strub
M.64.80.3a,b

362
LACE (alb flounce)
Flanders (Brussels), c. 1720
Linen bobbin lace; floral designs on
geometric ground.
17 x 129 in. (43.2 x 327.2 cm.)
Promised Gift of Anne Caldwell
TR.3620.1
See fig. 36

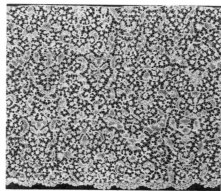

363
LACE (flounce)
Flanders (Brabant), mid-18th century (detail)
Linen bobbin lace; probably for church use.
15 x 144 in. (38.1 x 365.7 cm.)
Gift of Mrs. Vera W. Strub
M.64.80.2

364
LACE (alb flounce)
Flanders (Brussels), c. 1700
Linen bobbin lace.
12 x 108 in. (30.4 x 274.3 cm.)
Gift of Mrs. Beatrice Greenough
M.64.33.2
See fig. 35

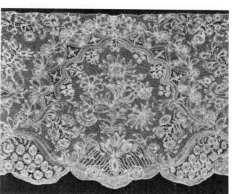

365
LACE (flounce)
Flanders (Brussels), late 17th or early 18th
century (detail)
Linen bobbin lace; slightly reworked from an
original alb flounce.
18 x 67 in. (45.7 x 170.1 cm.)
Gift of Mrs. Beatrice Greenough
M.64.33.3

366
LACE (dress robing)
Flanders (Brussels), c. 1710 (detail)
Linen bobbin lace, *point d'Angleterre*.
9 x 57¾ in. (22.8 x 146.7 cm.)
Costume Council Fund
M.64.85.9

367
LACE (pair of lappets)
Flanders (Brussels), c. 1720
Linen bobbin lace.
3¼ x 23½ in. (8.2 x 59.7 cm.)
Costume Council Fund
M.64.85.12a,b
See fig. 37

368
LACE (lappet fragment)
Belgium (Brussels), early 18th century
Linen bobbin lace, *point d'Angleterre*.
13½ x 4 in. (34.2 x 10.1 cm.)
Gift of Countess de Limur
54.103

369
LACE (bonnet back)
Flanders (Mechlin), second quarter of 18th
century
Linen bobbin lace.
10 x 10½ in. (25.4 x 26.7 cm.)
Gift of Mrs. Etienne Noir
A.4943.40.37

370
LACE (border)
Flanders (Mechlin), first half of 18th century
Linen bobbin lace.
2½ x 20 in. (6.4 x 50.9 cm.)
Gift of Mrs. Tibor Scitovszky
60.18.3

371
LACE (borders)
Flanders (Brussels), late 18th century
Linen bobbin lace.
a: 3¼ x 14 in. (8 x 35.5 cm.)
b: 3¼ x 25 in. (8 x 63.5 cm.)
Gift of Miss Beatrice Wood
60.41.35a,b; ex-coll. Dr. Esther Rosencrantz

372
LACE (border)
France (Valenciennes), c. 1745–50
Linen bobbin lace.
1½ x 28 in. (3.8 x 71.2 cm.)
Gift of Mrs. Irene Salinger in Memory of
Her Father, Adolph Stern
54.104.130

373
LACE (tucker or modesty piece)
France (?), c. 1700–1710 (detail)
Linen needle lace, *point d'Alençon.*
2⅜ x 31 in. (6 x 78.7 cm.)
Purchased with Funds Provided by
Mr. and Mrs. John Jewett Garland
M.63.15.2
Exh: N
Pub: 30, no. 18 (ill.); 34, p. 97, pl. 44

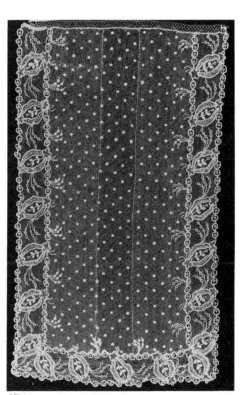

374
LACE (cravat)
France, c. 1795
Linen needle lace, *point d'Alençon.*
11 x 6½ in. (28 x 16.5 cm.)
Purchased with Funds Provided by
Mr. and Mrs. John Jewett Garland
M.63.15.3
Exh: N

375
PANEL (*The Pagan Paradise*)
Portugal, c. 1700 (detail)
Polychrome silk and metallic thread design of
exotic plants and animals brocaded on cream
silk satin ground; unusual use of border at top
and bottom.
35 x 14 in. (88.9 x 35.5 cm.)
Mr. and Mrs. Allan C. Balch Collection
M.55.12.73
Exh: A
Pub: 17, p. 45, pl. 71, no. 341 (ill.); 38, p. 151,
pl. 272

375a
PANEL (fragment)
Portugal, c. 1690–1700
Polychrome silk and chenille design of birds and
flowers brocaded on cream silk ground.
22 x 6 in. (55.9 x 15.2 cm.)
Gift of Museum Patrons Association
M.44.3.70

376

PANEL

France, 1737–39

Multicolored silk design of flowers, architecture, and a vista brocaded on dark olive figured silk ground.

36 x 20½ in. (91.4 x 52.1 cm.)

Museum Associates

M.55.12.55

Exh: D

Pub: 12, p. 11 (ill.)

See fig. 26

377

PANEL

Italy (Venice), c. 1730–70 (detail)

Polychrome and silver thread design of chandelier, bowls of fruit, peacock feathers, and draped cloth brocaded on pink silk patterned ground.

18 x 7½ in. (45.7 x 19 cm.)

Mr. and Mrs. Allan C. Balch Fund

M.55.12.54

Exh: B, D

Pub: 4, no. 87 (ill.); 12, p. 7 (ill.); 17, p. 47, pl. 73, no. 357 (ill.)

See plate 29

378

PANEL

France, c. 1755–65

Blue, cut and uncut, silk velvet design of floral and leaf motif on cloth-of-silver ground; padded silver bullion embroidery.

52 x 47 in. (132.1 x 119.4 cm.)

Gift of Miss Bella Mabury

M.55.20.2

Exh: G

Pub: 32, p. 44, no. 30 (ill.)

379

PANEL

France (Lyon), c. 1760

Polychrome silk and chenille design of floral bouquets and branches brocaded on cream twill satin ground; designed by Philippe de Lasalle (1723–1805).

37½ x 26½ in. (95.3 x 67.3 cm.)

Gift of Mrs. Frederick Kingston

M.59.11.2

Exh: D

Pub: 6, fig. 506 (ill.); 11, p. 13 (ill.); 26, p. 8 (ill.)

379a

PANEL (*The Peacock*)

France (Lyon), c. 1765

Multicolored silk and chenille brocaded on cream silk satin ground; fragment of furnishing fabric for wall panel; designed by Philippe de Lasalle (1723–1805).

28 x 24 in. (71.2 x 61 cm.)

Gift of Mrs. Frederick Kingston

M.59.11.1

Exh: N

Pub: 1, p. 211; 8, p. 231; 11, p. 10 (ill.); 22 (ill.); 30, no. 25 (ill.)

379b

PANEL (*The Pheasant*)

France (Lyon), c. 1765

Multicolored silk and chenille brocaded on pale green silk satin ground; designed by Philippe de Lasalle (1723–1805).

76 x 30½ in. (193 x 77.5 cm.)

Costume Council Fund

M.59.1

Exh: D, N

Pub: 1, no. 212, 214; 5, pl. 87, no. 1; 6, no. 508; 8, p. 231; 9, p. 212; 11, p. 12 (ill.); 23, p. 8; 30, no. 26 (ill.); 35, p. 393, no. 383

379c

MEDALLION (*The Chinese Astronomer*)

France, c. 1750

Polychrome silk brocaded on cream silk ground.

diam: 25 in. (63.5 cm.)

Purchased with Funds Provided by Mr. and Mrs. John Jewett Garland

M.59.6

Exh: N, P, F

Pub: 12, cover (ill.); Smith College Museum of Art, 1965, no. 32 (ill.)

380

PANEL

France, c. 1762–66 (detail)

Multicolored silk and metal thread design, of double meandering bands with floral bouquets and branches of blossoms, brocaded on pink silk ground.

41 x 20½ in. (104.1 x 52.1 cm.)

Costume Council Fund

M.59.27.2

381

PANEL

France, 1727–28

Polychrome silk and gold metallic thread design, of elaborate floral, leaf, and lace motif, brocaded on crimson silk satin ground.

63 x 35 in. (160.1 x 88.9 cm.)

Los Angeles County Fund

62.6.1

Exh: Q

See plate 32

382
PANEL
France, second quarter of 18th century
Polychrome silk floral and leaf double-meander design, with silver gilt stylized decoration, brocaded on salmon pink silk ground.
40 x 21 in. (99.1 x 53.4 cm.)
Costume Council Fund
M.63.16

383
PANEL
England, third quarter of 18th century
Multicolored silk and gold metallic thread design, of floral bouquets and leafy branches in double meander, brocaded on white silk ground with white alternating floral meander; Spitalfields.
90 x 21 in. (228.8 x 53.4 cm.)
Purchased with Funds Provided by
Mr. and Mrs. John Jewett Garland
M.63.1

384
PANEL
France, c. 1750–60
Purple and rose silk design of flowers, with green and silver metallic leaves and golden bows, brocaded on pale blue patterned silk ground.
52 x 21½ in. (130 x 54.6 cm.)
Gift of Mrs. Fred Kingston
M.60.36.2
Pub: 37, p. 185, pl. 92b (ill.)
See plate 29a

385
PANEL
France (Lyon), c. 1800
Cream silk pattern of cherubs, grotesques, and animals in Neoclassical design on blue silk ground.
74½ x 21½ in. (188 x 54.6 cm.)
Purchased with Funds Provided by
Mr. and Mrs. John Jewett Garland
M.61.15
Exh: Q

386
PANEL
France, c. 1762–66
Multicolored floral bouquets and garlands of bouclé and metallic threads brocaded on patterned, ribbed, apple green silk ground.
41 x 21 in. (104.1 x 53.3 cm.)
Costume Council Fund
M.67.87.1
Exh: N, Q
See plate 24

387
PANEL
Italy (Venice), c. 1712–31
Multicolored silk and metallic thread in abstract floral and geometric design brocaded on pink and white silk damask ground (Bizarre).
37 x 21 in. (94 x 53.3 cm.)
Costume Council Fund
M.67.87.2

388
PANEL
England, c. 1724–25
Polychrome silk and metallic thread in elaborately patterned lace and garland motif brocaded on yellow silk damask ground.
77 x 60 in. (197 x 150 cm.)
Gift of Elsie H. Brownstein
M.68.59.1

389
PANEL
France, mid-18th century
Polychrome silk and gold metallic thread in shaded floral and branch motif brocaded on green patterned silk ground.
56¾ x 41¼ in. (145 x 105.5 cm.)
Costume Council Fund
M.69.36.2
See plate 29b

390
PANEL (pair)
Holland, c. 1740
Orange, cream, pink, and lavender oversized flowers with trees, in twill brocade on dark green silk taffeta ground.
1: 45¼ x 17 in. (115 x 43 cm.)
2: 43¼ x 17 in. (110 x 43 cm.)
Costume Council Fund
M.70.63.1,2
Exh: N, Q
See plate 34

391

PANEL

China, c. 1690–1700

Multicolored pastel silk floral and abstract decorative motif brocaded on green silk satin ground; probably made in China for European market.

31 x 75 in. (78.7 x 190.5 cm.)

Costume Council Fund

M.63.52.3

392

PANEL

France (Lyon), c. 1730–70

Polychrome silk and gold metallic thread in symmetrical leaf and fruit pattern brocaded on scarlet silk ground; design attributed to Jean Revel (1684–1751); *ornement d'église* (?).

37 x 21 in. (94 x 53.3 cm.)

Costume Council Fund

M.64.84.1

Pub: 31, p. 95 (ill.)

See plate 28

393

PANEL

France, first quarter of 18th century

Yellow, blue, and cream silk in abstract diagonal pattern brocaded on deep pink silk ground (Bizarre).

38 x 22 in. (96.5 x 55.9 cm.)

Costume Council Fund

M.66.42.6

See plate 30

394

PANEL (furnishing fabric)

France (Lyon), c. 1780 (detail)

Green and cream silk medallion, and wreath pattern of doves, flowers, and string-of-pearls, brocaded on crimson silk ground; style of Philippe de Lasalle (1723–1805).

40 x 21 in. (101.6 x 53.3 cm.)

Costume Council Fund

M.66.41.1

395

PANEL

China, mid-18th century

Polychrome floral design of flowers and leaves painted on pale yellow silk ground; made for European market.

29½ x 45 in. (75 x 114.3 cm.)

Costume Council Fund

M.63.55.2

Exh: N, Q

See plate 23

396

PANEL

England (Norwich), mid-18th century

Blue, purple, yellow, and green wool brocaded on coral and white patterned wool damask ground.

38 x 18 in. (96.5 x 45.7 cm.)

Costume Council Fund

M.63.52.2

See fig. 23

397

PANEL

Italy (?), first quarter of 18th century

Rose, pale green, and lilac silk and metallic gold, in floral and geometric diagonal motifs, brocaded on blue silk patterned ground.

78 x 60 in. (198.1 x 152.4 cm.)

Gift of Mrs. Thomas O'Donnell

M.63.4.1

398

PANEL

England, c. 1740

Purple, green, and yellow silk in realistic shaded bergamot design brocaded on white silk patterned ground; attributed to Anna Maria Garthwaite (1690–1763); Spitalfields.

51 x 20 in. (129.5 x 51.1 cm.)

Costume Council Fund

M.81.69.2

See plate 25

399

PANEL

Holland (Haarlem), c. 1720 (detail)

White, red, pink, and green silk flowers and leaves brocaded on yellow diaper-patterned silk ground.

40½ x 17½ in. (102.9 x 44.4 cm.)

Costume Council Fund

M.81.69.1

See plate 31

400

PANEL

France (Lyon), 1730–32

Red, purple, and green silk and silver threads, in realistic hollyhock and pomegranate motif, brocaded on oyster silk ground; style of Jean Revel (1684–1751).

24¼ x 21¾ in. (61.6 x 55.2 cm.)

Costume Council Fund

M.81.69.7

See plate 26

401

PANEL

Italy or France, early 18th century

Polychrome silk and silver threads in design of flower beds, trees, rocks, strawberries, and thistles brocaded on cream silk and silver ground.

30½ x 21¾ in. (77.5 x 55.2 cm.)

Costume Council Fund

M.81.69.5

Exh: T

See plate 33

402

PANEL

France, second quarter of 18th century
Multicolored silk and metallic thread in stylized
leaf, bud, and fanlike motif brocaded on yellow
silk patterned ground.
55 x 22 in. (139.7 x 55.9 cm.)
Costume Council Fund
M.60.36.3

403

PANEL

Italy, 1762–66
Pink bouclé and polychrome silk, with gold
metallic strip in clumps of flowers and
meandering ribbons, brocaded on pink silk
patterned ground.
46¼ x 21 in. (117.5 x 53.3 cm.)
Costume Council Fund
M.81.69.4

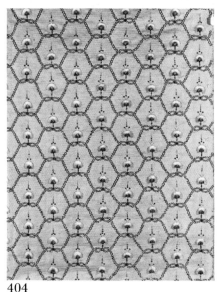

404

PANEL

Italy (?), c. 1776 (detail)
Red and white silk embroidery, with red
metallic sequins in hexagonal pattern
surrounding thistlelike flowers in satin stitch,
on yellow ribbed silk; pastel jewels in flowers and
hexagonal pattern.
24 x 18¼ in. (61 x 46.3 cm.)
Costume Council Fund
M.81.69.5
See plate 27

405

PANEL

France, early 18th century
Silver metallic thread in abstract pattern
brocaded on cream and blue ombré silk
patterned ground.
40 x 19 in. (101.6 x 48.3 cm.)
Costume Council Fund
M.81.69.3
See fig. 22

406

PANEL

France, c. 1760
Polychrome silk design of cinquefoil, flowers,
and stems in *droguet* style on mauve silk
diapered ground.
32 x 19⅛ in. (81.2 x 48.5 cm.)
Purchased with Funds Provided by
Mrs. Richard L. Narver
M.82.68

407

PANEL

France, c. 1735
Wine red and pink silk and metallic thread, in
leaf and bud motif *droguet* pattern, brocaded on
green silk ground.
38½ x 19½ in. (97.7 x 49.5 cm.)
Promised Gift of the Costume Council
TR.5208.1

408

PANEL

Italy (?), c. 1725–30
Polychrome silk floral, pomegranate, and stone
wall design brocaded on green silk satin ground.
42½ x 20¾ in. (108 x 52.7 cm.)
Promised Gift of the Costume Council
TR.5507.2

409

PANEL

England, c. 1730
Multicolored silk in shaded floral, berry, and
holly leaf motif brocaded on cream silk ground;
Spitalfields.
39½ x 20¼ in. (103.3 x 51.5 cm.)
Promised Gift of the Costume Council
TR.5236.46

410

PANELS (pair)

Holland, c. 1720
Blue, purple, pink, green, and yellow silk floral
sprays and leaves brocaded on cream silk satin
ground.
36¾ x 19½ in. (93.3 x 49.5 cm.)
Promised Gift of the Costume Council
TR.5236.40

411

PANEL (furnishing fabric)

France, c. 1800–1807
Gold and brown silk Neoclassical panel design
brocaded on deep red silk satin ground.
142 x 21 in. (327 x 53.3 cm.)
Costume Council Fund
M.64.84.2

412

BORDER

France, c. 1770 (detail)
Multicolored design of portrait medallions,
ribbons, swags, trees, and chained and kenneled
dogs in cut silk velvet on cream silk ground.
7⅝ x 39 in. (19.4 x 99.5 cm.)
Costume Council Fund
M.66.6
Exh: G
Pub: 5, pl. 83, no. 4 (ill.); 32, p. 41, no. 26a and
b (ill.)

413

FRAGMENT

France (Lyon), c. 1807
Natural dyes applied to velvet warp before
weaving; inscription "Vivat Borussorum
Regina"; profile portrait of Queen Louise of
Prussia by Gaspard Grégoire (1751–1846).
7½ x 5¼ in. (19 x 13.3 cm.)
Costume Council Fund
M.59.14
Exh: E, G
Pub: 23, pl. 49 (ill.); 32, no. 29 (ill.)

414
PANEL
England, c. 1720
Pink, yellow, green, and cream silk brocaded in
elaborately stylized pattern of figs and imaginary
fruit on blue silk satin ground.
43½ x 20¾ in. (110.4 x 52.7 cm.)
Purchased with Funds Provided by
Mr. and Mrs. Paul A. Erskin
M.82.5

415
PANEL
France, c. 1700–1720
Yellow, red, and green silk in stylized floral and
lace pattern brocaded on gold metallic ground.
77 x 58 in. (195.7 x 147.3 cm.)
Gift of Anna Bing Arnold
60.46.10
Pub: 28, p. 30, pl. 9

TAPESTRIES

416
PSYCHE CARRIED ON THE MOUNTAIN
France (Paris, Rue de la Chaise), before 1691
From the series *The Story of Psyche;* after a design
by Michel Coxcie (1499–1592).
Wool and silk; 19–20 warps per inch.
122 x 223 in. (309.9 x 586.7 cm.)
Gift of Mr. and Mrs. Richard Weininger
55.70; ex-coll. the Marchioness de Berenger
Pub: 21, vol. 8, no. 1, pp. 18–19 (ill.)
See fig. 45

417
THE TRIUMPH OF ALEXANDER
Flanders (Brussels), c. 1730–50
From the series *The Story of Alexander;* after a
design by Charles Lebrun (1619–1690).
Wool and silk; 19 warps per inch.
117 x 170 in. (297.2 x 431.8 cm.)
Gift of J. Paul Getty
51.36.5; ex-coll. Duc de Trevise
Pub: 7, pp. 170–71 (ill.); 15, p. 54 (ill.)
See fig. 42

418
LE REPAS (*The Repast*)
France (Beauvais), c. 1770–80
From the series *Jeux Russiens (Russian Games)*;
after a design by Jean-Baptiste Le Prince (1734–
81); under the directorship of André-
Charlemagne Charron; mark: lower right, fleur
de lis, "A. C. C. Beauvais."
Wool and silk; 23 warps per inch.
116½ x 276 in. (275.4 x 696 cm.)
William Randolph Hearst Collection
48.5.2

419
VENUS AND VULCAN
France (Beauvais), 1749
From the series *The Loves of the Gods*; after a
design by François Boucher (1703–1770); mark:
signed in reverse on chest at left center, "F.
Boucher, 1749."
Wool and silk; 19 warps per inch.
130 x 276 in. (244 x 696 cm.)
Gift of J. Paul Getty
49.2; ex-coll. Adolph Clément Bayard
Pub: 10, p. 40, no. 23 (ill.); 31, p. 92 (ill.)
See fig. 50, plate 48

420
THE ABDUCTION OF EUROPA
France (Beauvais), c. 1753–72
From the series *The Loves of the Gods*; after a
design by François Boucher (1703–1770); under
the directorship of André-Charlemagne
Charron; mark: lower right, "C. Beauvais."
Wool and silk; 22 warps per inch.
144 x 174 in. (365.7 x 442 cm.)
Gift of J. Paul Getty
51.36.8; ex-colls. de Valencay and Otto H. Kahn
Pub: 2, pp. 61, 68 (ill.); 18, pp. 14, 15 (ill.)

421
PSYCHE CONTEMPLATING THE SLEEPING CUPID
France (Gobelins), 1792
From the series *Scènes de Théâtre*; after a design
(1767) by Clément Belle; atelier Michel-Henri
Cozette; marks: lower right, "Cozette fils, 1792."
Wool and silk; 21–22 warps per inch.
148 x 120 in. (376 x 304.8 cm.)
Gift of J. Paul Getty
51.36.7; ex-colls. Jacques Seligmann and
Henry Walters
Pub: 24, pp. 22–23 (ill.)

422
HORSE TRAPPING
Spain, mid-18th century
Silver gilt metallic thread embroidery on deep
red silk velvet; attached to leather.
21¼ x 38¼ in. (53.4 x 97.2 cm.)
Gift of Mrs. Richard Jewett Schweppe
48.17a
See fig. 28

423
FIRE SCREEN
France, first half of 18th century
Multicolored wool chain stitch embroidery of
flowers surrounding small landscape on linen
canvas; ground filled with white bugle beads.
34 x 26 in. (86.3 x 66 cm.)
Costume Council Fund
M.82.25.2
See plate 44

424
QUILT (pieced)
United States (New England), second quarter of
18th century
Green, brown, red, and blue and brown plaid
natural dyed wool in star pattern; brown wool
lining; for four-poster bed.
104½ x 102½ in. (266 x 259.5 cm.)
Gift of Betty Horton
M.81.327.2

425
QUILT (pieced)
United States (New England), second quarter of
18th century
Pink glazed, olive green watered, and brown
wool in large alternating diamond pattern;
butternut-dyed wool lining; for four-poster bed.
103 x 88 in. (261.5 x 224 cm.)
Gift of Betty Horton
M.81.327.3

APPENDIX:
COSTUME AND TEXTILE CONSERVATION

PAT REEVES
TEXTILE CONSERVATOR
LOS ANGELES COUNTY MUSEUM OF ART

FERNANDE G. JONES
ASSISTANT TEXTILE CONSERVATOR
LOS ANGELES COUNTY MUSEUM OF ART

NANCY CONLIN WYATT
ANDREW W. MELLON
FOUNDATION FELLOW,
TEXTILE CONSERVATION,
LOS ANGELES COUNTY MUSEUM OF ART

CATHERINE C. McLEAN
ANDREW W. MELLON
FOUNDATION FELLOW,
TEXTILE CONSERVATION,
LOS ANGELES COUNTY MUSEUM OF ART

Many of the eighteenth-century costumes and textiles in this exhibition and catalogue have been treated in the textile department of the Conservation Center at the Los Angeles County Museum of Art. The Conservation Center's primary goal is the preservation and stabilization of works of art. In order to achieve this goal effectively, the following principles are used as guidelines:

1. All objects are treated with equal care and respect; the highest and most exacting standards are maintained.

2. Before beginning a treatment, the conservator should have an understanding of the work of art from an art historical and a scientific viewpoint.

3. Knowledge of the composition of materials and their aging properties is necessary. The conservator must be aware of the development of new materials and new techniques in order to continue to give the best possible treatment.

4. Conservation treatments are reversible.

When a textile comes to the laboratory for treatment, the first step is documentation of its condition. Black-and-white photographs are made, and then color slides. Generally, front-and-back overall photographs and detail photographs of any specific damage are taken as well. Careful examination of the textile is recorded in an examination report, which includes such information as a description of the textile, its dimensions, weave structure, and a fiber analysis. Its condition, including stains, accretions, losses, tears, fading, and insect damage, is documented and diagrammed.

Following examination, the conservator writes a proposal for treatment. This proposal is made in conjunction with preliminary tests and discussion with other conservators and the curator. Each textile is considered individually, for no two treatments are the same.

The treatment may take several hours, or it may involve several months of delicate work. Because so many eighteenth-century textiles and costumes are made of tightly woven silk, it is necessary for the conservator to use very fine needles and silk thread when working with them. After the treatment is completed, photographs are taken, a report is written, and recommendations for handling, display, and storage are made.

What follows are descriptions of a few of the many treatments carried out in preparation for this exhibition and catalogue. Before-and-after photographs accompany each record of condition and treatment.

FIG. 67
Yellow Silk Gown and Petticoat (cat. no. 44)
Before treatment, detail

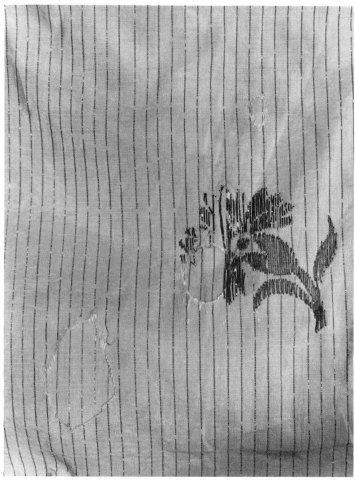

FIG. 68
Yellow Silk Gown and Petticoat (cat. no. 44)
After treatment, detail

FIG. 69
Yellow Silk Gown and Petticoat (cat. no. 44)
Petticoat overall after treatment

This pale yellow sack dress is a court dress once worn by a young girl. The gown and matching petticoat are pale yellow silk taffeta with metallic silver brocade and lace. (X-ray fluorescence spectroscopy indicates that the metal is nearly pure silver, with trace amounts of gold, copper, and lead.)

When received in the textile conservation laboratory, the costume was in very good condition, except for several holes buried in the folds of the petticoat. These holes had been previously mended with an adhesive and patches cut from the hem and inner seams of the costume. The adhesive was discolored and was so deteriorated that the patches readily peeled off.

Several spot tests were made before a suitable solvent that safely dissolved the adhesive was found. The solvent was applied locally to the stains on the petticoat and patches, and then blotted. Fortunately, the patches could be rearranged to cover all of the holes. The patches were sewn to the petticoat using a #12 needle and a very fine silk thread, dyed to match.

The costume was lightly steamed to remove all the creases. Then the sleeves and the flounce in the petticoat were padded with acid-free tissue paper to prevent wrinkling during storage.

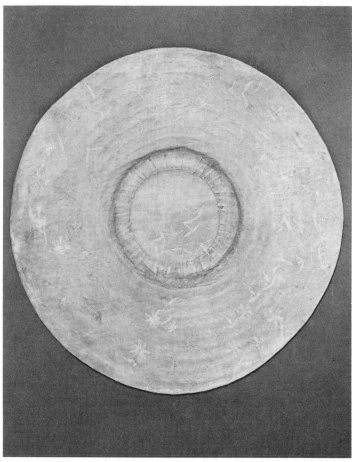

Above left
Fig. 70
Wood Chip Hat (cat. no. 191)
Before treatment

Above right
Fig. 71
Wood Chip Hat (cat. no. 191)
After treatment

This woman's hat of wood chip is covered with pink silk fabric, to which cut paper flowers and leaves are adhered. A fine net covers the hat. It measures sixteen and seven-eighths inches in diameter.

The conservation treatment was complicated because of the composite construction of the hat. Each layer had to be treated separately, yet none of the layers could be detached from the wood chip base.

Several areas on the brim of the hat where the wood had cracked were weak; one diagonal split measured three inches in length. The splits in the wood were repaired with thin strips of Japanese paper and a starch paste. A portion of the wood that was stained was cleaned with water and a cotton swab.

The pink silk fabric covering the wood chip was discolored overall, with dark stains along the rim for ten inches. As the fabric could not be removed, only the soiled area was cleaned. Before spot-cleaning, the stability of the dye was tested to insure that there would be no color loss. In this same area the pink silk was weak, and was reinforced on the underside with a lining of silk crepeline. The cut paper flowers and leaves adhered to the silk fabric were distorted, and, in several places, were no longer attached to the silk. They were reshaped and readhered to the silk with a starch paste.

The net covering the hat was in the poorest condition. It was not only discolored, but also had large areas of loss and was detached along the brim. The net was tested to determine if it could be cleaned; however, since the coating on the net proved to be soluble, no cleaning was attempted. The net was lined with a similar type of net and sewn around all areas of loss and at the edge. It was then attached to the pink silk fabric at the brim, turned to the underside of the hat, and sewn in place.

FIG. 72
Shoes (cat. no. 164)
Right: before treatment
Left: after treatment

These shoes are nine inches long and four inches wide. The heels are moderately high and curved, the toes pointed. Black satin crossover flaps, which cover the high tongue of the shoes, were originally fastened with a buckle. The shoes are bound on all edges with yellow silk grosgrain ribbon which matches the embroidery, and are lined in pink silk.

When received for treatment the shoes were in poor condition. The satin was split in many areas and some fabric was actually missing; the pink silk lining was almost totally disintegrated. The grosgrain ribbon binding, however, was intact.

After testing, the shoes were spot-cleaned with a dry-cleaning solvent. Patches of black China silk were inserted with forceps under the slits and missing areas. The original fabric was carefully realigned over the patches, and then steamed and pinned into place. All the patches were sewn with a #12 needle and a fine silk thread.

Even though the pink silk lining of the tongues and flaps was very deteriorated, it was retained, as original fabric or sewing is never removed. A suitable shade of pink China silk was washed and then sewn with matching silk thread over what remained of the original lining.

Finally, the shoes were stuffed with acid-free tissue paper and steamed into their original shape.

SELECTED GLOSSARY:
EIGHTEENTH-CENTURY COSTUME AND TEXTILE TERMS

Precise definitions of eighteenth-century terms are difficult to formulate chiefly because of the apparent lack of standardization of spelling and usage during the period. Efforts have thus been made to include here as many terms as possible. However, since this listing is intended to be a selective and not an all-inclusive one, only those terms which appeared regularly in the literature have been included. Variations in the spellings of authors' names, cities, and publication dates, as well as differences in book titles, have been standardized.

Quotations illustrating the definitions have been chosen to show the context of the usage, the period or periods during which the term was used, and to illuminate the social values placed upon dress in the eighteenth century. In order to include as much material as possible, it was necessary to cite authors' last names only. It should be noted that much of the documentation used here comes from the writings of women. They include: Jane Austen, Mary Delany, Madame D'Arblay (Frances Burney), the Countess D'Anois, and Lady Mary Wortley Montagu. Without their recorded observations, this compilation would have been far less complete.

Glossary terms have been divided into two sections: Costumes and Accessories, and Textiles and Lace. In the first section, the following abbreviations are used: (F) denotes items worn by females; (M) denotes those used by males; and (M/F) denotes those worn by both.

What is presented here is intended as a touchstone for further research. It is also hoped that readers will find as much delight in perusing these terms and their meanings as we did in discovering them.

COSTUMES AND ACCESSORIES		
ADONIS WIG	(M) Wig made of fine hair; very fashionable and very expensive. "A fine flowing adonis or white periwig." Graves, *Spiritual Quixote*, 1772.
BAG-WIG	(M) Wig in which the backhair was enclosed in an ornamental bag. "Pig-tailed lawyers and bag-wigged attorneys." Sheridan, *St. Patrick's Day*, 1775.
BALLOON HAT, LUNARDI	(F) Hat with large ballooned crown and wide brim; made of gauze or sarcenet over a wire or wood chip foundation. Popular from 1783–85; fashion resulted from the first balloon ascent on June 5, 1783.

BANDANA (M) Tie-dyed fabric; technique traditionally applied to silk but later to cotton. Fabric had a dark ground of red or blue and little white or yellow spots. Imported from India and used for neckcloths and snuff handkerchiefs.

BANDORE PEAK (F) Widow's headdress. Black bonnet curving to a point or peak over the forehead. "The buxom Widow, with Bandore and Peak." D'Urfrey, *Wit and Mirth*, 1719.

BANYAN (M) Loose-skirted coat, knee-length or longer, with a short back vent. In the 1780s often worn outdoors when made very fashionably and of costly material. "I have lost nothing by it but a banyan shirt, a corner of my quilt, and my bible singed." *Harleian Miscellany*, 1725.

BASKET BUTTONS (M/F) Buttons covered with interlacing pattern or a metal imitation of a basketweave.

BEARING CLOTH (M/F) Mantle or cloth used to cover an infant when carried to baptism.

BEDGOWN (M/F) Loose-sleeved dressing gown; negligee only worn in the bedroom for comfort. "Why must the wrapping bed-gown hide/Your snowy bosom's swelling pride?" Moore and Brooke, *Fables for the Female Sex*, 1744.

BEEHIVE HAT (F) Hat with tall rounded crown, beehive-shaped, with a narrow brim. Popular during the 1770s and 1780s.

BERGÈRE HAT (F) Large straw hat with flexible brim and low crown. First found in the peasant classes, but adopted by the bourgeoisie with their false "return to nature" influenced by the writings of Rousseau. Worn from 1730–1800.

BICORNE (M) Hat with back and front flap, fringed edge, and silk rosette or emblem on one side. Worn from 1775 on.

BINDER (M/F) Band of wool flannel worn tightly wrapped around babies, to give some support to the back. "Plain linen caps, with binders herringboned with coloured cruel [crewel]." Trimmer, *Two Farmers, An Exemplary Tale*, 1787.

BIRTHDAY SUIT (M/F) Court suit or dress worn for the celebration of the king's birthday. "So many birth-day suits were countermanded the next day." Swift, *Works*, 1727.

BOB-WIG (M) Wig with the bottom locks turned up into "bobs" or short curls; always worn for undress.

BODICE (M/F) Inner garment for the upper part of the body, quilted or strengthened with whalebone. A tight-fitting outer vest or waistcoat, either made in one piece with the skirt or separate. *See also* Stays. "[Pope] was invested in boddice made of stiff canvass, being scarce able to hold himself erect till they were laced." Johnson, *Lives of English Poets*, 1779.

BODKIN (F) Small pointed instrument made of bone, ivory, or steel; used for piercing holes in cloth. Also a pin-shaped ornament used by women to fasten the hair. "Their hair is set...set out with three or four rows of bodkins (wonderfully large, that stick out two or three inches from their hair)." Montagu, *Letters*, 1716.

BOOT CUFF — (M) Very deep, turned-back cuff on a man's coat; it frequently reached the bend of the elbow. Fashionable from 1727 to the 1740s. The term "boot sleeve" was applied to someone who wore a boot cuff. "These boot-sleeves were certainly intended to be the receivers of stolen goods." Fielding, *Miser*, 1733.

BOOTIKIN — (M/F) Soft boot made of wool and oiled silk; worn as a cure for the gout. "Booterkins made with oiled Silk, as they confine the perspirable matter, keep the part moist and suppled." Darwin, *Zoonomia, Or the Laws of Organic Life*, 1794.

BOSOM BOTTLES — (F) Small vessels of tin or glass worn by ladies to keep their bouquets fresh. Corsets were fitted with pouches to hold bosom bottles. Used during the second half of the eighteenth century. "Bosom Bottles, pear-shaped, flat 4 inches long, of ribbed glass for bouquets." *Boston Evening Post*, 1770.

BOSOM FRIENDS — (F) Chest protectors of wool, flannel, or fur, which also served as bust-improvers. In use in the late eighteenth and early nineteenth centuries. "The fashionable belles have provided themselves with *bosom friends* for the winter. Their province is to protect that delicate region from assault of every kind; and they may be had at all the furriers shops in town. A modern lady, with her feet in a *fur-basket*, and her *bosom-friend*, is as impregnable as the Rock of Gibraltar." *Norfolk Chronicle*, 1789.

BREAST-KNOT — (F) Ribbon bow or bunch of ribbons worn at the breast of a woman's gown. In use in the eighteenth and early nineteenth centuries.

BREECHES — (M) Pair of breeches; distinguished from trousers by coming only just below the knee.

BREECHES BALL — (M) Ball of composition for cleaning leather breeches. "An expenditure in shoe-strings, hair powder and breeches-ball." Austen, *Northanger Abbey*, 1797.

BRUTUS HEAD WIG — (M) Cropped head of hair, or brown unpowdered wig, disheveled in appearance. Inspired by the French Revolution. "'I suppose, Sir,' said a London hair-dresser to a gentleman from the country, 'You would like to be dressed in the Brutus style-all over frizzley, Sir, like the Negers—they be Brutus you know.'" Southey, *Letters from England*, 1807.

BUCKLED WIG — (M) Wig having tightly rolled curls (buckles) arranged horizontally above or about the ears. "What's a woman when her virtue's gone! A coat without its lace; a wig out of buckle." Fielding, *Tom Thumb*, 1730.

BUFFON — (F) Similar to a fichu; worn around the neck. "Buffonts, trimmed and plain, are in universal use still." *European Magazine*, 1783.

BULLY-COCKED — (M) Large broad-brimmed hat cocked in the style favored by bullies.

BUSK	(M/F) Strip of wood, whalebone, steel, or other rigid material inserted into the front of a corset, and used to stiffen and support it. "The want of which latter instrument of death [a dagger] I once saw supplied with a lady's busk; who had just presence of mind sufficient to draw it from her stays." Clarke, *Autobiography*, 1775. "Whale bone and busks, which martyr European girls, they know not." *Annual Register*, 1786.
CABRIOLE	(F) Ornament for a headdress in the shape of a carriage. Short-lived fad from 1755–57. "Those heads which are notable to bear a coach-and-six …make use of a post-chaise." *Connoisseur*, 1756.
CADOGAN	(M/F) Wig with a broad flat queue turned up on itself and tied around the middle; sometimes plaited. Said to be from the name of the 1st Earl of Cadogan (1675–1726). Worn from 1760 to the end of the century. "The duchess of Bourbon had introduced at the court of Montebeliard… [the fashion] of cadogans, hitherto worn only by gentlemen." O'Berkirch, *Memoirs*, c. 1780.
CALASH	(F) Collapsible pleated hood of silk, made with whalebone or cane hoops, which projected in front of the face. "Give no [theater] ticket to any that wear calashes." Wesley, *Works*, 1791.
CAPE	(M/F) Turned-down collar of a cloak; it hung loosely over the shoulders. "The cape so contrived as to make him appear very round about the shoulders." *St. James Chronicle*, 1763.
CAPUCHIN	(F) Cloak and hood; made in imitation of the dress of Capuchin friars. "Wrapping up their Heads in their Hooded-Gowns, they seemed to me to be Thieves disguised in Capuchines." D'Anois, *Ingenious and Diverting Letters of the Lady*, 1692. "Within my memory the ladies covered their lovely necks with a Cloak; this was exchanged for the manteel, this again was succeeded by the pelorine, the pelorine by the neckatee, the neckatee by the capuchine, which hath now stood its ground a long time." Fielding, *Covent Garden Journal*, 1752.
CARACO	(F) Thigh-length, waisted jacket worn as the bodice of a gown. Worn with a skirt, it was known as the "Caraco dress."
CARDINAL	(F) Originally made of scarlet wool with a hood. "You are capering about in your fine cardinals." Delany, *Autobiography and Correspondence*, 1745.
CAULIFLOWER WIG	(M) Closely curled bob-wig, commonly worn by coachmen; also, to dress a wig in a manner resembling a cauliflower. Used during the second half of eighteenth century. "Some Barber's leathern powder-bag/Wherewith he feathers, frosts, or cauliflowers/Spruce Beau, or Lady fair, or Doctor grave." Southey, *English Eclogues*, 1799.
CAXON	(M/F) Tie-wig, usually white or a pale color, but occasionally black. Worn with undress, chiefly by the professional classes. "Though that trim artist, barber Jackson,/Spent a whole hour about your caxon." Cawthorn, *Poems*, 1756.
CERUSE	(M/F) Cosmetic used to whiten the face; made of white lead and popular from the time of Elizabeth I (1558–1603). "At Paris the face of every lady

you meet is besmeared with unguent, ceruss, and plaister." *Connoisseur*, 1754.

CHEMISE
(M/F) Shirtlike undergarment, usually of linen. In the 1780s it began to be used as an overgarment. "A chemise of very clean gauze put over a dress of rose taffety." *Bath Journal*, 1789.

CHEMISE DRESS
(F) Dress with long fitted sleeves and a low neck gathered on a draw-string; usually worn with a sash. The English chemise gown, known as the "Perdita Chemise," was closed down the front from bosom to hem with buttons or a series of ribbon bows.

CHICKEN-SKIN
(F) Chicken-skin gloves were worn in bed to keep the hands white; used as late as the reign of George III (1760–1820).

CHIP HAT
(F) Hat woven of thin wooden strips; constructed in various styles. "A fashionable hat…a black one, if they are worn; otherwise chip." Cowper, *Letters*, 1784.

CLOCK
(M/F) Ornamental pattern in silk thread worked on the side of a stocking. "To knit all the Actions of the Pretender…in the Clock of a Stocking." Steele, *Tatler*, 1709.

COCK
(M) Way of tipping a hat, or the turn-up part of the brim. "The Variety of Cocks into which he moulded his Hat." Ludgell, *Spectator*, 1712.

COLMAR
(F) Fan fashionable in Queen Anne's time (1702–14). "The bride… with an air divine her Colmar ply'd." Pope, *Art of Sinking*, 1727. "Thinks we that modern words eternal are?/Toupet, and Tompion, Cosins, and Colmar/Hereafter will be called by some plain man/A Wig, a Watch, a Pair of Stays, a Fan." Bromston, *Art of Politicks*, 1729.

CORK RUMP
(F) Large, crescent-shaped pad stuffed with cork; used to extend the buttocks in the late eighteenth century. *See also* Rump.

CORSET
(M/F) Closely fitting inner bodice stiffened with whalebone, metal, or wood, and fastened by lacing; worn chiefly by women to give shape and support to the figure. "Corsettes about six inches long, and a slight buffon tucker of two inches high, are now the only defensive *paraphernalia* of our fashionable Belles." *Times*, 1795.

CRAPE
(M/F) To make the hair wavy and curly; to crimp, to frizzle. "The hour… for curling and craping the hair." D'Arblay, *Diary and Letters*, 1786. *See also* Crape in Textiles and Lace.

CUPOLA COAT, BELL HOOP
(F) Dome-hooped petticoat distended with whalebone or cane hoops to the fashionable size. "The cupola-coat allows all the freedom of motion… the compass of the coat serves to keep the men at a decent distance and appropriate to every lady a spacious verge sacred to herself." *Whitehall Evening Post*, 1747.

DEMI-HABILEMENT, HALF-ROBE, HALF-GOWN
(F) Low-necked, thigh-length tunic with short sleeves; worn over a round gown and pulled in at the waist by a narrow ribbon belt. Fashionable from 1794 to c. 1800.

DILDO	(M) Sausage-shaped curl of a wig. Worn throughout the late seventeenth and eighteenth centuries.
DOMINO	(M/F) Loose cloak, of Venetian origin, chiefly worn at masquerades by people not impersonating a character. Worn with a small mask covering the upper part of the face. "He [the King, Louis XV] order'd to have 20 dominos laid ready for him as…he was determined to go & change his Dress very often in order to Teize Mme. du Barri." Northumberland, *Diaries of a Duchess*, 1770.
DORMEUSE, DORMOUSE	(F) White undress day cap with puffed-up crown and deep falling flaps on each side (popularly known as "cheek wrappers").
DOWNY CALVES	(M) False calves. Pads woven into the calves of stockings to exaggerate and produce manly looking calves. Patented in 1788.
DRAGON'S BLOOD CANE	(M) Fashionable cane made from the frond stems of the dragon palm, a rattan palm from Malay. Used in the early part of the eighteenth century.
DUVILLIER WIG	(M) Very long and very tall dress wig named after famous French perruquier; also known as a falbala or furbelow wig. Worn in the early eighteenth century. "A long Duvillier full of powder"…"Huge Falbala periwigs." Steele, *Tatler*, 1709.
ECHELLE	(F) Arrangement of ribbons in the form of a ladder; a lacing of ribbons on the front of a stomacher. First appeared in the 1690s. Popularized by women in the French court of Louis XV.
ENGAGEANTES	(F) French term meaning sleeve ruffles; worn in graduating sizes in sets of one, two, or three. Used to accentuate the graceful movement of the arm. "Engageantes are double ruffles that fall over the wrists." *Ladies Dictionary: Being a General Entertainment for the Fair-Sex*, 1694.
ESCLAVAGE	(F) Necklace composed of several rows of gold chains, beads, or jewels falling in festoons over the bosom. Named for its resemblance to slave fetters. "How d'ye like the Style of this Esclavage?" Colman and Garrick, *Clandestine Marriage*, 1766.
ETUI, ETWEE	(F) Small ornamental case for articles, such as bodkins and toothpicks; before the eighteenth century, also a case for surgical instruments. "Gold Etuys for Quills, Scissars, Needles, Thimbles." Steele, *Tatler*, 1710. "The gold etwee, With all its Bright inhabitants…" Shenstone, *Works in Prose and Verse*, c. 1765.
EYELETS, OILETS	(M/F) Lacing holes for a lace, cord, or tape; bound with silk or heavy thread. Facilitates the joining of garments. "Peeping the curtains eyelet through." Colman, *Posthumous Letters*, 1764.
FALSE CALVES	*See* Downy calves.
FAN HOOP	(F) Hooped petticoat, pyramidal in shape, compressed in front and back to form a fan-shaped structure over which the skirt fell with a curve upon each side. Mentioned as early as 1713, but fashionable in the 1740s and 1750s. "Mrs. Mayoress…came sidling after him in an enormous fan-hoop." Cowper, *Connoisseur*, 1756.

FANTAIL HAT	(M/F) Tricorne hat, with a high, fan-shaped back brim, vertically cocked to resemble an open fan. Fashionable for riding and sometimes worn by women on horseback. Popular from 1775 to the end of the century.
FAUSSE MONTRE	(M) False watch worn when it was fashionable for a man to wear two watches. Often one of them was a sham, such as a snuffbox disguised as a watch.
FEARNOTHING	(M) Jacket resembling a sleeved waistcoat; made of thick woolen cloth called fearnothing, fearnought, or dreadnought. Worn by seafaring men, sportsmen, laborers, and apprentices.
FEATHER-TOP WIG	(M) Wig with a toupee made of feathers, usually drake's or mallard's. Worn by parsons and also sportsmen during the second half of eighteenth century. "Gentlemen's perukes for sporting made of drakes' tails." *Ipswich Journal*, 1761.
FICHU	(F) Shaped piece of lightweight fabric, often triangular, worn as a covering for the neck, throat, and shoulders.
FLANNELS	(F) Large flannel gown or wrap worn by bathers at the seaside and at spas such as Bath. "Oh! 'Twas pretty to see them all put on their flannels/And then take to the waters like so many spaniels." Anstey, *New Bath Guide*, 1766.
FLY FRINGE	(F) Fringe of cord with attached knots and bunches of floss silk; used to decorate gowns and stomachers.
FOIL BUTTON	(M/F) Silk pasted on paper and applied as a foil to the underside of a glass button. Patented in 1774.
FRIZZ-WIG	(M) Wig closely crimped all over. "This machine [a tye-periwig] has been in buckle ever since, and now all the servants in the family were employed to frizz it out for the ceremony." Smollett, *Expedition of Humphrey Clinker*, 1771. "It's not enough you read Voltaire,/While sneering valets frizz your hair?" Whitehead, *Goat's Beard*, 1777.
FROCK, FROCK COAT	(M) Derived from the French word *frac*, meaning man's coat. Double-breasted coat with large revers. The frock coat formed the foundation for our present-day evening and morning dress coats.
FROUZE	(F) Wig of crimped false hair worn by women to cover up baldness. In use late seventeenth and early eighteenth centuries. "This filthy Fruz I ne'er shall brook." *British Apollo*, 1710.
FULL-BOTTOMED WIG	(M) Massive wig, with center part and close curls framing the face, extending onto the shoulders. After c. 1730 worn on formal occasions and by the learned professions only. "My Banker ever bows lowest to me when I wear my full-bottom'd Wig." Budgell, *Spectator*, 1711.
FURBELOW	(F) Piece of self-fabric pleated and puckered, on a gown or petticoat, in the form of a flounce or swag. "Lady Revel…Discovers a purse in the Furbeloes of her Apron." Centlivre, *Basset-table*, 1706. "Here, Jane, settle the furbellows of my scarf." Johnston, *Chrysal: Or the Adventures of a Guinea*, 1760.

GALLOON   (M/F) Narrow, close-woven, ribbon or braid of gold, silver, or silk thread; used for trimming. "His livery is yellow, laced with a galloon of blue silk and silver." Hanway, *Historical Account of the British Trade*, 1753.

GOLOSH   (M/F) Wooden shoe or sandal fastened to the foot with thongs of leather; also a shoe with a wooden sole and an upper of leather or other soft material. "Improvements in women's clogs by a goloshoe or clog of an entire new make." Patent, 1779.

HAIR-LACE   (F) String or tie for binding the hair. "They say, a marry'd Woman has nothing of her own, but her Wedding-Ring and her Hair-lace." Swift, *Collection of Genteel and Ingenious Conversation*, 1738.

HALF-GOWN   *See* Demi-habilement.

HASP   (M/F) Clasp or catch for fastening coats; used instead of buttons. "A set of gentlemen who take the liberty to appear in all public places without any buttons on their coats, which they supply with little silver hasps." *Spectator*, 1711.

HEDGEHOG   (M/F) Woolly-style wig from France; worn high off the forehead. Particularly popular with the Macaronis in the 1780s.

HOUSEWIFE   (F) Pocket-case for needles, pins, thread, and scissors. "Women… spending their time in knotting, or making an housewife." Skelton, *Deism Revealed*, 1749. "To bring whatever he had to say into so small a compass that…it might be rolled up in my mother's housewife." Sterne, *Tristram Shandy*, 1762.

HUSSEY   (F) Phonetic reduction of housewife. *See also* Housewife. "So I…dropt purposely my Hussey." Richardson, *Pamela*, 1741.

INCHERING   Measuring a person in inches for making a garment. "Pd. for Inchoring the girls 2d. [pence]." *Walthamstow Records*, 1729.

INDISPENSIBLE   (F) Small satchel or bag carried by women, replacing the pocket. "A number of disputes having arisen in the Beau Monde, respecting the exact situation of ladies Indispensibles (or New Invented Pocket)." Gillray, *Print*, 1800.

INEXPRESSIBLES   (M) Euphemism for breeches or trousers. Also called ineffables, inexplicables, and unmentionables. "I've heard, that breeches, petticoats, and smock,/Give to thy modest mind a grievous shock,/And that thy brain (so lucky its device)/Christ'neth them inexpressibles, so nice." Wolcott, *Rowland for Oliver*, 1790. "A pair of old *inexpressibles*…contained seven thousand Guineas!…deposited in so vulgar a Garment." *Jerningham Letters*, 1800.

INKLE   (M/F) Wool or linen tape, sometimes white but usually colored, used as a cheap binding by the lower classes or as a trimming; sewn on in patterns. "His shoes were…ty'd with strings of a purple colour…but whether ribbon, or inkle, I know not." Harrod, *Antiquities of Stanford and St. Martin's,* 1781.

JAMBEE CANE   (M) Knotty, bamboo walking stick from Jambi in Sumatra. Popular during the early part of the eighteenth century. "Yours [a cane] is a true Jambee, and Squire Empty's only a plain Dragon [blood]. This Vertuoso has a Parcel of Jambees now growing in the East Indies." Steele, *Tatler*, 1709.

JASEY	(M) Cheap wig made of Jersey wool yarn; also a contemptuous name for a wig or bushy head of hair. "Dash my jasey, if I wasn't threatened with the pillory." Robinson, *Walsingham*, 1797.
JEMMY CANE	(M) Little switch carried under the arm; most fashionable in the 1750s and 1760s.
JOSEPH	(F) Lady's riding habit; when worn open it was popularly called a "flying Josie." It was buttoned all the way down the front and had a small collar. "Olivia would be drawn as an Amazon...dressed in a green joseph, richly laced with gold, and whip in her hand." Goldsmith, *Vicar of Wakefield*, 1766.
JUMP	(F) Type of underbodice worn by women, usually fitted to the bust; often used instead of stays. From 1740 on commonly used in plural form (a pair of jumps). "Now a shape in neat stays, now a slattern in jumps." *Satirical Songs and Poems on Costume*, 1762. "These springs are for ladies' jumps who do not choose to wear hard incommodious stays." Patent, 1784.
LAPPETS	*See* Pinner.
LEADING-STRING	(M/F) Strings which guided and supported children who were learning to walk. Sometimes in the form of reinforced cloth attached to the shoulders and hanging to the ankles. "In little time the Hell-bred Brat... Without his Leading-strings could walk." Otway, *Poet's Complaint of His Muse*, 1680.
LEVITE	(F) Loose dress which supposedly resembled the dress of the Levites. "A habit-maker...is gone stark in love with Lady Ossory, on fitting her with the new dress. I think they call it a Levite, and says he never saw so glorious a figure...but where the deuce is the grace in a man's nightgown bound round the belt?" Walpole, *Letters to Countess Ossory*, 1779.
MACARONI	(M/F) An exquisite of a class which arose in England about 1760. It consisted of young men who had traveled and affected the tastes and fashions prevalent in Continental society. A fop or dandy. "The Macaroni Club (which is composed of all the travelled young men who wear long curls and spying-glasses)." Walpole, *Letters, Earl Hartford*, 1764. "There is indeed a kind of animal, neither male nor female, a thing of the neuter gender, lately started up amongst us. It is called a Macaroni. It talks without meaning, it smiles without pleasantry, it eats without appetite, it rides without exercise, it wenches without passion." *Oxford Magazine*, 1770.
MAJOR WIG	(M) Military-style wig worn by civilians. It had a toupee and two corkscrew curls tied together at the nape of the neck, forming a double queue. Worn during second half of the eighteenth century. "His tye-wig degenerated into a major." Smollett, *Adventures of Ferdinand Count Fathom*, 1753.

MANTEEL	(F) Cape or mantle. "Ladies…covered their lovely necks with a cloak; this, being routed by the enemy (the vulgar), was exchanged for the manteel." Fielding, *The Covent Garden Journal*, 1752.
MANTLE	(M/F) Loose, sleeveless cloak of varying length. "Fools, indeed, drop the man in their account, And vote the mantle into majesty." Young, *Complaint; Or Night-thoughts on Life, Death and Immortality*, 1742.
MANTUA	(F) Loose gown, with an unboned bodice, joined to an overskirt with a long train. It was open in front, exposing a decorative underskirt called a petticoat. Worn on all social and formal occasions from the mid-seventeenth to mid-eighteenth century. "Brunetta…came to a public Ball in a plain black Silk Mantua." Steele, *Spectator*, 1711. "A Mantua of a better kind of calico." Defoe, *History and Remarkable Life of Colonel Jacque*, 1722.
MARCASITE	(M/F) Crystallized form of iron pyrite used to ornament buttons or accessories. "Half the ladies of our acquaintance…carry their jewels to town, and bring nothing but paste and marcasites back." Goldsmith, *She Stoops to Conquer*, 1773.
MECKLENBURG CAP	(F) Turban roll worn as an indoor cap, dating from the marriage of Charlotte of Mecklenburg to George III (1761).
MITTENS, MITTS	(F) Glove of lace or knitted work covering the forearm, wrist, and part of the hand, but not extending over the fingers. Dresses made of cotton or linen often had mitts of the same material buttoned to the shoulder of the gown; they were in fashion after the French Revolution. "On weekdays were black worsted mittens worn;/Black silk on Sundays did her arms adorn." Wolcott, *Works*, 1795.
MODESTY, MODESTY PIECE	(F) Veil for the concealment of the bosom. "Sometimes the Stomacher rises almost to the chin, and a modesty-bit serves the purpose of a ruff; at other times but half way, and the modesty is but a transparent shade to the beauties beneath." *Gentleman's Magazine*, 1731.
MUCKENDER	(M/F) Handkerchief, table napkin, or bib. "For thy dull fancy a muckinder is fit/To wipe the slabberings of thy snotty wit." Dorset, *To Howard on his Plays*, 1706.
MUFFETEES	(M/F) Small wrist muffs made in pairs, worn for warmth or to protect the wrist ruffles when playing cards. Also refers to mittens. "Pray buy my mother a pair of black silk French muftees for the hand…they must be with thumbs to them." Purefoy, *Letters*, 1748.
NECKCLOTH	(M) Cloth worn around the neck; a cravat, neckerchief. "His man…puffs out his neck-cloth with as smart an air as Mr. Anybody." Amherst, *Terrae Filius: or the Secret History of the University of Oxford*, 1721. "His countenance…turned…as pale as his neckcloth." Kippis, *Biographia Britannica*, 1784.
NECK-HANDKERCHIEF	(M/F) Kerchief worn about the neck. "So what will I do, but strip off my upper Petticoat, and throw it into the Pond, with my Neck-handkerchief." Richardson, *Pamela*, 1740.

NECKLACE	(F) Lace or ribbon for the neck. "Then I bought of a Pedlar…two Yards of black Ribband for my Shift Sleeves, and to serve as a Necklace." Richardson, *Pamela*, 1740.
NIGHTGOWN	(M/F) Loose gown worn at night in place of ordinary clothes; also a dressing gown. Originally worn by women as an evening dress. "Long hoods are worn close under the chin, tied behind…Nightgowns worn without hoops." Delany, *Autobiography and Correspondence*, 1756. "The Queen was in a hat and an Italian night-gown of purple lutestring." Delany, *Autobiography and Correspondence*, 1778.
NIGHT-RAIL	(F) Dress worn loose at the waist and closed only at the neck. Nightgowns, which the ladies adopted as a morning costume and for undress. "Does it not look as if she would have been an useful creature in the days of nightrail and notableness?" Richardson, *History of Sir Charles Grandison*, 1753.
NIVERNOIS HAT	(M) Small version of the tricorne hat; it had a broad spreading brim rolled over a flat crown. Named for the French writer Nivernois. Macaronis wore the hat perched idiotically in front of the head on top of an enormous wig. Popular in the 1760s.
NONE-SO-PRETTYS	(M/F) Narrow linen tape with designs woven in colors. "1 [piece] cotton romals, 4 ditto, none-so-pretties, 8lb. coloured thread." *Annual Register*, 1759.
OILETS	*See* Eyelets.
ORANGE-BUTTER	(M/F) Pomade used in the Dutch Colonies. "The Dutch way to make orange-butter—Take new cream two gallons, beat it up to a thickness, then add half a pint of orange-flower water, and as much red wine, and so being become the thickness of butter, it retains both the colour and scent of an orange." *Closet of Rarities*, 1706.
PANNIER	(F) Frame of whalebone, wire, or other material, used to distend the skirt of a woman's dress at the hips. From the French word for "breadbasket."
PAPILLOTTE	(M/F) Curling papers for the hair. "The wild Devonia still on fashion doats,/And turns thy satire into papillotes." *Refutation*, 1778.
PATCH	(M/F) Small piece of black silk or court plaster, often of fanciful shape; worn on the face or bosom either to hide a fault, or, more usually, to show off the complexion by contrast. First introduced towards the end of the reign of Charles I (1625–49). "Hours…pass'd in deep debate,/How curls should fall, or where a patch to place." Montagu, *Town Eclogues*, 1715. "Their hair plastered with pomatum, their faces patched to taste." Goldsmith, *Vicar of Wakefield*, 1766.
PATTEN	(F) Overshoe with a wooden sole mounted on an iron, oval ring; the wearer was raised off the ground and protected from mud and filth. "Good housewives…Safe thro' the Wet on clinking Pattens tred." Gay, *Trivia; Or the Art of Walking the Streets of London*, 1714.
PELERINE	(F) Small mantle or cape with the edges meeting at a point in front;

usually of lace or silk, or the same material as the dress. "Her neck suffers for it, and confesses, in scarlet blushes…this misfortune, however, she conceals under a handkerchief or pelerine, and high tucker." Haywood, *Female Spectator*, 1744.

PELISSE   (F) Long, lined mantle or cloak reaching to the ankles and having armholes or sleeves. "I don't know what you mean by a pompadour, unless it is what we call in this part of the world a pelisse; which in plain English is a long cloak made of satin or velvet, black or any colour; lined or trimmed with silk, satin, or fur, according to the fancy." Delany, *Autobiography and Correspondence*, 1755.

PERUKE   (M/F) French term for wig of false or artificial hair. "A fair peruke may adorn a weak head." Wesley, *Works*, 1757.

PETTICOAT   (F) Trimmed or ornamented skirt worn over or beneath the gown. Originally two words, "petty coat," meaning small coat. In daily usage often referred to as "coat." "There is not one of us but has reduced our outward Petticoat to its ancient Sizable Circumference, tho' indeed we retain still a Quilted one underneath." Steele, *Spectator*, 1711. "I hope you saw her petticoat, six inches deep in mud…and the gown which had been let down to hide it not doing its office." Austen, *Pride and Prejudice*, 1796.

PHYSICAL WIG   (M) Long wig swept back from the forehead, with or without a center part, standing out in a "bush" around the back of the head. Often hanging below the nape of the neck. Replaced the full-bottomed wig during the second half of the eighteenth century.

PIGTAIL   (M) Plait or queue of hair tied at the back of the head. "The French carpenter cannot saw his boards, without a long pig-tail and ruffled shirt." Tucker, *Light of Nature Pursued*, 1768.

PINCHBECK BUTTON   (M/F) Pinchbeck, an alloy of five parts copper and one of zinc, resembling gold, invented by Christopher Pinchbeck about 1700. Used to simulate more expensive gilt buttons from 1770 on. "He said…that the nobility and gentry run so much into Pinchbeck, that he had not dispos'd of two gold watches this month." Fielding, *Intriguing Chambermaid*, 1734.

PINNER   (F) Head covering with two long flaps, one on each side, either pinned in place with ends (lappets) hanging down or fastened at the breast. Nineteenth-century usage meant a pinafore or apron with a bib. "The pinners are double ruffled with twelve plaits of a side." Farquhar, *Sir Harry Wildair*, 1701. "The women…wear four pinners with great ribbons between, and eight lappets hanging down behind." Montagu, *Buccleuch Manuscripts*, c. 1720.

PLUMPERS   (F) Cork contrivances for expanding the cheeks; also referring to a means for expanding the skirts, like a side hoop or pannier. "Mrs. Button who wears cork plumpers in each cheek and never hazards more than six words for fear of showing them." Cowley, *Belle's Stratagem*, 1780. "With one blow of her fist she not only made several of her Teeth leap out of her Mouth, but also two little Cork plumpers." D'Anois, *Ingenious and Diverting Letters of the Lady*, 1692. "Old Mrs. Ashley has added a yard of whalebone to her plumpers merely on his account." Montagu, *Letters*, 1749.

POCKET   (F) Small bag or pouch worn on or under the clothing for carrying a coin purse or other small articles. "All the money I have...I keep in my pocket, tied about my middle, next my smock." Swift, *Mrs. Fr. Harris' Petit*, 1701.

POLONAISE   (F) Dress or overdress, from 1770 on, consisting of a bodice, with a skirt open from the waist down. Sometimes drawn up to reveal the petticoat. It is literally a "Polish robe" or redingote. *See also* Redingote. "The habit of the women comes very near to that of the men, a simple Polonaise, or long robe edged with fur." *Guthrie's New System of Modern Geography*, 1790.

POMPADOUR   (M/F) Word in constant use in the eighteenth century: pompadour shoes, laces, caps, aprons, sacks, stockings, and headdresses. It also referred to a rich silk taffeta with satin stripes and floral sprigs, as well as a shade of crimson pink. All were named after the Marquise de Pompadour, mistress of Louis XV (1721–1764). "I think there is a time of life...when very gaudy entertainments are as unbecoming, as pink colour and pompadours!" Delany, *Autobiography and Correspondence*, 1752. "No decent coif—but just before/Was grandly plac'd a pompedore [headdress]." *Universal Magazine of Knowledge and Pleasure*, 1756.

POMPON   (F) Jewel or ornament attached to a long pin; also a tuft or bunch of ribbon, velvet, flowers, or threads of silk, worn in the hair, on a cap, or dress. "'How do you like my pompon, papa?' continued my daughter... putting up her hand to her head, and showing me in the middle of her hair a complication of shreds and rags of velvets, feathers, and ribbands, stuck with false stones of a thousand colours." Chesterfield, *World*, 1753.

POWDER   (M/F) Powder, in the form of rice meal or wheat meal, applied to the face and hair. Increased in use during the reign of George I (1714–27). At first it was gray, but after c. 1720–25 white was more popular.

POWDERING-DRESS, POWDERING-GOWN   (M/F) Garment worn over ordinary clothes to protect them while the hair was being powdered. "In his hurry, he threw his powdering dress over his shoulders." Harris, *Letters of the First Earl of Malmesbury*, 1776.

PUDDING CAP   Padded roll, or skull cap, worn by children to protect the head from injury. "I displayed a black pudding upon mine [head], which my mother, careful soul, had provided for its protection in case I should fall." Nollekens, *Nollekens and his Times*, 1768.

QUEUE, CUE   (M) Long roll or plait of hair worn hanging down behind like a tail, either from the head or from a wig. Worn by the military in the seventeenth century; first appearing as civilian dress c. 1720. "The Cit, the Wit, the Rake cocked up in Cue." Cibber, *Epilogue to G. Lillo's London Merchant*, 1731.

RANELAGH MOB   (F) 1760s. Headdress of gauze or mignionet handkerchief folded diagonally, tied under the chin, with the ends pinned behind and allowed to hang down the neck. A babushka. Copied from style worn by the lower classes; fashionable form of undress in the second half of the eighteenth century.

REDINGOTE — (M/F) Corruption of English "riding coat." A double-breasted outer coat for men, with long, plain skirts not cut away in the front. A similar garment worn by women was sometimes cut away in the front.

ROBE À LA FRANÇAISE — *See* Sack.

ROBE À L'ANGLAISE — *See* Sack.

ROBE DE CHAMBRE — (F) Dressing gown or negligee robe. "Instead of which [knowledge] we have brought home the French *Coifure*, the *Robe de Chambre* of the Women, and *Toupé* and *Solitaire* of the Men." *Gentleman's Magazine*, 1731.

ROBING — (F) Trimming in the form of bands or stripes on a gown or robe. "Gold chains…were tacked on the robings of their gowns in loose scollops in the manner of a galloon." Delany, *Autobiography and Correspondence*, 1727. "I made Robings and Facings of a pretty Bit of printed Calico, I had by me." Richardson, *Pamela*, 1740.

ROLL-UP BREECHES — (M) Breeches worn with stockings rolled up over the knee. Unfashionable after 1730.

ROLL-UPS, ROLLING-HOSE — (M) Stockings worn with roll-breeches. "The altitude of square-toed shoe heels, the breadth of his milk-and-watered rollups." Mason, *Letters to Thomas De la Gray*, 1755.

ROUND DRESS, ROUND GOWN — (F) Dress with joined bodice and skirt, the latter closed all around and not open in front to expose an underskirt. Occasionally made with a slight train. Worn in late eighteenth and mid-nineteenth centuries. "I have bought a spotted muslin round gown." Bower, *Diaries and Correspondence*, 1796.

ROUND-EARED CAP — (F) White indoor cap which curved around the face following the hair line. Front had a single or double frill, the back was drawn together by a running string. Worn by servants c. 1730–70. "I bought of a Pedlar, two pretty enough round-ear'd Caps, a little Straw Hat." Richardson, *Pamela*, 1740.

RUCHE — (F) Frill or quilling of light material, such as ribbon, gauze, or lace, used to ornament some part of a garment or headdress.

RUMP — (F) Stuffed pad worn on the buttocks; very prominent in the 1770s and 1780s. Decreased in size at end of the century. *See also* Cork rump.

SACK, SACQUE — (F) Gown, originating in France, worn from 1720 to 1780. Also called robe à la française. The essential feature of the sack was the sack-back consisting of two box pleats, single, double, or treble, stitched down on each side of the back seam from the neckband to just below the shoulders. From there, it was left loose to merge into the fullness of the skirt below. From 1720 to 1730 the gown fell loose all around, sometimes confined by a girdle. From 1730 the bodice was shaped to the figure in front. From 1750 the skirt was open in front revealing a decorative petticoat or underskirt which was part of the garment. From 1770 the box pleats were sometimes sewn down to the waist and the garment was called robe à l'Anglaise. "I can assure you, my Lady Traill has had a sacque [made] from this piece this very morning." Goldsmith, *Citizen of the World*, 1762. "I can't bear a sacque [because it has gone out of fashion]." D'Arblay, *Diary and Letters*, 1782.

SCRATCH BOB   (M) Bob-wig covering only the back of the head; possibly named because the wearer could scratch the head. Worn from 1740 to end of the eighteenth century. "His long lank greasy hair may be exchanged in Middle-Row for a smart bag [wig] or a jemmy scratch." *Connoisseur*, 1755.

SHIFT   (M/F) Garment of linen or cotton. Term applied indifferently to men's and women's underclothing in second half of the century. Also referred to outer garments. Before 1700 a shift was often called a smock. "A Lady's Shift may be metamorphosed into Billet-doux." Addison, *Spectator*, 1712. "But remember that Julia and Rosara...fail not to bring with them checqu'd shifts to appear in at church." Brooke, *Old Maid*, 1756.

SIDE HOOPS   (F) English term for pannier. *See* Pannier.

SILK HAT   (M) Hat invented by John Hettierington, a London haberdasher, and first worn by him on Jan. 15, 1797, which provoked a riot. The satinlike silk surface was on a felted base of rabbit hair. This rival to the beaver hat became the top hat, the supreme headgear of the gentleman from c. 1830 on.

SKIRT   (M) Lower part of a man's gown or robe. "I saw the skirts of his garments ascending up those steps in the rock." Radcliffe, *Italian...*, 1797.

SLAMMERKIN, TROLLOPEE   (F) Loose gown or dress. Mrs. Slammekin, who is described as affecting a careless undress, is a character in Gay's *Beggars' Opera* (1727). It is more probable that the colloquial word suggested the name for the character, rather than the other way around. "A burgess's daughter...who appeared in a Trollopee or Slammerkin, with treble ruffles to the cuffs." *Connoisseur*, 1756.

SLEEVE-KNOT   (F) Ribbon bow worn on the sleeve just above the bend of the elbow.

SLIP-SHOE   (M/F) Slipper with a flat heel. The term "slip-shod," coined c. 1570, referred to the shuffling step resulting from walking in slip-shoes. Worn from sixteenth to mid-eighteenth centuries. "A Gentleman...having strain'd his Ankle...went lame and slip-shoo'd for at least a Year and a half." Baynard, *Genuine Use of Hot and Cold Baths*, 1702. "I...was Slip-shoe'd and without Stockings, being just as I turn'd out of my Cabin." Roberts, *Four Years' Voyages of Capt. G. Roberts*, 1726.

SMALL-CLOTHES   (M) Euphemism for breeches; worn from 1770 to mid-nineteenth century. "The immensity of their breeches, (for, in spite of the fashionable phrase, it would certainly be a perversion of terms to call them small-clothes.)" Hunter, *Travels*, 1796.

SNUFF

(M/F) Preparation of powdered tobacco inhaled through the nostrils; came into general use in England in 1702. "The makers of snuff, who...employ by far the greatest number of hands of any manufacture of the kingdom." Swift, *Reasons Against...Drugs*, 1702.

SOLITAIRE

(M) Black ribbon worn over a stock collar, usually with a bag-wig. Broad solitaires were draped around the neck and either tied in a bow under the chin, tucked into the shirt-front, pinned into place, or loosely knotted and allowed to dangle. A narrow solitaire was worn snugly and tied in a stiff bow in front. "The beau, almost throttled in a large solitaire...was thought to appear most charming." Tucker, *Light of Nature Pursued*, 1768.

SPANISH PAPER

(F) Red color which the ladies of Spain used to paint their faces. It was made up into little books and a leaf was torn out and rubbed on the cheeks; the vermillion powder on the paper was transferred to the face. In use at the end of eighteenth century.

SPENCER

(M/F) Type of wig; also a short, double-breasted overcoat without tails worn in the latter part of the eighteenth century and the beginning of the nineteenth. Derived from the family name Spencer. "The uniform 'diamond' of a card was filled up by the flying dress...of the little capering figure in the spencer wig." Hogarth, *Analysis of Beauty*, 1753. "So cold that Mrs. Custance came walking in her Spenser with a Bosom-Friend." Woodforde, *Diary of a Country Parson*, 1799.

STALK BUTTON

(M/F) Button with shank made of catgut; used in the first half of the eighteenth century.

STAYS

(M/F) One of the strings holding up the brim of a shovel hat; also a cap string passing under the chin. More usually, a laced underbodice, stiffened by the insertion of strips of whalebone, metal, or wood. The use of the plural is due to the fact that stays were originally, as they still are, made in two pieces laced together. "The rich Stays her Taper Shape confine." Gay, *Araminta, a Town Eclogue*, 1713. "I know no Reason...that a White Wig should lower to hoary Hair, or a brush'd Beaver strike to a Carolina-Hat with Stays." Swift, *Right of Precedence between Physicians and Civilians*, 1720. "The stay he has an invincible aversion to, as giving a stiffness that is void of all grace." *Gentleman's Magazine*, 1731.

STEENKIRK

(M/F) Neckcloth having long laced ends hanging down or twisted together and passed through a loop, ring, or buttonhole. According to Voltaire, the original cravate à la Steinkerke simulated the appearance of negligence, in allusion to the disordered dress of the French nobles when hastily summoned to the battle. "A Fashion makes its Progress much slower into Cumberland than into Cornwall...The Steenkirk arrived but two months ago in Newcastle." Addison, *Spectator*, 1711.

STOCK

(M) Replaced the cravat or high neckcloth after c. 1735–40. It was tied around the neck without hanging ends. A black silk ribbon was often tied over the stock in a bow in front after 1745–50. *See also* Solitaire. "He lay in his Stock, which was so tight about his Neck, that it near strangled him." *Gentleman's Magazine*, 1731. "My neckcloths being all worn out, I intend to wear stocks. In that case, I shall be obliged to you if you will buy me a handsome stock-buckle." Cowper, *Letters*, 1781.

STOCK-BUCKLE	(M) Buckle which fastened the stock. "The Stock with buckle made of plate/Has put the cravat out of date." Whyte, *Poems*, 1742.
STOMACHER	(M/F) Waistcoat worn by men; also an ornamental triangular covering for the chest worn by women over the corset. "Embroidered stomachers generally worn by gentlemen in these countries." Evelyn, *Diary*, c. 1697. "Which seem'd to adorn her Bosom far more than the richest Stomacher made of Diamonds or Pearls could do." Dorrington, *Philip Quarll*, 1727. "Sometimes the stomacher rises almost to the chin." *Gentleman's Magazine*, 1731.
SULTANE	(F) Rich gown trimmed with buttons and loops, fashionable in the late seventeenth and throughout much of the eighteenth century. "My lady will travel in her Sultane, I suppose." Gay, *Distress'd Wife*, 1732.
SURTOUT	(M/F) Long, loose overcoat with one or more spreading collars called "capes." Became known in the nineteenth century as a box coat. Worn by men 1680–1840s; after 1790, also worn by women. "He was forced constantly to wear a surtout of oiled cloth, by which means he came home pretty clean." Arbuthnot, *Law is a Bottomless Pit, Exemplified in the Case of ...John Bull*, 1712.
TETE DE MOUTON	(F) Headdress of close frizzly false curls; in French literally means "sheep's head." "I beg she will not leave off her *tete de mouton* and her *pannier*." Suffolk, *Letters To and From*, 1737.
TIE-WIG	(M/F) Wig with tied-back queue.
TITUS WIG	*See* Brutus wig.
TOMPION	(M/F) Watch made by Thomas Tompion, a noted watchmaker in the reign of Queen Anne (1702–14).
TOUPEE	(M/F) Curl or artificial lock of hair on the top of the head. "Love in his lac'd coat lies,/And peeps from his toupee." Fielding, *Grubstreet Opera*, 1731. "Little Girls have their Heads dressed a foot high so that their Faces seem to be just half way between the top of their Toupets and their Feet." Northumberland, *Diaries of a Duchess*, 1774.
TRICORNE	(M/F) Cocked three-cornered hat with brim turned up on all three sides; made of black or dark felt. Edges decorated with gold braid, fringing, or ostrich fronds.
TUCKER	(F) White edging, usually frilled, of lace, lawn, muslin, or soft material; worn around the top of a low-necked bodice. "The Butcher's Lady thinks, that living in style, is manifested in putting on her best bib and tucker on holidays." Williams, *Life of Late Earl of Barrymore*, 1793.
TURBAN	(F) Headdress resembling the oriental turban, elaborately trimmed. Worn in the late eighteenth century. "Assuring her [the cap] was grown so old-fashioned, that not a lady's maid...would not be seen in it, she offered to pin her up a turban." D'Arblay, *Camilla*, 1796.
UNDRESS	(M/F) Informal or ordinary dress not usually worn in public. Also called

deshabille. "How he surpriz'd a famous Miss of the Town, dining at her Lodgings in an Undress." Brown, *Works*, c. 1703. "He had ben on the bed, but was not risen and in his undresse." Evelyn, *Diary*, c. 1697. "The Men to continue in Black full trimmed…Undress light grey Frocks." *London Gazette*, 1767.

VANDYKE	(M/F) Broad lace or linen collar with a deeply cut edge, in imitation of the style of collar frequently depicted in portraits painted by Vandyke. "Vandyke dress" was a form of costume worn for portraits in the eighteenth century. "Circling round her ivory neck/Frizzle out the smart Vandyke;/Like the ruff that heretofore/Good Queen Bess's maidens wore." *Gentleman's Magazine*, 1755.
WAISTCOAT	(M/F) Short, sleeveless undergarment worn about the upper part of the body; intended to be partly exposed to view. Term also applied to plainer wool functional garment. "Her night-cloaths tumbled with resistless grace,/And her bright hair play'd careless round her face;/Reaching the kettle, made her gown unpin,/She wore no waistcoat, and her shift was thin." Montagu, *Town Eclogues*, 1747.
WHALEBONE	Elastic horny substance which grows in a series of thin parallel plates in the upper jaw of certain whales in place of teeth. Used as stiffening in stays and dresses. "Have you got the whalebone petticoats among you yet? …A woman here may hide a moderate gallant under them." Swift, *Journal to Stella*, 1711.
WRAP-RASCAL	(M) Loose overcoat or great-coat. *See also* Surtout.

TEXTILES AND LACE

ALAMODE	Thin, light, glossy silk; usually black. "To wear Hatbands of Black *English* Alamode covered with Black Crape." *London Gazette*, 1702.
ALEPINE	Cloth of mixed fiber, either wool and silk or mohair and cotton.
ALLEJAH	Corded silk fabric from Turkestan. Early eighteenth century.
ANTWERP LACE	Bobbin lace with a vase as the central motif. Popular in the late seventeenth and eighteenth centuries.
ARMOZEEN	Stout plain silk, usually black, used for clerical gowns and mourning scarves. "Lady Dysart's clothes were pink armazine trimmed with silver." Delany, *Autobiography and Correspondence*, 1733.
BAIZE	Coarse woolen cloth with a long nap. "70 yards of red bays…for under petticoats." *Account of Workhouses*, 1732. "The Well of a Carriage is lined with linen or baize." Felton, *Carriages*, 1801.
BARRACAN	Coarse, thick, corded wool fabric resembling camlet; warp of silk and wool, weft of Angora goat's hair. In the eighteenth century it was often watered.
BARRAS	Canvas or linen imported from Holland and used for neckcloths.

BEAVER	Felted cloth used for overcoats, gloves, and hats. "Their carpets and bevers…retain the electrical virtue, and prevent its spreading to the floor." *Gentleman's Magazine*, 1756.
BINCHE LACE	Similar to Brussels lace, except that Binche is a continuous thread lace. The design is closely sprinkled with snowflakelike motifs. Named after the city of Binche.
BLONDE LACE	Silk bobbin lace; usually the color of raw silk. "Raving about gauze, Blon, Brussels, and ruffles." *London Magazine*, 1760.
BOBBIN	Long, thin spindle used for making lace; made of wood, bone, or ivory.
BOBBIN LACE	Lace made with bobbins on a pillow. Each bobbin supplies a single strand of thread; these strands are twisted around pins and each other to form bobbin lace.
BOMBASINE	Twilled or corded dress material of silk and wool worsted; sometimes also of cotton and worsted, or of worsted alone. Black often used during mourning. "Black bombazeen will do very well in a sack." Delany, *Autobiography and Correspondence*, 1747. "In Sorrow's dismal crape or bombazeen." Wolcott, *Works*, 1789.
BRAWL	Blue and white striped cloth manufactured in India.
BRILLIANETTE	Glazed woolen textile, striped and flowered; sometimes referred to as calamanco.
BRILLIANT	Silk fabric. "Many woollen stuffs, and stuffs mixed with silk, and even silks themselves…such as brilliants…and bombazines." *Spinster*, 1719.
BROCADE	Textile woven with a pattern of raised figures, originally in gold and silver. "Stiff in Brocard, and pinch'd in stays." Prior, *Phyllis' Age*, c. 1720. "At present, any stuff of silk, satin, or even simple taffety, when wrought, and enriched with flowers…obtains the denomination of brocade." Chambers, *Cyclopoedia*, 1728.
BRUSSELS LACE	Fine bobbin lace made in Brussels and its environs; noted for the evenness of its texture, and the delicate accuracy of its forms. English merchants sold smuggled Brussels lace under the name of *point d'Angleterre* in order to avoid illegality. "Her head dress was a Brussels lace mob." Richardson, *Clarissa*, 1748.
CADDIS	Cotton wool or floss silk, used in padding; also worsted yarn or wool ribbon. "Soft half-worn Linen, which the French call *Charpie*, the English, *Lint*, and we *Caddiss*." *Medical Essays and Observations*, 1738.
CALAMANCO	Woolen textile, plain, striped, checked, or figured and glazed. "A tawny yellow jerkin, turned up with red calamanco!" Sterne, *Tristram Shandy*, 1760.
CAMBRIC, CAMBRESINE	Fine white linen, originally made at Cambray in Flanders.

CAMLET	Fabric originally made of silk and angora goat hair, later with wool and silk. "Here [Leyden, Flanders] they make...camblets, tho' inferior to those of Great Britain." Nugent, *Grand Tour*, 1756.
CANTALOON	Worsted woven of fine single yarns.
CHENILLE	Velvety cord with soft threads of silk and wool standing out at right angles from a core, like hairs of a caterpillar. Used in trimming and bordering dresses and furniture. "Lady Huntingdon's...petticoat was black velvet embroidered with chenille." Delany, *Autobiography and Correspondence*, 1738.
CHENILLE LACE	French bobbin lace with a silk honeycomb ground filled with thick stitches and outlined with white chenille.
CHERRYDERRY, CARRODARY	Indian cotton fabric similar to gingham.
CHEYNEY	Worsted or woolen fabric with pattern printed on warp threads prior to weaving; this gives the effect of a shadow. From the Persian *chini*.
CHINTZ	Painted or printed calicoes of cotton and linen imported from India; usually glazed. "Let a charming Chintz and Brussels lace Wrap my cold limbs." Pope, *Moral Essays*, 1732.
COLBERTEEN LACE	Needle lace with a square ground. Named for Monsieur Colbert (1619–1683), superintendent of Louis XIV's manufactories. By the mid-eighteenth century it became unfashionable. "[She] Scarce knows what difference is between/Rich Flanders lace and Colberteen." Swift, *Cadenus and Vanessa*, 1713.
CORDUROY	Thick corded cotton material, with a pile similar to velvet. "An old brown coat, and old corduroy breeches." *Hull Advertiser*, 1795.
CRAPE	Thin transparent gauzelike fabric, plain woven, with a minutely wrinkled surface. "Proud Roxana, fir'd with jealous rage,/With fifty yards of crape shall sweep the stage." Swift, *Works*, 1721.
CUTTANEE, COTTONY	Fine East Indian linen used for shirts and cravats; also a silk with metallic stripes.
DAMASIN, DAMASELLOURS	Silk brocaded with metal threads.
DAMASK, DAMASCUS	Silk, wool, or linen reversible fabric richly figured with designs; ground and pattern distinguished by contrasting luster. "All ye bed and hangings are of fine damaske made of worsted." Fiennes, *Diary*, 1710. "He looked at the tablecloth, and praised the figure of the damask." Goldsmith, *Bee*, 1759.
DENIM	Stout cotton twill. Shortened from *serge de Nimes*, which was named after the town in Southern France. "A pair of Flower'd Serge de Nim Breeches." *London Gazette*, 1703.

DIMITY	Fine ribbed cotton fabric woven with raised stripes or figures; made first in Damietta, India. Used undyed for beds, bedroom hangings, and for garments. "A half bedstead as the new mode, dimity with fine shades of worsted works well made up." Fiennes, *Diary*, c. 1710. "His waistcoat was a white dimity, richly embroidered with yellow silk." Fielding, *Life of Jonathan Wild the Great*, 1743.
DITTO	*See* Suit of ditto.
DOWLAS	Heavy linen, originally from Brittany, used for shirts and smocks by the poorer classes. "Throw o'er your Dowlass Shirt a Morning Gown." Bull, tr., *Dedekind's Grobianus*, 1739.
DRAB	Thick strong wool cloth, usually twilled; dull brown or gray color. "To smile on a Brocade more than upon a Brown Drap." *Freethinker*, 1718.
DRAP DE BERRY	Wool cloth woven at Berry in France. "Fools never wear out—they are such drap de Berri things!" Congreve, *Way of the World*, 1700.
DRAWBOYS	Name given to figured materials which first required the use of boys to regulate the treadles of the looms; superseded by the Jacquard loom (1801).
DRESDEN LACE	Technically, a form of drawn fabric work embroidery. Executed on fine linen or cotton with a diversity of patterned ground stitches. Usually associated with Dresden, but often produced in France.
DRILL	Stout twilled linen.
DRUGGET	Coarse wool, or mixture of wool and silk or wool and linen; used for clothing.
DUCK	Strong untwilled linen or cotton fabric, lighter and finer than canvas; used for small sails and men's outer clothing, especially sailors'. From the Dutch word *doeck*, meaning linen or linen clothes. "What is to be done for tents, I know not. I am assured that very little duck can be got in this country." Jefferson, *Writings*, 1780.
DUFFEL	Coarse wool cloth with a thick nap, originally made in Flanders. "They likewise make here the Duffield Stuffs, a Yard and three Quarters wide, which are carried to New England and Virginia, and much worn even here in Winter." Defoe, *A Tour Through the Whole Island of Great Britain*, 1769.
DURANCE	Durable wool cloth made in Norwich; sometimes called everlastings.
DUROY	Coarse wool fabric resembling tammy. Though the words are similar, it is not the same as corduroy.
ELL	Measurement of length; the measurement rarely meant the same length. The English ell = 45 in.; the Scottish = 37.2 in.; the Flemish = 27 in. From an old Teutonic word which originally meant arm or forearm. "102 Ells dantzig make 50 ells english." Hanway, *Historical Account of the British Trade*, 1753.

ENGLISH POINT LACE	*See* Brussels lace.
FEARNOTHING, FEARNOUGHT, SHEPHERD'S CLOTH	Stout wool cloth, used chiefly on board ship for outside clothing in the most inclement weather. *See also* Fearnothing in Costumes and Accessories. "A Magellanic Jacket made of a thick woollen stuff called Fearnought." Cook, *Voyages*, 1772.
FUSTIAN	Coarse cloth made of cotton and flax, with a short pile or nap, usually dyed olive or another dark color. *See also* Jean. "For all my bit of a fustian frock...I have more dust in my fob, than all these powdered sparks put together." Smollett, *Adventures of Ferdinand Count Fathom*, 1753.
GAUZE	Thin, semitransparent silk textile invented at Gaza in Palestine. In the eighteenth century it was made also of linen. "A Vandyke in frize your neck must surround./Turn your lawns into gauze, let your Brussels be blond." *Satirical Songs and Poems on Costume*, 1754.
GENOA VELVET	Brocaded silk velvet from Genoa.
GIMP	Silk, worsted, or cotton twist wrapped over cord or wire and used as trimming. "Unmov'd by Tongues, and Sights he walk'd the place,/Thro' Tape, Toys, Tinsel, Gimp, Perfume, and Lace." Parnell, *Poetical Works*, 1717.
GINGHAM	Cotton or linen cloth woven of dyed yarn in stripes, checks, or patterns. "Ladies of taste are prodigiously fond of the Ginghams manufactured there [Manchester]." *British Magazine*, 1763.
GROGRAM	Coarse fabric of silk, mohair, and wool, or all three mixed; often stiffened with gum. "She did more Execution upon me in Grogram, than the greatest Beauty...has even done in Brocade." Addison, *Spectator*, 1712. "The charmful Village-Maid, With Innocence and Grogram blest." Thompson, *Poems*, 1757.
GROS DE NAPLES	Heavy silk fabric with ribbed ground; made originally in Naples. *Gros de Tours*, a similar fabric, was originally made in Tours.
HARRATEEN	Linen fabric used for curtains, bed furniture, and other household items. "Ready-Made Furnitures...either of Harrateen, Cheney, Flower'd cotton, Checks." *General Advertiser*, 1748.
HESSIAN	Strong coarse cloth made of a mixture of hemp and jute. In modern usage called burlap.
HOLLANDS	Fine linen cloth first imported from Holland; after the eighteenth century the name was applied to any fine linen.
INDIAN	Drawn muslin lace, often called Indian work, or muslin fabric.
JEAN	Twilled cotton cloth; a type of fustian.
KENTING	Fine linen made originally in Holland; imported into Ireland in mid-eighteenth century, but later made there.

KERSEY	Coarse narrow cloth woven from long-strand wool; usually ribbed. "English broad-cloth, and red Kersey they highly esteemed." Cook, *Voyages*, 1772.
KINCOB	Indian cotton gauze; generally embroidered with gold or silver.
KNOTTING	Fancy threadwork made by tying knots in thread; used for bordering garments. "Next to mere idleness, I think knotting is to be reckoned in the scale of insignificance; though I once attempted to learn knotting." Boswell, *Life of Samuel Johnson*, 1784.
LAWN	Fine linen, resembling cambric, used as early as the reign of Queen Elizabeth I (1558–1603). "If you can get fine lawns, bring them with you, for they are rare." Auckland, *Journal and Correspondence*, 1793.
LINSEY-WOLSEY	Coarse woolen cloth first made at Linsey in Suffolk, England; popular in the Colonies. "Martha...delighted to be cloathed in good Linsy Woolsy, the work of her own hands." Bage, *Barham Downs*, 1784.
LIVERY LACE	Worsted braid woven with the household coat of arms; worn on servants' uniforms.
LOOM LACE	Lace woven on a loom; an imitation of bobbin or point lace.
LOVE, LOVE-RIBBON	Thin silk with narrow satin stripes; used for ribbons. "A black velvet cloak with a love coarsley run round it." *London Daily Advertiser*, 1751. "I made her and Annie new caps, which I trimmed with rosettes of black love-ribbon." Sherwood, *History of the Fairchild Family*, c. 1805.
LUTESTRING, LUSTRING	Glossy silk fabric; also a dress or ribbon made of this material. "She was dressed in a flowing Negligee of white Lutestring." *Women of Fashion*, 1767.
MANCHESTER VELVET	Cotton velvet. "Blue Manchester velvets, with gold cords...are generally the uniform of Bum-bailiffs." *London Chronicles*, 1762.
MECHLIN LACE	Bobbin lace with the pattern outlined by a flat thread on a net ground. Produced at Mechlin, Flanders. "Mechlin the queen of lace." Young, *Love of Fame*, 1728. "His shirt which was of the finest cambric, edged with right Mechline." Smollett, *Adventures of Roderick Random*, 1748.
MEDLEY	Wool cloth made of different colors. "These fine Spanish Medley Cloths are mix'd coloured Cloths, which all the Persons of Fashion in England wear." Defoe, *A Tour Through the Whole Island of Great Britain*, 1769.
MIGNONETTE LACE	Light, fine bobbin lace, fashionable for headresses in the second half of the eighteenth century. "He had on...a pair of Mignonette Ruffles with a narrow edging." Northumberland, *Diary of a Duchess*, 1772.
MOREEN	Worsted wool with a watered surface in imitation of moiré. "A high, long old fashioned room, with a dark blue morine bed at the end of it." Smith, *Marchmont*, 1796.
NAINSOOK	Cotton fabric; type of muslin from India or a garment made of this

fabric. "Nor could I find a man in the whole parish who understood any thing about nainsook and bandannoes." *Spirit of the Public Journals*, 1804.

NANKEEN Cotton cloth, originally made at Nanking, China, from a yellow variety of cotton. "Make his breeches of nankein,/Most like nature, most like skin." *Satirical Songs and Poems on Costume*, 1755.

NEEDLE LACE Lace stitched entirely with a needle on a parchment pattern.

ORRIS LACE Bobbin lace with designs in gold or silver threads. "His coat was wonderfully lace with gold orace." Scott, *Test of Filial Duty*, 1772.

PADUASOY Corded or grosgrain silk fabric worn by both sexes; also a garment made of this material. "Let him his active limbs display/In camblet thin, or glossy paduasoy." Jenyns, *Art of Dancing*, 1730.

PERSIAN Thin, soft silk used for linings. "She had an exceeding pretty…dress, made of pink persian." D'Arblay, *Early Diary of Frances Burney*, 1777.

POINT LACE Needle lace often named after the place of manufacture: *point d'Alençon, point d'Argentan, point de France, point de Venise*. Except in the case of *point d'Angleterre*, a bobbin lace.

POPLIN Mixed woven fabric, consisting of a silk warp and worsted weft, with a corded surface; it was plain, watered, or brocaded. In use after 1685. "The mixed goods, or tabinets and poplins [Irish] have been long celebrated." Morse, *American Universal Geography*, 1796.

PRINTED FABRICS Printing of textiles using woodblocks. First used for printing calico in London in 1676.

PRUNELLA Strong wool worsted cloth; used for graduate, clergy, and barrister gowns. "Worth makes the man, and want of it, the fellow;/The rest is all but leather or prunella." Pope, *Essays on Man*, 1734.

RAS DU MORE Silk resembling armozeen. *See also* Armozeen.

RASH Smooth textile made of silk (silk rash) or worsted (cloth rash).

RATTEEN Thick twilled wool cloth, usually friezed or with a curled nap, but sometimes dressed. "We'll rig in Meath-street Egypt's haughty queen,/ And Anthony shall court her in ratteen." Swift, *Works*, 1721. "I recommended him to have a brown rateen, which at that time was much wore." Bellamy, *Apology for Her Life*, 1785.

RUSSEL, RUSSET Coarse homespun wool cloth of a reddish brown, gray, or neutral color; used for the clothing of peasants and country folk. Also worn in the Colonies. "O how I wished for my grey russet again, and my poor honest dress, with which you fitted me out." Richardson, *Pamela*, 1740.

SARSENET Very fine and soft silk, plain or twilled, in various colors; also a dress made of this fabric. Term used since the thirteenth century. "The palest Features look the most agreeable in white Sarsenet." Addison, *Spectator*, 1712. "I, remember, too, Miss Andrews drank tea with us that evening, and wore her puce-coloured sarsenet." Austen, *Northanger Abbey*, 1818.

SATINETTE	Satin woven of silk, or silk and cotton. "*Sattinet*, or *Sattinade*, a very slight, thin Sattin, chiefly used by the Ladies for Summer Night-gowns, etc. and ordinarily striped." Chambers, *Cyclopoedia*, 1728.
SERGE	Wool twill fabric, primarily used for clothing. "*Serge*…a Woollen cross'd Stuff, manufactured on a Loom with four Treddles, after the Manner of Rateens, and other cross'd stuffs." Chambers, *Cyclopoedia*, 1728.
SHAG	Cloth with a velvet nap on one side, usually of worsted, but sometimes of silk. Used as early as 1632. "The Indians make a most elegant cloathing …as fine as a silk shag." *Philosophical Transactions of the Royal Society*, 1781.
SHAGREEN	Untanned leather of horse, ass, shark, or seal skin. It had a rough granular surface and was frequently dyed green. Also a silk fabric with a grained ground. "I…bought eighteen yards of very pretty white silk for Trott, something in the nature of shagreen, but a better colour than they ever are." Delany, *Autobiography and Correspondence*, 1728.
SILESIA	Thin coarse linen with a glazed surface; used for neckcloths and cravats. Originally manufactured in Silesia, Germany.
SNAIL	Short for chenille. *See also* Chenille. "I have brought down a screen to work in snail for the Duchess." Montagu, *Letters*, 1744.
SOOSEY	Striped fabric of silk and cotton imported from India.
STUFF	Woven material of any kind, though usually referring to a woolen fabric. "*Stuff*, in Weaving, is any Sort of Commodity made of Woollen Thread, etc. but in particular Manner those thin light ones that Women make or line their Gons of or with." Dyche and Pardon, *New General English Dictionary*, 1735.
SUIT OF DITTO	Suit of clothes having all the pieces made of the same material and color. "A snuff-coloured suit of ditto with Bolus [clay] Buttons." *Connoisseur*, 1755.
SWAN'S-DOWN, SWANSDOWN	Down, soft underplumage of the swan; used for dress trimmings, powder puffs, muffs, and pelerines. Also a soft, thick, close woolen cloth. "The blankets of the finest swansdown." *Sporting Magazine*, 1801.
SWANSKIN	Thin twilled flannel with a downy surface; used for linings and blankets. "*Swanskin*, a sort of fine Flannel, so call'd on account of its extraordinary Whiteness." Phillips, *New World of English Words*, 1706.
TABBY, TABINE, TAFFETA	Silk taffeta of uniform color, waved or watered. Also a dress or gown, or padding or quilting to improve the figure. "The Duke of York who was dressed in a pale blue watered tabby." Walpole, *Letters to the Earl of Strafford*, 1760. "Ward, at the Cat and Gridiron, Petticoat-lane, makes tabby all over for people inclined to be crooked." Foote, *Knights*, 1747.
TABINET	Watered fabric of silk and wool resembling poplin. "Poplins, some which, called tabinets, have all the richness of silk." *Philosophical Survey of the South of Ireland*, 1778.
TAFFETA	*See* Tabby.

TAMBOUR	Circular frame, formed of one hoop fitting within another, in which silk, muslin, or other material is stretched for embroidering. Also a type of embroidery worked in chain stitch on a frame. "When I saw you first sitting at your tambour, in a pretty figured linen gown." Sheridan, *School for Scandal*, 1777.
TAMMY, TAMIN, STAMIN	Fine worsted cloth of good quality, often with a glazed finish. "Her riding dress a light drab, lined with blue tammy." *Annual Register*, 1758.
THUNDER AND LIGHTNING	Wool cloth, apparently of glaring colors. "He had on a coat made of that cloth they call thunder and lightning." Goldsmith, *Vicar of Wakefield*, 1766.
TIFFANY	Thin transparent silk; also a transparent gauze, muslin, or cobweb lawn. "A shepherdess's hat, of pale blue silver tiffany." Sherwood, *History of the Fairchild Family*, 1788.
TUFTAFFETA	Taffeta with a pile or nap arranged in tufts.
TUFTED DIMITY	Fustian with a tufted surface; used for underpetticoats.
TULLE	Fine silk bobbin net first made by machinery in 1768 at Nottingham. Named for Tulle where the fabric was first manufactured. Used for women's dresses, veils, hats, and accessories.
VALENCIENNES LACE	Similar to Binche, except finer and more closely worked. Lace resembling Valenciennes was made in Belgium as well. *See also* Binche lace.
VELVERET	Variety of fustian with a velvet surface. "The Cotton Trade…has been greatly improved of late…by the Invention of Velverets." Defoe, *A Tour Through the Whole Island of Great Britain*, 1769. "I shall presently see landscapes beautifully diversified with…plains of Plush…vallies of Velveret, and meadows of Manchester." Canning, *Microcosm*, 1787.
WORSTED	Cloth made of long-strand wool combed straight and smooth before spinning. First made at Worstead in England in the reign of Henry I (1100–1135). "Woollen yarn and worsted are prohibited to be exported under the same penalties as wool." Smith, *Wealth of Nations*, 1784.

BIBLIOGRAPHIES

THE ELEGANT ART OF DRESS

Arnold, J., *Patterns of Fashion*, London, 1964.
Boehn, M. von, *The Eighteenth Century*, trans. J. Joshua, *Modes and Manners*, 4 vols., London, 1935, vol. 4.
Bradfield, N., *Costume in Detail, 1730–1930*, New York, 1968.
Buck, A., *Dress in Eighteenth-Century England*, New York, 1979.
Ciba Review, The Society of Chemical Industry in Basel, Switzerland, 1937–82.
Cunnington, C.W. and P., *Handbook of English Costume in the Eighteenth Century*, Philadelphia, 1957.
Davenport, M., *The Book of Costume*, New York, 1948.
Diderot, D., *L'encyclopédie, ou dictionnaire raisonné des sciences, des arts et des métiers*, Paris, 1751–65.
Ewing, E., *History of Children's Costume*, New York, 1977.
Fairholt, F.W., *Costume in England*, London, 1860.
Halls, Z., *Men's Costume 1580–1750*, London, 1970.
————, *Women's Costume 1600–1750*, London, 1970.
————, *Women's Costume 1750–1800*, London, 1972.
Ham, E., *Elizabeth Ham, by herself, 1783–1820*, ed. E. Gillett, London, [1945].
Heideloff, N., *Gallery of Fashion*, London, April 1794–March 1803, vols. 1–9.
Journal des Luxus und der Moden, ed. F.J. Bertuch and G.M. Kraus, excerpts from *Journal für literatur, kunst, luxus und mode*, Leipzig, 1967–68.
Köhler, C., *A History of Costume*, ed. and aug. E. von Sichart, trans. A.K. Dallas, London, 1928.
Kybabva, L., O. Herbeyova, and M. Lamarova, *Pictorial Encyclopedia of Fashion*, trans. C. Rosoux, London, 1968.
Leloir, M., *Histoire du costume de l'antiquité à 1914*, 12 vols., Paris, 1935–49, vols. 10–12.
McClellan, E., *Historic dress in America, 1607–1800*, Philadelphia, 1904.
Nienholdt, E., *Kostümkunde*, Braunschweig, 1961.
Pauw, L.G. de, and C. Hunt, *Remember the Ladies: Women in America, 1750–1815*, New York, 1976.
Payne, B., *History of Costume from the Ancient Egyptians to the Twentieth Century*, New York, 1965.
Piton, C., *Le costume civil en France du XIIIᵉ au XIXᵉ siècle*, Paris, 1926.
Pottle, F.A., ed., *Boswell's London Journal 1762–1763*, New York, 1950.
Purefoy, H., *Purefoy letters, 1735–1753*, London, 1931.
Richardson, S., *Pamela*, New York, 1958.
Squire, G., *Dress, Art and Society, 1560–1970*, New York, 1974.
Stewart, J., *Plocacosmos: or the Whole Art of Hair Dressing*, London, 1782.
Waffen-und Kostümkunde; Zeitschrift der Gesellschaft für historische Waffen-und Kostümkunde, Munich, 1959–82.
Woodforde, J., *The Diary of a Country Parson*, ed. John Beresford, 5 vols., Oxford, 1968.

THE ELEGANT ART OF MOVEMENT

Aresty, E.B., *The Best Behavior*, New York, 1970.
Baur-Heinhold, M., *The Baroque Theatre: A Cultural History of the 17th and 18th Centuries*, trans. M. Whittall, New York, 1967.
Casanova, J., *The Memoirs of Jacques Casanova de Seingalt*, trans. A. Machen, 6 vols., New York, [1959–61].
Chesterfield, P.D.S., *The Letters of Philip Dormer Stanhope, 4th Earl of Chesterfield*, ed. B. Dobrée, 6 vols., London, 1932.
Clark, K., *Civilisation*, New York, 1969.

Courtin, A., *The Rules of Civility*, 12th ed., London, 1703.

Gay, P., *Age of Enlightenment*, The Great Ages of Man, New York, 1966.

Hecht, J.J., *The Domestic Servant Classes in 18th Century England*, London, 1956.

Hilton, W., *Dance of Court and Theater: The French Noble Style: 1690–1725*, Princeton, 1981.

Hogarth, W., *The Analysis of Beauty*, ed. J. Burke, Oxford, 1955.

Laver, J., *The Age of Illusion: Manners and Morals: 1750–1848*, New York, 1972.

Levron, J., *Daily Life at Versailles in the 17th and 18th Centuries*, trans. C.E. Engel, New York, 1968.

————, *The Man of Manners: or Plebeian Polish'd*, 3rd ed., London, [1768].

Nivelon, F., *The Rudiments of Genteel Behavior*, London, 1737.

Petrie, A., *Rules of Good Deportment, or of Good Breeding*, Edinburgh, n.d.

————, *The Polite Academy*, 8th ed., London, [178–].

Rameau, P., *The Dancing Master*, rep. ed., trans. C.W. Beaumont, New York, [1970].

Russell, D.A., *Period Style for the Theatre*, Boston, 1980.

Scott, A.F., comp., *Every One a Witness: The Georgian Age: Commentaries of an Era*, London, 1970.

————, *The Spectator*, Cincinnati, 1857.

Swann, J., *Shoe Buckles*, Northampton, 1981.

The Tatler, 4 vols., London, 1804.

Tomlinson, K., *The Art of Dancing*, London, 1735.

Towle, M., *The Young Gentleman and Lady's Private Tutor*, Oxford, 1770.

Turberville, A.S., ed., *Johnson's England: An Account of the Life and Manners of His Age*, 2 vols., Oxford, 1933.

Turner, E.S., *What the Butler Saw: 250 Years of the Servant Problem*, New York, 1967.

Waugh, N., *Corsets and Crinolines*, London, 1954.

————, *The Cut of Men's Clothes 1600–1900*, New York, 1964.

————, *The Cut of Women's Clothes 1600–1930*, London, 1968.

White, T.H., *The Age of Scandal*, London, 1950.

————, *The Scandalmonger*, London, 1952.

Wildeblood, J., *The Polite World*, London, 1973.

Wood, M., *Advanced Historical Dances*, London, 1960.

THE ELEGANT ART OF WOVEN SILK

Bertholon, P., *Du commerce...*, Montpellier, 1787.

Godart, J., *L'ouvrier en soie*, Lyon, 1899.

Honour, H., *Chinoiserie: The Vision of Cathay*, [London], 1961.

Joubert de L'Hiberderie, A., *Le Dessinateur, pour les fabriques d'étoffes, d'or, d'argent et de soie...*, rev. ed., Paris, 1774.

King, D., ed., *British Textile Design in the Victoria and Albert Museum*, 3 vols., Tokyo, 1980, vols. 1, 2.

Levey, S., "Lace and Lace Patterned Silks: Some Comparative Illustrations," *Studies in Textile History*, Toronto, 1977.

Rothstein, N., "Dutch Silks: An Important but Forgotten Industry of the 18th Century or a Hypothesis?" *Oud Holland*, 79:3, 1964.

Smith, G., *The Laboratory, or School of Arts*, 6 vols., London, 1756, vol. 2.

Thornton, P., *Baroque and Rococo Silks*, London, 1965.

————, "Jean Revel: Dessinateur de la Grande Fabrique," *Gazette des Beaux Arts*, July 1960, pp. 71–86.

THE ELEGANT ART OF EMBROIDERY

Berz, *Journal and Correspondence*, London, 1865, vol. 1.

Campbell, R., "Survey of the London Trades," *London Tradesman*, 1747.

Encyclopédie méthodique, Paris, 1785.

Galerie des modes, Paris, 1778–87.

Havard, H., *Dictionnaire de l'ameublement de la décoration, depuis le XIIIᵉ siècle jusqu'à nos jours*, Paris, 1887.

Johnson, S., *The Idler*, London, 1758.

Macky, J., *A Journey Through England*, London, 1722.

Postlethwayt, M., ed. and trans., *The Universal Dictionary of Trade and Commerce*, London, 1757.

Saint-Aubin, C. de, *Art of the Embroiderer*, 1770, trans. N. Scheuer, Los Angeles, 1983, (in press).

THE ELEGANT ART OF LACE

Guignet, P., "The Lacemakers of Valenciennes in the 18th Century: An Economic and Social Study of a Group of Female Workers under the Ancient Regime," *Textile History*, vol. 10, 1979, pp. 96–113.

Malotet, A., *La dentelle à Valenciennes*, Paris, 1927.

Mercure de France, vol. 16, March 1729, rep. ed., Geneva, 1968.

Molomenti, P., *La Storia di Venezia nella vita privata*, 3 vols., Bergamo, 1929, vol. 2.

Paris, Archives Nationales, KK378, "Registre pour la tenue journalière des atours de la garde-robe et autres détails des chambres des enfants de France."

————, KK523, "Journal des dépenses d'une dame de la cour, 1783–1792."

————, O1830/18, O1830/114, O1830/176, "Garde-robe du roy, maison du roi."

_____, 011043, "Papiers du Grand Maître des Ceremonies."

_____, 013259, "Habillement des différentes personnes qui ont assisté aux cérémonies du sacre en 1722."

Reisert, G.A.H. de, *Modes et usages au temps de Marie-Antoinette: livre-journal de Mme. Eloffe, marchande de modes, couturière lingère ordinaire de la reine et des dames de sa cour*, 2 vols., Paris, 1855.

Venice, Museo Correr, 2254/2, "Inventario generale di casa Tron."

THE ELEGANT ART OF TAPESTRY

Ananoff, A. and D. Wildenstein, *François Boucher*, 2 vols., Lausanne, 1976, vol. 2.

Badin, J., *La Manufacture de tapisseries de Beauvais depuis des origines jusqu'à nos jours*, Paris, 1909.

Coural, J., "Notes documentaires sur les ateliers parisiens de 1597 à 1662," *Chefs-d'oeuvre de la tapisserie parisienne 1597–1662*, exh. cat., Orangerie de Versailles, 1967.

Delesalle, H., "Les Tapisseries des 'Jeux Russiens,'" *Bulletin de la société de l'histoire de l'art français*, Apr. 1944, pp. 127–32.

Fenaille, M., *État général des tapisseries de la manufacture des Gobelins depuis son origine jusqu'à nos jours, 1600–1900*, 6 vols., Paris, 1903–23, vols. 1, 2, 4.

Galerie Jean Charpentier, *Adolphe Clément Bayard Collection Sale*, sales cat., Paris, June 22, 1937.

Geffroy, G., *Les Gobelins*, Les musées d'Europe, Paris, 1924.

Gobel, H. *Wandteppiche: Romanischen Länder*, 3 vols., Leipzig, 1923, vol. 2.

Guiffrey, J., *Histoire de la tapisserie*, Tours, 1886.

_____, "Les Manufactures parisiennes de tapisserie au XVIIᵉ siècle," *Mémoires de la société de l'histoire de Paris et de l'Ile-de-France*, vol. 19, 1892, p. 98.

Guiffrey, J., E. Muntz, and A. Pinchart, *Histoire générale de la tapisserie*, 3 vols., Paris, 1878–85, vol. 1.

Hunter, G.L., *The Practical Book of Tapestries*, London, 1925.

Jamot, P., *Duc de Trevise Sale*, sales cat., Galerie Jean Charpentier, Paris, May 19, 1938.

Jarry, M., *World Tapestry: From Its Origins to the Present*, New York, 1968.

Los Angeles County Museum, *Bulletin of the Art Division*, 4:2–3, summer 1952.

Los Angeles County Museum of Art, *Handbook*, 1977.

Standen, E.A., "Some Exotic Subjects," *Apollo*, 113:233, July 1981, pp. 44–54.

Weibel, A.C., "The Story of Psyche," *Wadsworth Atheneum Bulletin*, 3:1, spring 1957, pp. 13–15.

Weigert, R.A., *La tapisserie et le tapis*, Paris, 1964.

THE ELEGANT ART OF FANCY DRESS

Aspinall, A., ed., *The Correspondence of George, Prince of Wales 1770–1812*, 8 vols., London, 1963–71, vol. 1.

Boucher, F., "An Episode in the Life of the Académie de France à Rome," *Connoisseur*, Oct. 1961.

Bretagne, P. de, *Réjouissances et fêtes magnifiques qui se sont faites en Bavière l'an 1722...*, Munich, 1723.

Halsband, R., ed., *The Complete Letters of Lady Mary Wortley Montagu*, 3 vols., Oxford, 1965–67.

Lowe, A., *La Serenissima: The Last Flowering of the Venetian Republic*, London, 1974.

Magazine à la mode, London, 1777.

Montagu, E., *The Queen of the Blue-Stockings: Correspondence 1720–1761*, ed. E.J. Climenson, 2 vols., London, 1906, vol. 1.

Moore, J., *A View of Society and Manners in France, Switzerland and Germany*, 2 vols., London, 1779, vol. 2.

_____, *A View of Society and Manners in Italy*, 2 vols., London, 1781, vol. 2.

Nevinson, J.L., "Vandyke Dress," *Connoisseur*, Nov. 1964.

Pilon, É., and F. Saisset, *Les fêtes en Europe au XVIIIᵉ siècle*, Saint-Gratien, 1943.

Ribeiro, A., "The Exotic Diversion: The Dress Worn at Masquerades in Eighteenth-Century London," *Connoisseur*, Jan. 1978.

_____, "Mrs. Cornelys and Carlisle House," *History Today*, Jan. 1978.

_____, "Turquerie: Turkish Dress and English Fashion in the Eighteenth Century," *Connoisseur*, May 1979.

Russel, J., *Letters from a Young Painter abroad to his Friends in England*, 2 vols., London, 1750, vol. 1.

Vaudoyer, J.L., "L'Orientalisme en Europe au XVIIIᵉ siècle," *Gazette des beaux-arts*, 1911, p. 98.

Walpole, H., *Letters*, ed. P. Toynbee, 16 vols., Oxford, 1903–5, vol. 1.

KEY TO EXHIBITIONS

A. LACM, Jan. 23–Feb. 28, 1944, *2,000 Years of Silk Weaving*.

B. LACM, Nov. 22, 1955–Feb. 13, 1956, *Silken Masterpieces*.

C. LACM, Nov. 13, 1957–Mar. 16, 1958, *English Costumes of the Georgian Period*.

D. LACM, Nov. 15, 1960–Feb. 12, 1961, *Rococo, 18th-Century Costumes and Textiles*.

E. LACM, June 20–Sept. 17, 1961, *Painted and Printed Textiles*.

F. Smith College Museum of Art, May 10–June 7, 1965, *An Exhibition of Chinoiserie*.

G. LACMA, Mar. 21–May 15, 1966, *Velvets East & West from the 14th to the 20th Century*.

H. LACMA, Mar. 31–June 10, 1967, *Over and Underwear*.

I. LACMA, Mar. 26–June 30, 1968, *The Bridal Tradition: 1800–1960s*.

J. LACMA, Aug. 27, 1968–Feb. 23, 1969, *Brocade/Woven Embellishment*.

K. LACMA, Aug. 4–Oct. 26, 1970, *Patterns in Fashion*.

L. Huntington Library Exhibition, May 3–June 28, 1971.

M. LACMA, Nov. 14, 1972–Jan. 21, 1973, *Block, Brush, and Stencil.*

N. LACMA, May 14–Oct. 20, 1974, *Fabric and Fashion: Twenty Years of Costume Council Gifts.*

P. LACMA, Apr. 8–June 29, 1975, *A Decade of Collecting.*

Q. LACMA, Mar. 4–Aug. 24, 1975, *The Grand Tour.*

R. LACMA, Oct. 10, 1978–July 1, 1979, *The Splendid Silk Dress.*

S. LACMA, July 3–Aug. 29, 1979, *Recent Acquisitions.*

T. LACMA, Oct. 15–Nov. 15, 1981, *Recent Acquisitions.*

U. LACMA, Apr. 8–Oct. 31, 1982, *600 Years of Embroidery from the Permanent Collection, 1380–1980.*

Note: The Los Angeles County Museum (LACM) became the Los Angeles County Museum of Art (LACMA) in December 1961.

KEY TO PUBLICATIONS

1. Abegg, M., *Apropos Patterns for Embroidery Lace and Woven Textiles*, Bern, 1978.

2. Badin, J., *La Manufacture de tapisseries de Beauvais depuis des origines jusqu'à nos jours*, Paris, 1909.

3. Boucher, F., *20,000 Years of Fashion: The History of Costume and Personal Adornment*, New York, 1967.

4. *Catalogue des étoffes* (Besselière collection), exh. cat., Paris, 1912.

5. Cox, R., *Les Soieries d'art: depuis les origines jusqu'à nos jours*, Paris, 1914.

6. Falke, O. von, *Decorative Silks*, New York, 1922.

7. Fenaille, M., *État général des tapisseries de la manufacture des Gobelins depuis son origine jusqu'à nos jours, 1600–1900*, 6 vols., Paris, 1903, vol. 2.

8. Flemming, E., *An Encyclopedia of Textiles from the Earliest Times to the Beginning of the 19th Century*, New York, 1927.

9. Flemming, E., and R. Jacques, *Encyclopedia of Textiles; Decorative Fabrics from Antiquity to the Beginning of the 19th Century, Including the Far East and Peru*, New York, 1958.

10. Galerie Jean Charpentier, *Adolphe Clément Bayard Collection Sale*, sales cat., Paris, June 22, 1937.

11. Holt, E.I., "Brocaded Silk Panels by Philippe de LaSalle," Los Angeles County Museum, *Bulletin of the Art Division*, 11:1, 1959, pp. 10–14.

12. _____, "Rococo Costumes and Fabrics in the Museum Collection," Los Angeles County Museum, *Bulletin of the Art Division*, 12:2, 1960, pp. 3–14.

13. Holt, S.P., "A System of Record-Keeping," Los Angeles County Museum, *Bulletin of the Art Division*, 8:1, 1956, pp. 12–13.

14. _____, "English Costumes of the Georgian Period," Los Angeles County Museum, *Bulletin of the Art Division*, 9:2, 1957, pp. 1–24.

15. Jamot, P., *Duc de Trevise Sale*, sales cat., Galerie Jean Charpentier, Paris, May 19, 1938.

16. Köhler, C., *A History of Costume*, ed. and aug. E. von Sichart, trans. A.K. Dallas, London, 1928.

17. Los Angeles County Museum, *2000 Years of Silk Weaving*, exh. cat., 1944.

18. _____, *Bulletin of the Art Division*, 4:2–3, summer 1952, pp. 14–15.

19. _____, "Further Acquisitions," *Bulletin of the Art Division*, 6:3, supplement, summer 1954, pp. 41–42.

20. _____, "New Acquisitions: Costumes and Textiles," *Bulletin of the Art Division*, 6:4, fall 1954, p. 35.

21. _____, *Bulletin of the Art Division*, 8:1, winter 1956, pp. 18–19.

22. _____, "Costumes and Textiles," *Bulletin of the Art Division*, 10:4, 1958.

23. _____, *Painted and Printed Textiles*, exh. cat., 1961.

24. _____, "The French Period Rooms," *Quarterly*, 12:4, 1955, pp. 22–23.

25. _____, *Quarterly*, 13:4, summer 1957, p. 9.

26. _____, "Rococo," *Quarterly*, 17:3, summer 1961, pp. 8–9.

27. Los Angeles County Museum of Art, "Recent Acquisitions, Fall 1969–Spring 1973," *Bulletin*, 19:2, 1973, p. 56, no. 66.

28. _____, "Three Decades of Collecting: Gifts of Anna Bing Arnold," *Bulletin*, vol. 26, 1980, pp. 30–31.

29. _____, *A Decade of Collecting*, exh. cat., 1975.

30. _____, *Fabric and Fashion: Twenty Years of Costume Council Gifts*, exh. cat., 1974.

31. _____, *Handbook*, 1977.

32. _____, *Velvets East & West from the 14th to the 20th Century*, exh. cat., 1966.

33. Moore, D. (Langley-Levy), *The Woman in Fashion*, London, 1949.

34. Powys, M., *Lace and Lace-Making*, Boston, 1953.

35. Schmidt, H.J., *Alte Seidenstoffe: ein Handbuch für Sammler und Liebhaber*, Braunschweig, 1958.

36. Seligman, G.S., and T. Hughes, *Domestic Needlework: Its Origins and Customs throughout the Centuries*, London, 1926.

37. Thornton, P., *Baroque and Rococo Silks*, London, 1965.

38. Weibel, A.C., *Two Thousand Years of Textiles: The Figured Textiles of Europe and the Near East*, New York, 1952.